A dì 6 Agosto 18..

Io Fe Anti: M.o Bianchi Curat...
...rascritta Famiglia è ...
...pe e Soccorso. Ed in...

A dì 29 Agosto —— 1810

Visitata, personalmente la Casa della quì descritta Famiglia unitamente al Sig. Castello Quaratesi
ho ritrovato, che la medesima è miserabilissima spende composta di quattro individui, due deeg
non guadagnano, cioè il Padre, e la figlia minore, ajutando questa al Padre che fa l'arte, n
che da molto tempo non ha favoro; bisognou più sopra ogni altra cosa sono di letto non c
altro che una piccola materassa posta delle Scegiole sopra la quale sono obbligati a star
Dietro a questa dimostrazione, non dubito punto, che la Beneficenza non accorderà a que
miserabile famiglia un Letto grande, parendomi, che meglio non si possa adattare un tal
sussidio Rima

I Deputati P. Micelli
Castello Quaratesi

A dì 3 Settembre 1810.

Esaminato l'esposto da Sigg. Deputati crederei che attesa la miserabilità
di questa Famiglia dai medesimi SS.ri Deputati descritt
Ed attesa l'età delle due figlie della Supplicante, ciò
più che necessario accordarli un letto mezzano ff le
Medesime, rimettendomi

Luigi Caffee ecc Capo dell' Ufizio Ausilia

The Poor in
Western Europe

in the Eighteenth and Nineteenth Centuries

STUART WOOLF

The Poor in Western Europe

in the Eighteenth and Nineteenth Centuries

METHUEN

LONDON AND NEW YORK

First published in 1986 by
Methuen & Co. Ltd
11 New Fetter Lane, London EC4P 4EE

Published in the USA by
Methuen & Co.
in association with Methuen, Inc.
29 West 35th Street, New York NY 10001

Printed in Great Britain at the
University Press, Cambridge

Typeset by Vision Typesetting, Manchester

British Library Cataloguing in Publication Data
Woolf, S.J.
The poor in Western Europe
in the eighteenth and nineteenth centuries.
1. Poor – Italy – History
I. Title
305.5′69′0945   HC310.P6
ISBN 0-416-39330-6

Library of Congress Cataloging in Publication Data
Woolf, S.J. (Stuart Joseph)
The poor in western Europe
in the eighteenth and nineteenth centuries.
Bibliography: p.
Includes index.
1. Poverty. 2. Poor – Italy – History – 19th century.
I. Title.
HC310.P6W66   1986   305.5′69′094   86-5331
ISBN 0-416-39330-6

Contents

Note

Only the introductory essay in this collection has not previously been published; but many of the others have been published in places sometimes of difficult access to the English reader. I owe thanks to the publishers for permission to reprint them in this English edition. Essay 2 appeared in a considerably different version in *Storia d'Italia, Annali* I, *dal feudalesimo al capitalismo*, Turin, G. Einaudi Editore, 1978; essay 3 in the *Annuario dell'Istituto Storico per l'Età Moderna e Comtemporanea*, vols. 23–4, 1971–2; essay 4 in *Social History*, 1:1, 1976; essay 5 in G. Politi, M. Rosa and F. Della Peruta (eds), *Timore e carità. Atti del convegno 'Pauperismo e assistenza negli antichi stati italiani' (Cremona, 28–30 March 1980)*, Biblioteca Statale e Libreria Civica, Annali 27–30, 1976–9, Cremona, 1982; essay 6 in G. Lepschy (ed.), *Su/Per Meneghello*, Milan, Edizioni di Comunità, 1983; essay 7 in *Annales E.S.C.* (1984) 2; essay 8 as a European University Institute Working Paper, no. 85/131, Florence, 1985. I further wish to thank the Social Science Research Council for assistance through its grant HK 6583, with essays 7 and 8.

As several essays are based on an identical source, I have removed the most obvious and superfluous repetitions. I have also removed the appendix listing communes and figures from essay 4 and those Italian terms from essay 6 which have become superflu-

vii

ous in a wholly English text. In one or two major instances I have added bibliographical references to works that have appeared subsequent to the original publication of the article. Otherwise I have left the texts of the articles without changes (except for chapter 2), not because I do not think that they could not be improved, but because I believe that a historian should not interfere surreptitiously with texts that, for better or worse, have joined the historical record. For purposes of the same record, I should perhaps add that the chapters are printed in the order in which they were written; the exceptions are the introductory essay, written for this edition, and chapter 2 which has been placed before the others because of its broader time-span and the different set of problems with which it is concerned.

The following abbreviations are used:

ANP, Archives Nationales, Paris
Arno, Prefettura dell'Arno
ASF, Archivio di Stato, Florence.

'O'Grady,' I said, when he had detached himself from the mob, 'What can be done for them?'

O'Grady said, 'Forget it. They're the incurably poor. You can't do anything for them. A hundred dollars a week and they'd still be poor. This is the only society we have, the only one we know. It's a money society. So if they're poor, they're inadequate. If they're inadequate they're mentally ill, by the definition of our society. Their illness can't be fixed by effort *or* dollars. Only by will. Their will. And they won't.' He smiled, pleased at being able to talk down at me.

D. Ireland, *The Flesheaters* (1972)

I

❦

Introduction:
the poor and society in western Europe

1 The poor today and in the past

The dramatic changes of the past few years, in which the affluent
society in the western world has shown itself incapable of upholding
the welfare state, have once more drawn attention to the issue of
poverty, in its moral, social, economic and political aspects. To the
historian, as significant as the everyday material evidence of poverty
have been the contradictory responses the presence of the poor has
evoked among the more fortunate, ranging from fastidious irri-
tation and outright hostility to charitable solidarity. Twenty years
ago, to insist on the survival and indeed generation of poverty
amidst affluence generally aroused indifference or disbelief among
the public, with the exception of social administrators, welfare
workers, some social scientists – and the poor themselves.
Compared to the levels of absolute poverty and high mortality
endemic in the Third World, surrounded by the physical evidence
of multiple and sophisticated official welfare bodies (buildings,
printed forms, employees), such indifference is easily explained.
The rapidity of the change in attitudes (an unusual experience for
the historian of mentalities) has offered illuminating analogies and
indicators to a range of historical problems intrinsic to the study of
poverty and the poor: the cyclical character of poverty as a collective
phenomenon, the dependence of individual and family on economic

I

conjunctures outside their control, the social perception of the poor both of the causes of poverty and of the appropriate means to deal with it. It would be mistaken to force the analogies too far. Much of the contemporary discussion among social scientists has been concerned with measurements of poverty dependent on quantitative data such as national income, virtually non-existent in western societies until the systematic collection of statistics beginning in the nineteenth century; or with the workings of the welfare state, whose origins can be traced back barely one hundred years and whose philosophy and realities only came to the fore after the Second World War. Hence there may be little apparent tie between the problems and perspectives of the current debate and the historical discussion – except in the persistence of the problem of poverty. For example, the definition of long-term unemployment, in a valuable comparative study of the 1960s,[1] as lasting between two months and two years and averaging about six months, affecting predominantly the unskilled worker, has little applicability to the study of European societies before (and well into) the twentieth century when regular employment was the privilege of only the skilled minority of the working population. Conversely, one of the principal groups to attract charitable concern and expenditure over the centuries – abandoned infants and children – now plays a relatively small part in a would-be all-embracing philosophy of welfare. It is to the credit of sociologists and economists such as Titmuss, Townsend, Abel-Smith, Atkinson and their Continental peers[2] to have established the concept that poverty is relative to the prevailing standards of the particular period and society. But, precisely for that reason, much of the theoretical debate of contemporary social scientists about poverty and national welfare schemes is of little direct relevance to the discussion of medieval, early modern or even industrializing societies, where existing or potential poverty was the norm, expectations and institutional responses incorporated different social values, and welfare policies remained, well into the nineteenth century, municipally based. Contemporary industrial society, with its connotations of unprecedented levels of average *per capita* wealth, rapid social mobility, high urbanization, excellent communications and falling fertility rates, has changed the dimensions and scale of the institutional means of dealing with poverty and modified the priorities among the categories of those regarded as entitled to support.

Nevertheless, the continuities in identification of the composition of the poor, as in stereotyped public attitudes towards them, remain strong. Today, as in past centuries, the overwhelming majority of those identified as poor consist of children under fifteen, old people often living alone and female-headed families. Their condition of poverty relates to precise phases of particular vulnerability in their life or family cycle. The old have superseded the young as a primary object of concern, subsequent to the dramatic shifts in the age structure of the population: in mid-nineteenth-century England and Wales, the ratio of the 25 to 59 cohorts to those over 60 was 5.5 to 1, in 1951 3.2 to 1, in 1971 2.2 to 1. But, as Richard Smith has pointed out, however dramatic the change in the most recent decades, over the long term major realignments of the population age structure, and consequential adjustments of poor-relief policies, have occurred at various periods in the past.[3] Even more striking is the consistent presence of widows, with or without family: that two-thirds of all households categorized as in a condition of poverty should have been headed by women in the 1960s, whether in the London borough of Bethnal Green or in the urban United States,[4] would not have surprised anybody engaged in charitable activities since the sixteenth century or earlier. As easily recognizable in the early modern and modern periods would have been the sudden sharp increase in numbers of homeless and starving individuals in cities during winters of economic recession, or the permanent presence of urban under-employed families on the edge of starvation, transmitting their poverty and social exclusion to their children in a cycle of deprivation.[5]

It would not be difficult to identify similar continuities in popular attitudes towards the poor, ranging from concern about specific groups – certain types of handicapped people or aged women – to blanket condemnation of the work-shy. Oscar Lewis's culture of poverty, with its stress on solidary patterns of behaviour and aberrant values of down-town youths acquired through common experiences and close proximity, is not so remote – in its mythology as much as its perceptions, and particularly in its insistence on the separateness from the dominant values of society – from the stock-in-trade descriptions of rogues, vagrants and petty criminals that circulated across western Europe from the sixteenth century.[6] And the historically consecrated distinction between deserving and undeserving claimants continues to be applied by social security bureaucrats, some more humanely, others more disapprovingly, according to personal humours and instructions from above.[7] Indeed, the categories of persons regarded with approval or disapprobation in terms of access to assistance have remained surprisingly unaltered over the centuries, to the present day.

There are then strong resemblances as well as differences in the nature of poverty and its treatment today and in the past. Whether this derives from an identity of problems, or when specific aspects and attitudes arose, is beginning to emerge from the rapidly growing literature on the history of poverty.

2 How many were the poor?

Who and how many were the poor are obvious and obligatory questions for all students of poverty. Economists have shown how arbitrary are all quantifications of the poor because of their necessary dependence upon an artificially defined poverty line.[8] But in many respects the answers that can be provided for pre-statistical societies are not merely inadequate or incomplete, but for at least two reasons misleading. Firstly, the sources which list the poor or offer other means of estimating their numbers indicate, through their categories, a static state of being poor, which tends to ignore or mask the fluidity and gradualness of the process by which people decline, sometimes more than once, into a condition of poverty. All western societies have contained a core, of varying size, of permanently poor unable to sustain themselves and their families; indeed, recent studies point to such a condition of poverty as likely to be passed on from generation to generation.[9] But in most cases, only in exceptional circumstances did individuals or families fall abruptly from self-subsistence to poverty; far more common was an experience – and nagging awareness – of poverty at recurrent periods of the individual and family life-cycle. The very fluidity and relativity of the condition of being poor denies the fixity of all categorizations.

Secondly, the sources which define and (increasingly from the eighteenth century) count the poor were drawn up for varying and contradictory purposes. It can be deceptive to derive estimates of the poor from the classes on fiscal rolls paying no (or very low) taxes or rates, as they offer only broad and crude indications of differentiations within the overall body of the labouring classes, and were aimed at tax capacities, not assessments of need. Estimates calculated from wages linked to food prices are usually based on a series of assumptions that may exaggerate the level of poverty, as frequently only the monetized wages of the adult head of household are known. Censuses of the poor, carried out in one or another town, tended to be drawn up at moments of crisis and could easily be conditioned by restrictive definitions of socially acceptable poverty. Even in periods when listings of the poor were drawn up on the basis of local personal knowledge – from the sixteenth and especially the seventeenth century, and then mainly for the towns, not usually for the rural areas – their numbers as a proportion of the local population could vary significantly according to the criteria employed. In seventeenth-century England, the burghers of Salisbury tended to limit their lists primarily to children and the aged, unlike their peers at Norwich and Ipswich who were sensitive to the needs of poor married couples with children, with the result that the household size as well as the overall numbers of the Salisbury poor look smaller than those in the other two cities.[10] In early nineteenth-century France and Italy, listings of the poor were even more variable, ranging from inclusion of regular migrants in mountain villages to highly restrictive counts of solely urban homeless widows and orphans.[11] The concept of who was poor depended in each instance on the categorization (necessarily) employed in order to draw up the list; and there is a subtle danger, only too easily ignored by historians, in mistaking a terminological continuity of categories for a substantial continuity in reality.

Bearing in mind these reservations, some attempt at quantification, however approximate, remains necessary. The conceptual distinctions introduced by Gutton and Pullan for urban poverty offer a useful approach, and case studies of early modern cities in England, France and Spain provide figures with similar orders of magnitude. The 'structural' poor, incapable of earning a living for reasons of age, illness or physical handicap and hence wholly dependent on assistance or begging, amounted to between 4 and 8 per cent of the populations of Salisbury, Norwich, Odense, Lyons, Toledo, Venice, Florence, Rome and many other cities of north and central Italy from the fifteenth to the eighteenth centuries. The urban 'conjunctural' or 'crisis' poor, usually dependent on low wages or casual employment and hence immediately affected by fluctuations in bread prices, amounted to about 20 per cent. A third concentric circle (to use Pullan's metaphor) of artisans, small retailers and petty officials, who can be identified with the householders assessed at minimum tax rates, could fall easily and repeatedly beneath the level of subsistence, for personal family reasons or as a result of trade stoppages, so swelling the proportion of the urban poor, at crisis moments, to include as many as 50 to 70 per cent of all households.[12]

The figures available in the sources inevitably relate almost exclusively to the cities and disproportionately to moments of crisis. The sixteenth and eighteenth centuries, periods of relatively rapid growth of the population and more limited increase in agricultural production, are privileged for precisely this reason. But in societies where, until well into the nineteenth century, over 70 per cent of the population lived outside the cities, estimates of the rural poor, if available, would be of equal or greater significance. That they should not be available (except at times of harvest failure, and then only in small and strongly organized states like England) marks once more the limitations and ill-balanced nature of our sources, the product of formal, literate bureaucracies within the cities, obliged to define codes of comportment *vis-à-vis* the poor by the norms of their urban culture. Hence it is far more difficult to apply Pullan's image of concentric circles of poverty to the rural areas of Europe.

At the centre there can have been few villages which did not contain a core of structurally poor, above all of widows and the physically or mentally handicapped. The problems arise with the outer concentric rings, which require a different definition from those of the cities. European agriculture, through the centuries, has been conditioned on the one hand by the nature and fertility of the terrain, on the other by the patterns of landholdings and types of agrarian contracts. In mountainous or infertile areas (such as the Pyrenees, Massif Central, Alps, Apennines or Wales), where independent smallholdings were the norm but the climate drastically limited subsistence agriculture, a second concentric circle can be drawn, characterized by the regular annual migration of 50 per cent and even up to 90 per cent of the village populations to more fertile regions where job opportunities were greater.

More problematic is the next ring, geographically partly overlapping the migratory areas, but where climatic and pedological conditions were less severe. In such areas, often in the hills, smallholders or tenant farmers could often maintain their economic independence by unremitting labour and carefully deployed family and inheritance strategies. But other families, in the same or other areas (for example, in Brittany, Venetia or Ireland), were forced into growing debt and ultimate loss of their land either because the smallholdings had been subdivided into plots too minute to sustain them, or because contractual arrangements as tenants or cottagers left them insecure. It is almost meaningless to quantify such families, as their proportions in each region varied over the centuries, although it is reasonable to conclude that, with the commercialization of agriculture, their numbers were growing between the fifteenth and eighteenth centuries. In terms of poverty, it is arguable that these smallholders and tenant farmers were barely distinguishable from the day labourers of the fertile plains of northern France, the eastern Po valley or Sicily. In some regions, part of the population responded by turning to rural industry, particularly textile production. But, as the recent spate of research on proto-industrialization has shown, over the medium term the condition of these rural industrial workers – even more dependent than their urban counterparts on the vagaries of distant markets – was no better and often worse than that of the peasants. In late eighteenth-century France (when economic conditions were deteriorating), according to Hufton, one-third, maybe one-half, of the population was poor or indigent: a large proportion of these belonged to the migratory and smallholding concentric circles.

A final ring can be drawn to include the victims of periodic and frequent harvest failures, pestilence or military incursions. Plague, which persisted into the seventeenth century, and constant warfare, which affected vast areas of western and central Europe between the fifteenth and the seventeenth centuries, devastated entire rural areas, leaving their inhabitants vulnerable to the violence of disbanded or marauding soldiers. The 1520s, 1590s, 1630s, 1640s, 1650s, 1690s, 1710s, 1720s, 1764–6, 1811–12, 1816, 1847 were years of particularly widespread and devastating dearth and mortality crises in western Europe, but until the later eighteenth century, when government intervention finally improved the regional flow of foodstuffs, poor or disastrous harvests could easily occur on average every four or five years. At such times, to escape famine, plague or military foray, the peasants fled from the countryside.[13]

The result of this permanent outflow from the countryside was that the cities experienced the constant passage of temporary or permanent needy migrants – between 1000 and 1500 passed through seventeenth-century Lyons each month.[14] At times of famine the numbers of the poor dependent on charity in the city would suddenly swell out of all proportions: in late sixteenth-century Bergamo, the Misericordia, normally responsible for assisting 5000–7000 poor, found itself in times of famine aiding 15,000–20,000 persons, 10 per cent of the entire population of the province.[15] It was this pressure of the rural population on their resources that led to the hardening attitude of civic authorities from the 1520s, which was meant to stem the tide of peasants from the surrounding countryside (and proved ineffective), but which established a permanent discrimination against all non-residents.

3 Poverty and the economy

The terms 'poor' and 'indigent' are, of course, highly ambiguous and changed significantly over the centuries, as well as according to the context in which they were employed. But by the sixteenth century and emphatically by the eighteenth, they had acquired primarily economic connotations to describe the labouring classes, including those with a minimal capital in the form of a smallholding or loom. Among the innumerable descriptions and definitions

Introduction

offered by all writers on the poor it is worth citing that of Jeremy Bentham because he captures so fully this direct link between poverty and the economy: 'Poverty is the state of everyone who, in order to obtain *subsistence*, is forced to have recourse to *labour*. Indigence is the state of him who, being destitute of property . . . is at the same time, either *unable to labour*, or unable, even for labour, to procure the supply of which he happens thus to be in want.'[16] The weakness of Bentham's definition is that, by identifying the poor simply with the labouring classes, poverty risks becoming no more than the absence of capital or property; it is the indigents of Benthamite terminology who correspond to the poor discussed in this essay.

With the exception of specific groups, such as the Franciscans, who chose voluntary pauperism, or the shamefaced poor, whose status in society placed them in a special category of the relatively poor, in all periods the nature of the economy and specifically the labour market conditioned the levels and composition of poverty. The involution of the guilds in the fourteenth and fifteenth centuries created a permanent category of apprentices, *valets* and *compagnons*, alongside the far larger numbers of unskilled within and outside the guilds; the commercialization of agriculture in the early modern period reduced smallholders and those with insecure tenure to the condition of day labourers or migrants; the growth and strength of the urban guilds in the early modern period excluded the rural immigrants from access to skilled trades, crowding them into the casual labour market and domestic service; the extension of textile industries to the countryside, like the competition of mechanization and industrialization, had similar effects in the pauperization of broad segments of both rural and urban workers. It is, of course, possible to point to periods and regions with contrasting trends, and it would be important to analyse over the long term the impact of economic and particularly technological changes on relieving poverty (rather than to assume optimistically, as did social scientists and historians in the 1950s and 1960s, that such a relationship exists).

Virtually total lack of capital or property was what made the labouring classes so directly dependent on economic fluctuations. For dowries, the prerequisite for marriage for all girls, can hardly be

9

regarded as the *ancien régime* equivalent of inheritable property, as their small value restricted their function at best to that of working capital, sometimes adequate initially to set up household by conversion into equipment or stock, but depreciating (precisely because of such a conversion) over the family cycle. In the countryside, vicinity of growing urban markets, and especially improvements in communications could help the favoured few, free of strict contractual obligations and with enough land to produce above subsistence needs. Outside agriculture, periods can be identified, usually relatively short, when real wages rose, through a fall in prices or increases in wage rates, as (for example) after the passage of plague (which occurred in repeated bouts between the fourteenth and the seventeenth centuries) or in Britain in the 1850s and 1860s; but generally, over the long term, the wage-price terms of trade tended to work against dependent workers.

More significant were the incidental effects of structural changes in the pattern of employment on categories of persons in specific locations. We are accustomed to argue in terms of mechanization causing unemployment among those with obsolescent skills, such as nineteenth-century handloom weavers. But technological change (or rapid expansion of production without technological change, as in building) cut both ways, also creating some employment and, perhaps more important, offering greater job security and higher wages for those involved: the urban palaces built and decorated for rulers and nobles from the Renaissance on, or the massive eighteenth-century expansion of production of silk cloths or quality furniture are all examples of luxury goods where a widening market provided a degree of expansion in artisan employment in *ancien régime* societies, as did mechanized textile production in the early nineteenth century and engineering and shipbuilding in Britain in the 1850s. The scale of job creation must have increased significantly with the shift away from luxury production and the rapid nineteenth-century growth of a comfortable, often wealthy middle class throughout western Europe. But equally significant from the point of view of the relief of poverty was the shift in the categories of those employed: young women and children in the early industrial revolution making a possibly unprecedentedly large contribution to the family economy; the casually employed with the rapid expansion of services in the *belle époque* prior to the First World War; in both cases, categories particularly liable to fall into a condition of poverty. It could also be argued that if the massive increase in rural and urban proto-industrial employment created a process of proletarianization over the medium term, increasing investment in equipment in some sectors (such as silk or, later, engineering) made employers less likely to employ and dismiss casual labour and hence could increase job security; in this sense, civic authorities played an analogous role as governments after 1918, by offering incentives and putting pressure on employers not to dismiss labour during trade crises. To point to such relationships is not to argue that increasing employment reduced relative inequality, nor to deny the close dependence of levels of poverty on the transformations of the European economy. From the late Middle Ages until a fairly mature stage of industrialization in each nation-state, the waves of pauperism can be measured, albeit loosely, against the rhythms and crises of the pre-industrial and industrializing agrarian and manufacturing economies.[17]

4 Family and Poverty

If the dimensions and scale of pauperism varied according to the short-term conjunctures and longer-term transformations of the economy, the causes of poverty at the individual level and identity of the poor display a remarkable continuity across the centuries. In both cities and countryside, the evidence on wage levels and annual number of days' employment is overwhelming in its conclusion that a large majority of labourers could barely earn enough for minimum subsistence for themselves and their families, and then only for a limited period of their working lives. A skilled artisan might hope to work 190 full days and 70 part days anually in late medieval Paris, and 290 days in eighteenth-century Lyons; masons in seventeenth-century Milan might work for 250 to 270 days, but poor weather and the increasing number of religious festivals made 200 days more likely; an agricultural labourer, according to Vauban, could only count on 180 days. The range of wage rates could be enormous, with skilled miners earning ten times as much as unskilled, or (perhaps more normally) master masons earning twice as much as *valets*.[18] Women's wages were never more than half those of men and, like children's earnings, were almost always below subsistence level. To write of wages in this fashion is, of course, anachronistic, as throughout the history of the *ancien régime* (and later, indeed in minor forms, to the present day) payment was a composite affair, both monetized and in kind, sometimes for the period served, sometimes for piecework, partly through written or verbal contract, partly customary. How is one to calculate the eighteenth-century Pyrenean harvester's wage of a small cash payment, seven meals a day for himself and gleaning rights for his wife?[19]

What is unequivocally clear is that it is inappropriate, probably until the later nineteenth century, to think in terms of the individual wage-earner, when subsistence depended on the family economy, even at the level of the skilled artisan. The relative contribution of individual members of the family or household varied according to both age and sex, and the particular organization of production. In monetary terms, the contribution of women and children in seventeenth- and eighteenth-century rural textile workers' families was probably greater than in urban skilled artisan households and certainly greater than in peasant sharecropping or smallholding families; in the early phase of the industrial revolution, the earnings of women and children as a proportion of the domestic economy increased significantly.[20] Outside agriculture, textile production has inevitably (given its leading role in the economy) tended to dominate discussion of the internal roles of members of the household economy; and, taken together with the far older debate on father-son transmission of skills within guilds, it gives the probably misleading impression of a rational combination of family roles in terms of the production process. In fact, we know very little about the range of job-skills and temporary or casual occupations within the family. At the more skilled levels, did specific production processes (particularly outside textiles) or institutional networks, such as guilds or confraternities, offer possibilities of work for the wife, widow and children of a male earner? In seventeenth-century Venice, artisans increasingly joined more than one guild to counteract the negative employment consequences of the decline in manufacturing production.[21] At lower levels, lack of skills – in the past as today – by condemning all members of the family to low wages and uncertain employment, necessitated adaptability and willingness to change occupation frequently, in what Hufton has aptly defined as an 'economy of makeshifts'. Heavy physical labour, on roads, fortifications or porterage, was left to the unskilled and poorest, whose wives and children engaged in a multiplicity of activities at home and in the neighbourhood. But as various studies have shown, such adaptability and the economy of makeshifts was the norm for the greater proportion of the labouring classes, precisely because of the vulnerability of the family economy, even that of the skilled artisan. Indeed, the rural worker, whether agricultural or manufacturing, was psychologically better equipped to deal with short-term crises than was the urban artisan, given the wider variety of resources within his region upon which his family could fall back and a greater familiarity with temporary migration. The *ancien régime* urban weaver, like the nineteenth-century artisan shoemaker, could find his livelihood abruptly cut off; and, despite his appeals for civil public works at such moments of severe conjunctural crisis, could then discover that he was too weak to undertake heavy physical labour.[22] Servants, who constituted 10 per cent or more of urban populations in the eighteenth and nineteenth centuries, were in a special position so long as they 'lived in', since regular subsistence was provided; but they found themselves as poorly equipped as urban artisans once such protection was removed through age, dismissal or simply misfortune.[23]

The vulnerability of the family economy resulted from the absolute lack of reserves. As Gutton has shown, on the basis of Lyons probate inventories, the value of furnishings, tools or retailer's goods rarely amounted to more than 50 to 60 livres, equivalent to a silkworker's earnings in six weeks; and much of this might be owed for rental of his room, a major cause of poverty for urban workers, irrespective of country or period. In the countryside the possession of a small plot of land offered no greater guarantee.[24] The cost of food and wine in the sixteenth and seventeenth centuries may have taken up to 60 to 80 per cent of an artisan family's income; a family of four consumed 7 to 8 pounds of bread daily, which cost almost half the daily earnings of a Lyons labourer in the 1730s.[25] It is hardly surprising that even an economy of makeshifts should have collapsed so easily. If migration, begging and occasional appeals to charity all constituted supplementary (or even primary) sources of income for the family economy, indebtedness, for rental, materials or food, and recourse to the pawnshop usually marked the last, precipitous stages of the decline from poverty to indigence. The readiness of charitable organizations to redeem debts or pawned objects, as in general the relative willingness to give short-term assistance to families, were not casual but resulted from society's awareness of the fragility of the family economy.

The breakdown of this economy could occur for a variety of reasons, both economic and private, outside the family's control: disastrous harvest, trade interruptions, quarantine, death or prolonged illness of the male head of household or birth of an additional child. But a structural element, which has become very apparent with the recent literature on family demography, was often the small size of labouring-class families in Europe – however paradoxical this may seem in terms of Malthusian population theories. Richard Smith has noted very recently that Malthus wrote his essay in a period of abnormally high fertility, when viewed in a long-term perspective; but, of course, images and accusations that poverty breeds children do not necessarily bear much relationship to long-term populations trends, and were not unusual already in the mid-seventeenth century, when the fertility rate was not rising rapidly.[26]

The problem has been obscured in the literature by a confusion between size of family and size of household. As Wrigley and Schofield have demonstrated for England, fertility rates and hence completed family size varied considerably over the centuries; at the same time, Laslett and his colleagues of the Cambridge History of Population Group have proved the existence of a long-term pattern of nuclear and normally small family units characteristic of England and (they claim boldly) of all north-west Europe since at least the fourteenth century. But, as was clarified by the debate over the use of censuses, numbers listed as members of a household do not equate to the completed size of families.[27] For without prospective inheritance of property, or the labour requirements of a farm to hold kin together (as in the case of rural stem-families and sharecroppers), there were pressing subsistence reasons for kin households to remain small. For our present purposes, it is enough to note three means by which families achieved this aim: firstly, the relatively late age at marriage of both men and women, with increasing evidence that changes in age responded sensitively to economic conditions; secondly, linked to high infant mortality, the ample use of foundling hospitals by working families, at least from the eighteenth century, as temporary or permanent deposits for 'excess' babies; thirdly, the early departure of children from the household to earn their own living.[28] There are areas of dispute over the relationship between particular economic situations and size of family, such as whether rural proto-industrial activities made it less likely for teenage children to leave the household. But the evidence from urban censuses and listings for families regarded as poor points to a small average size, unusually above four, and certainly smaller than among the wealthier strata of urban dwellers; and this seems to be generally true of towns in Italy, France or England from the late medieval period at least until into the nineteenth century.[29]

The implications of this absolute predominance of small nuclear households among the poor, where kinship ties weakened with departure from the home, have been explored by Richard Smith.[30] At repeated phases of the life cycle, individuals and families without capital or reserves were likely not to earn enough for subsistence. Children up to the age of 15 constantly dominate lists of beggars for this reason; parents were under the greatest pressure on resources because of the encumbrance of small children, given the late age at marriage, between the ages of about 35 and 45, even though the husband was probably at the height of his earning capacity; in these same years, surviving grandparents, by now in their late sixties, would no longer be able to earn their keep. In this sense, ths small size of household of labouring families, unable to rely on kin support, introduced a structural likelihood of poverty through inadequate earnings for most phases of the individual life cycle, except during late adolescence and the early years of marriage. It is hardly surprising that the same age-groups – children, families with small children and the old, especially widows – should have been identified as indigent constantly over the centuries throughout western Europe, in Italian, French, English or Spanish treatises, from the sixteenth century to Seebohm Rowntree's investigation of

York in 1900; nor, given the decline in fertility since the late nineteenth century in an otherwise unchanged context of nuclear households, that the aged should have assumed a greater importance as a category of welfare concern than in most periods in the past.

English demographic historians affirm the particularity, to England and by extension to north-west Europe, of the independent small nuclear household, and its implications for social relations. They argue that the egocentrism of such nuclear households worked against kin solidarity in early modern English villages, even if relatives were resident close to those in need of assistance, and that perhaps more important were less formal ties of neighbourliness and friendship.[31] In support of their argument, the evidence of the town of Odense (Denmark) in the eighteenth century points to a similar loss of contact among kin, with parents unaware of where their children lived.[32] Nevertheless, it is not contradictory to propose that, at the level of labouring families without property or capital, the English 'model' was not confined to north-west Europe, particularly given the evidence of considerable mobility within both rural and urban populations. There were few means of maintaining kin ties over considerable distances and the level of accepted ignorance is, to our eyes, remarkably high: in early seventeenth-century Cremona, for instance, a husband and wife, married for twenty years, did not even know each other's surname, birthplace or exact age; nor was the wife unduly perturbed that the pedlar husband should suddenly leave without saying where he was going or when he would return.[33] The fundamental distinctions would seem to be those based on wealth and settlement: among the pedlars of the Oisans valley, kin networks functioned over a wide area, but among the successful pedlar families; similar self-defensive mechanisms within the urban parish might operate at the level of street solidarities, but presumably only where the inhabitants were accepted through settlement in the neighbourhood.[34] Public reputation, vouchsafed by parish priest, local spokesman, neighbour or midwife, was the operative mechanism, dependent on personal relations. The propertyless migrants or newcomers, whether individuals or (usually fragmented) families must surely have had greater difficulties in turning for help to kin or neighbour; and for the same reason – absence of mediators – were exposed to greater difficulties in their approaches to institutional charity or were more vulnerable to accusations of transgressions of the law.

5 Attitudes towards the poor

Concepts of poverty have shifted far more than the composition of the poor over the centuries, even since the early modern period. They are revealing indicators of the deeper values and often irrational motivations underlying both popular and élite attitudes, and are important to discuss because of their practical implications for the nature and limits of the assistance which society was prepared to provide at various periods for those unable or unwilling to maintain themselves. Many of the multiple usages of the term *paupertas* during the Middle Ages would have been recognized with difficulty, if at all, by the committed pamphleteers of the sixteenth century: 'poverty' was rarely an absolute, but was relative, a quality – of impecuniosity, infirmity, misfortune, pity, contempt, disgust – and the 'pauper' was the antonym of the 'mighty' (*potens*), the 'armed' (*miles*), the 'citizen' (*cives*) and, increasingly, of the wealthy (*dives*). But to be poor was at the same time a condition of grace, through the religious connotation of the 'poor of Christ'; although already by the latter part of the thirteenth century poverty aroused repugnance as degrading to man's dignity.[35] By the late Middle Ages the multiplicity of meanings had been reduced essentially to two – the economic and the religious contexts. But the use of the term remained ambivalent, oscillating ambiguously between religious merit and physical disgust, between moral concern for the victims of the uncertainties of life or fate and growing hostility to the potential menace represented by beggars and vagrants. As wealth generated social differentiation, attitudes to poverty changed; and with the social unrest from the thirteenth century, worries about public disorder increased. The growth of pauperism and hence geographic mobility consequential upon the economic difficulties and wars in the fourteenth and fifteenth centuries, increased fear of the unknown 'foreigner' and so acted as a constraint on the earlier open welcome for the pilgrim; the Franciscan doctrine of absolute poverty was judged contradictorily as a benediction but also as a source of corruption.

The fifteenth century witnessed the full emergence of that fundamental and age-old distinction between deserving and undeserving (dating back to the Justinian Code) which was to condition all future attitudes to the poor. In this discriminatory philosophy begging was attacked on both moral and practical worldly grounds, through its equation on the one hand with idleness, on the other with dishonesty. Some historians identify, more or less closely, the moral critique of mendicants as work-shy with the capitalist ethic, and cite the scholastic distinctions of the archbishop of Florence, St Antonino (1389–1459): voluntary poverty merited praise as a renunciation of worldly goods, but involuntary poverty resulting from material conditions was no virtue in itself and likely to lead to temptation and sloth, if encouraged by indiscriminate almsgiving.[36] It is difficult to propose any rational explanation for the practical attack on beggars and vagrants as rogues and tricksters exploiting the ingenuous Christian's compassion, except in terms of the growing numbers of vagrants, and magnification of examples of fraud in communities and societies traditionally accustomed to the passage of pilgrims and begging friars, in which the very complexity of symbolic values facilitated deception. Symptomatic of the diffusion of this unreasoned apprehensive response was the invention, by the Bishop of Spoleto's vicar in 1485, of the mirror image of a resident, respectful, pious society – an entire counter-culture of organized professional beggars, the *cerretani* who lived off the credulity of honest folk.[37]

Through the fifteenth century, charity, as the favoured instrument of spiritual improvement, manifested itself at new levels, from England to Italy, but with a discriminatory worldliness as to the objects of its concern. It is not accidental that this new wave of charity was channelled particularly through institutional structures – confraternities, hospitals, almshouses, civic pawnshops – rather than directly as largess to the poor, since this shifted the onus of discrimination away from the compassionate donor. Charity became more markedly urban and, through ecclesiastical initiative or with episcopal and royal support, led to an initial reorganization of the medieval network of small hospices, whose revenues had often been misappropriated, in favour of large new hospitals. Not surprisingly, given their precocity of development and accumulation of wealth, the cities of northern and central Italy provided the most elaborate and sophisticated infrastructures of support, both public and private – the first civic pawnshops (*monti di pietà*) in Europe, foundling hospitals, confraternities specializing in assistance to specific groups (such as the shamefaced poor) or moments of the life-cycle (marriage dowries, funerals).[38]

All historians of charity have stressed how this growth of municipal initiative (which was to dominate the following centuries) supplemented and co-ordinated rather than replaced the earlier medieval foundations. Indeed, particularly in the countryside or outside the city walls, the minute hospitals, with perhaps only a couple of beds, continued to accept the poor, just as the hospices gave overnight board to pilgrims and the monasteries provided free food to all who presented themselves, without discrimination. There was no sudden shift from a 'medieval' to a 'modern' approach to poverty. The wanderer or *errant* remained welcome; nor indeed in societies in which migration performed so central a function would anything else have been conceivable. Perhaps more interestingly, in the context of that separation of popular from élite culture attributed by some historians precisely to the early modern period, the official attempts to impose an aggressively hostile policy towards mendicants were often sabotaged by popular solidarity with the beggars.[39]

Nevertheless, the intellectual framework within which poverty was subsequently to be conceived, right through until the present century, had been set by the end of the fifteenth century. In this sense, the treatises and recommendations of the subsequent periods offer little more than variants on known themes, whereas the real innovations are to be found in the institutional means elaborated to execute the consequences of this schema. A practical consequence of this development, for the historian of the poor, is that the records relate almost exclusively to the cities. Except for England and the Scandinavian countries, the resources and hence the activities of charitable structures were at a far lower level in the countryside than in the cities and unable to cope with the pressure of populations often permanently close to, and periodically below, bare subsistence; the historian can only observe the outflow of peasants from their villages towards the towns at every harvest crisis, and explore the informal self-defensive mechanisms (of neighbourhood, kin and other such networks familiar to social anthropologists) which undoubtedly existed in the countryside but have left barely perceptible traces in the documentation.

With the increase of pauperism, a substantial local clientele of poor existed in permanence within the cities, a demand on resources and a potential threat to public order. What is often left unclear is that the partition line between those who merited assistance and the unworthy was marked by length of settlement. In societies structured around explicit values of honour, status and family, functioning through mechanisms of patronage, protection and recommendation, residence was a necessary condition of confidence and trust, through personal or indirect knowledge of the character, comportment and needs of the individual. It explains the establishment of organizations to assist the shamefaced poor in the fifteenth century. For who was better known or better recommended than the respected noble, merchant or artisan, whose misfortune threatened his ability to uphold his status in this society of orders, and hence who merited discreet (and sometimes substantial) assistance so that he be not shamed in the eyes of his peers? But even in such instances, a little worldly guile was not out of place, as the request for alms for such worthy recipients as the Shakespearian Antonio of Venice had been known to inspire dishonest rogues to anticipate the rounds of the genuine collectors.[40] For at the other side of the residential divide was the unknown begging vagrant, potential disturber of the peace, vector of disease, a likely trickster. In societies structured around corporative organizations, in which clientelism acted as a coagulant, the unknown individual without domicile, property, social or institutional ties, without guarantor, the *sans aveu*, could not but create suspicion.

6 Institutional charity and the deserving poor

Major institutional changes came in the early sixteenth century and were to continue in successive waves until the early nineteenth century; after a prolonged pause, they were then to resume at the turn of the century, with generalized state action in forms and on a scale habitually regarded as marking the beginnings of the welfare state. The chronology of these institutional passages differed somewhat across western Europe, as the motive forces behind such reforms (private, municipal, ecclesiastical and state) varied in will and capacity to persuade or impose them on the local populations. Such successive new structures to deal with the question of the poor have on occasion been regarded erroneously as stepping stones along a teleological path towards the welfare state. At their most visible, formally institutional level, they should, on the contrary, be considered as groping and contradictory attempts, translated into massive material efforts, to come to grips with a perennial problem, opaquely perceived and distorted through the lens of deeply rooted cultural norms and moral prejudices. However, they can and should also be considered as the terrain on which mechanisms of interpersonal social relations of reciprocity were played out, not separate from but constitutive elements of a social order in which to give and to receive were necessary expression of clientelistic ties based on values of family, status, honour and deference.[41]   In this sense, given that such values knew no political boundaries but were common to western Europe, it is not surprising that their institutional expression should also have assumed a supranational character. The abundant literature on the institutional changes shows unequivocally the cosmopolitan character of each wave, moving across countries with often remarkable rapidity and similarity, evidence of an emulative spirit diffused rapidly through the circulation and translation of certain key works. It would be possible (albeit at a somewhat abstract intellectual level) to construct a history of charity in western Europe by interpreting the municipal reforms of the 1520s and 1530s through Juan Luis Vives's *De subventione pauperum* (1526), the state-backed *renfermement* of the 1690s–1720s through the Jesuit Father Guévarre's *La Mendicité abolie* (1693), and the nineteenth-century reversion to private charity, with the state as backcloth, through Joseph Marie De Gérando's *Le Visiteur du pauvre* (1820); each of these works was translated, adapted and plagiarized into all the major European languages and reprinted numerous times. It is in this sense that, however schematically, it seems legitimate and appropriate to discuss the institutional history of charity on a European rather than on a national level.

The first major reform of the charitable system from the 1520s to the 1540s was characterized by its strongly municipal nature and by a remarkable identity of aims and methods. The civic authorities took over responsibility for charity from the church, and attempted to centralize and rationalize resources, channelling them towards specific groups (especially minors), while ordering the expulsion of foreigners, prohibition of begging, restriction of the traditional acceptance of pilgrims and segregation of the able-bodied in workhouses. From Wittenberg in 1522 the movement spread through south and west German cities, through Flanders (where the Ypres statutes acted as prototype) to northern and western France (with the Lyons Aumône Général as model for all France), to Venice, Verona, Genoa and Bologna, mostly in the 1530s and 1540s; by the mid-sixteenth century similar centralizing structures had been adopted, at municipal and even state level, in Protestant Europe, in England (1531 and 1536 Poor Laws), Holland, Germany and Scandinavia. Historians have offered various explanations for this major shift from the multiple, fragmented and indiscriminate forms of charity provided by the church and funded by centuries of accumulated legacies to the would-be co-ordinated and highly discriminatory policies of the civic authorities. The ambitiously comprehensive quality of the change was certainly intimately related to the religious intensity of the two Reformations, Catholic and Protestant; its discriminatory character provided a common basis, identifiable in the shared hostility to beggars of the humanist Erasmus, the Catholic Vives and Luther himself. Recently it has been argued that the obligation to work, central to the reforms, was a practical disciplinary response of the authorities of the Flemish textile cities at a particular moment of shortage of unskilled labour, when the wage–price relationship was so negative that begging seemed a preferable alternative to the workers. At the same time, the new institutions were usually linked in an immediate fashion to dearth, with consequential high prices, pressure of rural migrants and threats to public order and public hygiene.[42]

The trend towards civic control or at least co-ordination of charitable bodies was to continue until the end of the *ancien régime*. It was particularly marked in northern and central Italy, where urban patriciates jealously protected their traditional influence, and in England, where the affirmation of strong central authority was dependent upon recognition of the local initiatives of justices of the peace. But even in seventeenth-century France the absolute state lacked the means to enforce its regulations over charity and begging and could do little more than delegate to the municipal authorities, while in Spain and its empire, including southern Italy, there was an embedded reluctance on the part of the state to intervene in activities regarded as properly appertaining to the church and civil society. Hence one can identify national variants in the pattern of institutional developments, related to the incapacity or unwillingness of the (central) state organs to intervene or impose their power. Indirectly throughout the early modern period, and directly at moments of emergency, the state was present, through such mechanisms as the regulation of wages, the marketing and pricing of grain, or measures to restrict vagabondage. But the history of charity, until the late eighteenth century, must be sought in the cities and among religiously inspired groups.

Some cities – Lyons, Venice, London, Norwich, Salisbury, Amsterdam – were to develop highly sophisticated structures of assistance for the poor, utilizing existing religious organizations or creating separate ones. Thus sixteenth-century Venice, perhaps the most successful example of co-ordination between state and voluntary organizations, structured a comprehensive system of relief around the *Scuole Grandi*, guilds and confraternities, supplemented by repressive regulations against vagabonds and compulsory taxation at times of pestilence.[43] Early seventeenth-century London, where prolonged residence was not in practice employed as a filter, like eighteenth-century Amsterdam or Odense, created a thick network of assistance comparable to that of our contemporary welfare state.[44] Knowledge and imitation of the innovations in these 'model' cities spread to other towns through a spirit of emulation. Thus the authorities of the Lyons Aumône Général gave advice to their peers elsewhere in France; a wave of new hospital foundations for beggars (*Mendicanti*) swept through northern and centtral Italian cities between 1575 and 1610; the municipal brewhouse set up at Salisbury in 1623 as a means of funding poor relief was seen as an example to be imitated by other towns in southern England.[45]

To separate civic activities from those of voluntary religious associations is artificial and historically false in the sixteenth and seventeenth centuries, for characteristic of the wave of new institutions and experiments is their religious inspiration. Pullan has argued convincingly about the impulse given by the Catholic Reformation to the sixteenth-century renovation of charity. Already before the Council of Trent devout laity in Italy turned to previously neglected groups, creating hospitals for the incurably sick, and responded to the diffusion of new diseases, such as syphilis, by the redeployment of disused leper settlements. The Tridentine church was characterized by what Pullan calls the 'new Catholicism', the creation by aggressive new religious orders of specialized institutions aimed at saving the souls of the living, whether repentant prostitute, converted Jew or idle beggar, by segregation for a period within an enclosed institution, in order to modify habits and outlook and so reintegrate those treated as outcasts in an industrious Christian society.[46]

What is striking in the multitude of new foundations of the sixteenth and early seventeenth centuries – and probably characteristic of the Mediterranean Christian societies – is the particular concern for female honour, whether of children, unmarried girls or married women. The operations of these female conservatories reveal the continuous intimate connections with the urban societies responsible for their creation. Institutions existed for women whose virtue was endangered by the absence of adequate family protection, as orphans, daughters of poor or indecorous parents, wives of vicious husbands, abandoned spouses or widows; indocile girls and wives could be enclosed against their will by relatives; victims of seduction could redeem themselves or at least give birth in decent secrecy; poor, virtuous, physically attractive girls (as the regulations of the Bologna Barraccano conservatory specified) could earn their (substantial) dowry by spending seven years in an institution. The aim was not to exclude these women from contact with society by segregation, as Foucault would argue – although care was taken within the institutions to separate the women by categories of purity and sexual knowledge – but to achieve their secure and willing reinsertion into society, on the one hand by instruction in practical skills and induction of deferential attitudes, on the other by identification of socially appropriate protective benefactors and reliable husbands in the civic society of orders outside their walls. To achieve this end, the conservatories were extremely flexible in the periods of time for which they were prepared to accept responsibility for their charges, from a few days or weeks to many years, or indefinitely in the case of girls for whom appropriate arrangements could not be made. In the course of the seventeenth and eighteenth centuries, in some Italian cities at least, these female conservatories would seem to have developed into an interlocking and co-ordinated municipal system, with girls and women moved between institutions according to requirements of protection, instruction, correction or space.[47]

Confraternities, both lay and religious, continued to extend the range of charitable activities throughout the seventeenth century, perhaps more in France than in Italy through the successful activities of St Vincent de Paul and, in the final decades, of the missionary Jesuits, fathers Guévarre, Chaurand and Dunod. But an identical religious fervour permeated the charitable activities of the Puritan magistrates of English towns in the first half of the seventeenth century and resulted in largely similar practices: expulsion of non-residents, assistance to deserving groups, obligatory work for able-bodied beggars as a moral and practical measure, to resist sin and acquire self-discipline; the major difference – clearly a consequence of the Protestant Reformation – would seem to be the absence of so elaborate a network of assistance as on the Continent. The tensions and conflicts resulting from the religious disputes in mid-century Puritan England, compared to the Counter-Reformation piety and uniformity of Catholic Europe, perhaps explain the earlier decline in England of the intensity of disciplinary powers over morals by the late seventeenth century noted by Valerie Pearl.[48]

The institutional experiences of the sixteenth and seventeenth centuries are remarkable in terms of the material and human investment they involved. Their records provide evidence of a generalized recognition among the ruling classes of a new scale of poverty, unprecedented pressure on resources and the exclusion of substantial groups from a social order ideologized as static. Not all cities grew at the same time, or at all; but growth could be substantial and rapid: Lyons increased from 50,000 to 70,000 (1500–50), Marseilles from 30,000 to 66,000 (1550–1650), London from 40,000 to 200,000 (1500–1600), Rome from 55,000 to 105,000 (1500–1600).[49] The new and remodelled institutions were the mechanisms which, it was believed, could absorb these pressures.

Underlying the experiences of the leading (and many minor) cities was the ideal of a 'total' system, requiring lay centralization and more extensive powers than hitherto. Thus the Lyons Aumône Général of the 1530s was responsible for hospitalizing the aged and infirm, training and apprenticing children, distributing outdoor relief to prisoners, the shamefaced and deserving poor, as well as disciplining beggars with its own beadles and prison.[50] The ideal was never realized and the comprehensive proposals rarely survived the practical experiences of the first years, not least because to translate such imaginative vision into an ongoing practical reality, after a much publicized debut, required resources disproportionate to the generosity of the citizens.

More substantial, particularly in Catholic Europe, was the complementary and cumulative effect of the religious and civic creation of specialized institutions through collective effort to assist specific sectors of the population identified as real or potential outcasts from the social order. The hospitals, hospices, confraternities, congregations and conservatories for the incurable and foundlings, the orphan and imperilled virgins, the foreign 'nations' and local shamefaced poor, the imprisoned and condemned, the endangered girls and widows, were the material product of a careful process of categorization and selection of individuals identified as requiring attachment to an institution prior to (or as a substitute for) membership of a social order.[51] The powers attributed to themselves by the authorities in order to achieve these ends could be extensive, from taxation of householders (an option rarely exercised outside England or Scandinavia), and summary judicial procedures, to forced removal of children from pauper families to apprentice or seclude them elsewhere.[52] The periods of protection could vary, from days or months to the entire span of infancy and puberty and even longer for girls. The constant purpose remained that of passive reinsertion into a Christian world of structured work and social orders.

It would be mistaken to interpret the intensity of institutional innovations in the sixteenth and seventeenth centuries as marking a rupture either in social attitudes towards the poor or in the social mechanisms by which charity operated. There is a constancy through the centuries in the diffuse conviction that the charitable act entailed a personal relationship between donor and recipient: acting as guarantor to the poor of the neighbourhood, the foundation of institutions to endow female descendants of the lineage, the payment of board and lodging of a specified individual in a hospice or conservatory, are all examples of a quintessentially personal view of charity.[53] There is a similar continuity, well into the nineteenth century (and, some would argue, much later) in the conviction that charity should not be allowed to vault the gulf between the ranks of a society of orders (or, subsequently, of a society based on wealth), but on the contrary should function as a reinforcement of the existing social order. The quality and quantity of charity was proportionate to the social level of the recipient, from the material living conditions within the institutions, or the repression of love affairs that ignored the social divide by reclusion of the lower-class woman in a conservatory, to the whole organization of assistance to the shamefaced poor.[54] The social mechanisms to achieve this end implied clear roles for both donor and recipient, structured around a nexus of individual selection; patronage, protection and mediation provided obligatory channels of access to charity, enhancing the social and even political position of the benefactors, while increasing the uncertainty and insecurity inherent in the normal working lives of the poor. The stability of the system was ensured by unremitting concern to uphold the moral and economic independence of the basic unit of society – the family. In this context, the institutions of charity played a dual role, not only to substitute for the absence of family (for orphans, the sick and aged, etc.), but to bolster the public reputation of individual families by offering physical locations in which scandal (particularly of a sexual nature) could be hidden. Far from the separation from society argued by Foucault, the very process of individual selection for admission and discharge from institutions – whose ideal function was to inculcate the traditional values of deferential submission – necessitated a constant interplay between the charities and all levels of local society. At most the institutional method provided symbolic evidence of a fastidious desire to remove those assisted through segregation, particularly if they appeared not to understand their role.

7 Vagrants and beggars

Vagrants and beggars provided the most visible and decried category of individuals apparently unwilling to be integrated. There were, of course, exceptions – the respectable incapacitated or octogenarians, who possessed a place within the social order, legitimated by formal licence; indeed in early seventeenth century Rome, the crippled and blind had formed their own guild, claiming a monopoly of begging in the city.[55] But by the seventeenth century the ambivalent attitude which had persisted since the middle ages and through most of the preceding century had been replaced by outright hostility, which was reflected directly in the image of the repulsive threatening beggar of a Callot or Caravaggio or the cheating rogue bands of Cervantes and *gueuserie* literature. The turning point would seem to coincide with the alarming abandonment of the countryside by the peasantry, in the 1590s in Italy, the 1620s in France. The solution, advocated everywhere and practised, with variants, for over three centuries, was to attempt to repress vagrancy and mendicity by enclosing and putting to work those caught begging without permission. Certainly no distinction can be made between Protestant and Catholic cities and states in this increasingly harsh treatment of beggars.

The policy of *renfermement* (enclosure) has attracted a considerable literature because of its multiple implications, practical, ideological and symbolic. Whether or not one agrees with Foucault's highly ideological insistence on the unbroken continuity of workhouses, asylums, prisons and factories, there can be little doubt about the symbolic significance attributed by contemporaries to segregation, played out in the ceremonial processions of children and beggars at the opening of each new institution. Indeed so rooted was segregation as a cultural response to poverty from the mid-sixteenth to the eighteenth century that it would seem to have been accepted voluntarily by families in distress at moments of crisis, who applied to enter the new beggars' hospital in Florence in 1621 and even the *dépôt de mendicité* in Genoa in 1811.[56] The *alberghi dei poveri*, striking architectural monuments constructed in the major Italian cities from 1560 to the late seventeenth century (at Bologna, Milan, Turin, Venice, Florence, Genoa, Naples), like their French equivalents of the seventeenth century, encapsulated the ambiguity of purpose, in which assistance and punishment were coupled within these hospital-prisons. For the massive buildings were not reserved exclusively for vagrants, but were conceived of as all-embracing general hospitals for the deserving categories of society (young, aged, sick and incapacitated), as well as the reprobate able-bodied. Indeed, until the end of the *ancien régime* these enclosed institutions were viewed by a patriarchal society as an ultimate sanction, to which unruly children or wives could be consigned temporarily, in a final admission of defeat by the head of household.[57]

Less clear was what was expected of these institutions. Work was always regarded as an essential requirement for all who were capable of it, not just in the great hospitals, but throughout the charitable system. This already created contradictions for a society of orders, as manual labour was degrading for poor nobles or the category of shamefaced, so requiring explicit exemption in their case.[58] But what work was expected to achieve shifted considerably in meaning. In the latter sixteenth century, labour contained a strong moral content because of its rehabilitating qualities, a means of counteracting and escaping from the sinful dangers of idleness. At the same time, especially in the seventeenth century, and more in England and France than in Italy, a mercantilist literature (in the writings of, for example, Matthew Hale and Laffémas) saw workhouses as the key to a utopian future of prosperity through the labour of segregated beggars increasing production of goods and so replacing imports, while also limiting loss of population through migration. By the late seventeenth century, with the renewed wave of *renfermement* successfully urged on French, Piedmontese, Tuscan and Papal cities by unflagging Jesuits, and exemplified in England by the houses of correction, the earlier quality of labour as the means to achieve redemption through self-discipline, had been overlaid by a far simpler and harsher approach where segregated work was primarily the appropriate instrument of punitive correction. The *dépôts de mendicité* of later eighteenth-century France and the Napoleonic years, like the English workhouse after the 1834 Poor Law, eliminated the religious-moral connotations of labour, replacing them with an illusory expectation of the possibility of self-balancing budgets through beggar's labour.

The ideal of work was perhaps inevitable in such highly commercialized societies, where direct state intervention or indirect support were regarded (until the eighteenth century) as occupying a central role. At the same time, it was riddled with ambiguities. On the technical side, the cost of materials and managerial and marketing inexperience compounded the physical infirmities, lack of skills, and psychological reluctance of the enclosed; in any case the inmates frequently were subjected to periods of *renfermement* as short as one month or less, destroying the continuity on which work discipline could be based.[59] The realities of the workhouse militated against the possibility of sophisticated processes of production or the fabrication of high quality goods. Hence the objects produced tended to be simple or limited to the earlier phases of the production process: hemp-spinning and weaving for textiles; nail production as metalwork, etc.). But the underlying problem was deeper and connected, in one form or another, to the relations between institutional production and the market. It is possible that in the eighteenth century work assumed a new importance within the buildings, as outside entrepreneurs saw in workhouse production a means of avoiding corporative restrictions or experimenting with new techniques. Certainly the municipal authorities, at least in silk centres (such as Lyons or Bologna), conceived of their large expensive institutions as a means to cushion local unemployment during trade crises, and hence were relectant to spend resources on enclosing unknown drifting vagrants.[60] But whether outside entrepreneurs were allowed to employ workhouse inmates as cheap labour, or the institutions provided temporary employment or paid skilled masters to train the children under their care, the result was to introduce distortions in what were already partially protected and imperfect labour markets and production lines, and arouse accusations of unfair competition from independent guild producers. 'Giving alms no charity and employing the poor a grievance to the nation', Defoe declaimed, adding his voice to what was a clamorous polemic, particularly during the eighteenth century.[61]

In reality, in only one respect – that of training the young – was employing the poor generally accepted as of advantage to the nation. But even here the charitable institutions were ambivalent, oscillating between provision of a skill (such as lacemaking) within the house, or sending out their wards to be apprenticed. Both routes were used in the constant attempt to provide the young with the technical training judged appropriate to survive economically once they left the institution; although we have no way of gauging their success, since the orphans vanished from the record on leaving the institution.

Renfermement production would seem generally not to have competed in the open market, but to have operated through a separate parallel semi-closed market mechanism, supplying the army, navy and other public institutions with part of their requirements (sails, uniforms, beds, etc.). In this context, bearing in mind their social obligations and costs, it could be worth calculating the economic returns of workhouse production by employing accountancy procedures analogous to those for present-day nationalized service industries.

Because of the symbolic significance of the organization of *renfermement* institutions as microcosms of capitalist production, the productive activities of these workhouses have attracted more attention in the literature than they merit economically. For viewed within the overall context of assistance to the poor, it seems likely – even in the heyday of *renfermement* – that far greater sums were spent by municipal and other authorities in procuring temporary unskilled work for the crisis poor, such as building or levelling fortifications or constructing roads.

8 Outdoor relief and social welfare

Until recent years, outdoor relief (*à domicile, a domicilio*) received far less attention in the literature than its institutionalized counterpart, perhaps because the archival sources for the latter are richer and generally more easily accessible. The exception was always England, where outdoor relief became the norm earlier and on a more continuous and widespread scale than anywhere on the Continent. Hence in England parish relief acted as the catalyst for the radical attack on charity which was to lead to the 1834 Poor Law (and which has long proved a fertile terrain for historical debate), whereas on the Continent it was the overall cluster of charitable institutions which were opposed by Enlightenment critics. The contrast is revealed clearly by a comparison of Sir Frederick Eden's *The State of the Poor* (1796) with Lodovico Ricci's *Riforma degli istituti pii della città di Modena* (1787).

To discuss outdoor and institutionalized assistance as if they were non-communicating sectors is, of course, artificial. Continental hospitals traditionally gave outdoor help, while English parishes would pay for hospitalization. The dowry for the pauper girl, that ubiquitous symbol of *ancien régime* charity, was to be found in both sectors. Above all, outdoor relief was complementary and not in opposition to institutionalized charity; indeed social linkages and networks functioned to reinforce the complementarity, with recipients of outdoor assistance, such as bread doles, the more likely to obtain a bed in old age.[62] Nevertheless, there were two essential differences. Firstly, the institutions existed to punish as well as to assist (according to their specializations), whereas recipients of outdoor relief were by definition meritorious. Secondly, outdoor relief existed in order to uphold directly the independence of the household (and hence the uniform willingness to redeem pawned tools), whereas the institutions proffered a mediated support or even an alternative to the family. The implication of these distinctions was that mechanisms existed in both sectors to identify the genuinely worthy. But for outdoor relief such mechanisms were applied by probably a more diffuse range of mediators – parish priests, confraternity officials, local notables, street spokesmen, overseers of the poor – whose criteria of merit were not homogeneous.[63] The resulting dispersion of judgement helps explain the stridulous criticism against such relief in societies structured around clientelistic relationships, perpetually gnawed by suspicions of deceit, and hence distrustful of any sign of charitable laxity.

Some categories were normally exempt from such criticisms, particularly aged widows and the shamefaced poor, who (when it is possible to identify them) would seem to have consisted mostly of women, especially widows.[64] In fact, irrespective of country or period, the categories identified as meriting relief are those one would expect in terms of the family cycle – the aged and islolated, families whose earning capacities were reduced either temporarily (through illness, interruption of employment or small children) or permanently (without a male head), and widows. The differences are to be found in the forms and organization of assistance.

Only in some Protestant countries, such as England, Holland and Denmark, was the wealthy minority forced by law more or less continuously to maintain the poor majority. In England, the great Elizabethan Poor Laws of 1598 and 1601 established a system of obligatory rates, assessed and exacted at the parish level, to support the poor; in eighteenth-century Denmark poor relief was financed by town rates and, at the end of the century, by excise and income tax. There could hardly be a greater contrast with the Catholic Continent, where in the Napoleonic years outdoor relief agencies were dependent on alms and a tax on theatre ticket sales.[65]

A consequence of this compulsory transfer of income was that the recipients might be assisted for as extensive a period as thirty years without interruption, although with variations in the amounts of money and other forms of relief they received. Research in recent years has illustrated in detail how, at its peak in the seventeenth century, the system functioned with remarkable flexibility and humanity in both countryside and town.[66] The prerequisites of this success were a degree of consensual authority at the parish level without parallel on the Continent, and a personal knowledge derived from topographical vicinity; in the City of London (although not in the newer, larger and less integrated extra-mural suburbs) the parishes rarely contained more than 200 houses, covering an area of 120 square yards.[67] By the later eighteenth century, population growth and economic change were fast destroying the consensual basis.

On the Continent, outdoor relief became more organized and widespread precisely in the eighteenth century. As in England its

33

efficacy was dependent on the reliability of local knowledge, and hence on the parish priest. It is difficult to compare these Continental experiences, as almost everywhere relief was not provided by public authorities but by charitable organizations; in consequence, whereas the records of the English or Danish poor-relief agencies relate to the entire population of a delimited area, the parish, their Continental equivalents were usually only concerned with a highly specific sector or group of the population but normally (in towns) with responsibilities for areas greater than a single parish. In Amsterdam, as in Denmark, there seems to have been a system of outdoor relief comparable to the English one, indeed with a form of wage supplementation calculated by family needs similar to the notorious Speenhamland system.[68] Elsewhere the fact that outdoor assistance remained structured around voluntary organizations (albeit supported partly by state funds) implied relief only over the short term.

Outdoor relief was attacked wherever it assumed an appearance of regularity as corruptive and demoralizing. Even in cases when it was accepted as necessary (to avoid death by starvation), as at Genoa in 1594, care was taken to spell out that a bare minimum should be given, lest the recipient become a 'good-for-nothing'.[69] By the late eighteenth century radical critics claimed that the existence of relief increased the numbers of poor – a rationally cloaked repeat of the sixteenth-century accusations, based on the moral assumption that the able-bodied poor were naturally idle, unless forced by necessity to work. In fact, what little evidence we have on England, Amsterdam and Odense, from the mid-seventeenth to the mid-eighteenth centuries, leaves little doubt that outdoor relief never represented more than a proportion, usually varying between a fifth and a third, of the contemporaneous earnings of an employed male labourer.[70] The harshness of late eighteenth- and early nineteenth-century attitudes, in England as much as on the Continent, was a logical development of the Enlightenment faith in utility tempering humanitarianism. Philanthropy and *bienfaisance* (a term introduced by the abbé de Saint-Pierre in the early eighteenth century) were necessarily discriminatory if they were to be useful and effective. In consequence, the whole concept of outdoor relief, while not destroyed,

34

underwent drastic revision which was to characterize its application until the later nineteenth century. A striking feature of this development was the increasingly important role of the state, which assumed a new centrality in a variety of ways: as repressive agent of the ill-intentioned and idle; as ultimate patron of the genuinely needy, preferably as guarantor of employment possibilities, occasionally as direct provisioner of public works (as in the *ateliers de charité*); as collectors of information about the poor. It is not accidental that our sources become particularly rich in the eighteenth century, but is a direct consequence of the recognition that the problem of the poor was properly within the purview of the state. In Protestant countries, such recognition had come much earlier, already in the sixteenth century, and, where backed by strong state authority, had led to the utilization of lower ecclesiastical personnel to collect demographic information and the authorization of compulsory taxation. On the Continent, only with that late eighteenth-century cult of useful knowledge, in which statistics were to provide a reasoned basis for official action, were enquiries at a range of levels (within the dioceses as well as by lay authorities) and collection of quantifiable information to develop, until they became the hallmark of Continental poor policy, culminating in the strongly humanitarian Revolutionary Committee of Mendicity. Bentham, in his writings on the poor, constantly lamented the absence of such quantifiable information in England, which only began to be collected and discussed by the statistical societies in the mid-nineteenth century.[71]

This enhanced role of the state was to lead to notable and, in the nineteenth century, highly influential debates about the proper relationship between public and private charity. On the Continent, as in so many fields, Revolutionary and especially Napoleonic legislation accentuated the direct responsibility of the state, not merely to provide repressive institutions (*dépôts de mendicité*, prisons), but to control that other pole of the welfare system, outdoor relief. But even in England regulation of the poor became the specific issue over which state intervention was to be legitimated, with the powers over local authorities entrusted to central bureaucrats by the 1834 Poor Law.

Private philanthropy or *bienfaisance* was to assume renewed respectability, particularly after the fall of Napoleon and the passing of the English Poor Law, with the swing away from excessive government and the recognition of the inevitable existence of poverty in economically and socially mobile societies. The degree of withdrawal by public authorities varied from state to state – far more in Piedmont than in Austrian Lombardy,[72] greater in England than in France. For philanthropists such as De Gérando, the most influential Continental writer on *bienfaisance* of the Restoration, the apparent scientific inevitability of pauperism propounded by the Malthusians needed to be combated as unacceptable to Christian morality. But already by the end of the eighteenth century private *bienfaisance* had absorbed the lessons of the Enlightenment in its accentuated concern to distinguish true from false indigence and to modernize philanthropy by the application of useful science to the problems of the poor. It is significant that the only Continental experience to interest English philanthropists, such as Sir Thomas Bernard, was that of Rumford, with his economic recipes and heating methods for the needy. De Gérando was obsessed with the need to identify the truly poor from the false, but also not to allow the level or forms of charity to discourage the recipient from work.[73] The method by which this was to be achieved was the classic one of a direct and personal relationship between the two parties, a fusion of Christian charity and patronage. De Gérando was concerned with the recipients of charity, of whom he had a strongly traditional vision; but although he did not offer any social definition of the benefactors, his entire argument, framed within the context of a highly commercial and partly industrialized society, pointed towards a major social change in the charitable field – the particular role of the middle-class wife.[74] Personal visits to the homes of the poor, as to prisoners, was to characterize *bienfaisance* in the nineteenth century, from De Gérando to Octavia Hill and the Charity Organization Society, in an effort to render philanthropy selectively effective, while encouraging the principle of self-help.

The shift away from this emphasis on the individual rather than the category, on voluntary charity rather than state aid, which occurred in the last quarter of the nineteenth century, remains in good part to be explored in detail, particularly on the Continent. The evidence of pauperization accompanying the unprecedented economic changes from the 1840s needs little emphasis. On the Continent, traditional forms of charity, such as dowries or bread doles, began to be recognized as irrelevant to a transformed context of poverty.[75] In England, the massive exclusion from outdoor relief of able-bodied men (by the 1850s a mere 7000 were assisted, compared to perhaps 100,000 in 1800), followed by an almost missionary drive against all out-relief after 1870,[76] must have highlighted increasingly the total inadequacy of private philanthropy.

Any study of the reasons for the emergence of the social welfare policies of the late nineteenth century would contain a checklist including at least the following: the appalling living standards of the poor, in terms of housing, clothing and diet, revealed ever more systematically in the accumulation of information, from the private 'moral statistics' of the 1830s and 1840s to the official policing of public hygiene that accompanied urban expansion through the century; the topographical segregation resulting from the growth of the suburbs and social dislocation of domicile and casual work in the slum quarters of the great cities, which rendered impractical the earlier assumptions of personal relationships; the social realities documented in the investigations of a Booth or a Jacini; the uncomfortable realization of the high mobility and real or potential class basis of the excluded; the articulation of new demands through trade unions and socialist parties. Once the case for social reform had been accepted, from the 1880s, public policy was directed on the one hand towards the provision of obligatory insurance schemes, on the other towards regulation and bureaucratization of casual labour. It is not difficult to link this dual path of public action with the structural historical causes of poverty – phases of the life-cycle and job opportunities. Insurance offered an effective if inadequate cushion against the disastrous consequences of accident, sickness or, especially, old age; casual labour marked the lower end of that continuum of uncertain employment which characterized the broad stratum of independent labouring families, prone to fall temporarily into poverty. In this sense, welfare policies – following the analyses of (usually unofficial) investigators such as

37

Booth and Rowntree in England – responded at least approximately to the historical realities of poverty, above all to an awareness of the inadequacies and often the inappropriateness of the family as a universal panacea.

9 Attitudes of the poor towards their condition

Many problems in so vast and amorphous a subject as the history of poverty and the poor remain to be explored: perhaps the most prominent, and probably the most difficult, is how the poor viewed poverty, charity and *bienfaisance*. For charity has never been neutral, but has mediated social relations. The unrelenting moral pressure of benefactors has interposed thick layers of ideological preferences and prejudices between the poor and the historian. Nineteenth-century concepts of respectability still permeate our attitudes towards dependence on charity.

The difficulties of casting the poor as the subjects rather than the object of any study of poverty do not merely derive from the hackneyed observation that, historically, they do not often speak. There is the subtler problem of the recurrent identity of poor and labouring classes: precisely because the condition of being poor was experienced by an unquantifiable but substantial proportion of the labouring classes (and modern working class), and the possibility of such an experience was always present, it is tempting to subsume the culture of poverty into that of popular culture. Undoubtedly, poverty was a central theme of early modern popular culture, exemplified in the imagery of the 'world turned upside down' or the *paese di Cuccagna* stories. But there is a specificity about the poor – those whose experiences were predominantly of poverty – which escapes the historian. At best it is possible to approach the poor through the solidarity expressed on occasion by the labourers and housewives who felt closest to their condition – the tacit acceptance of petty rural theft, the defence of the beggar against arrest. At moments of crisis it is possible to go further, as in the women-led grain riots, which combined a worried awareness of poverty with the expectations of E.P. Thompson's 'moral economy'. But we have no means of knowing whether such incidents represented a general attitude, or whether the mobility of so many of the poor did not normally work against the solidarity of resident labouring families.

At another level, it is as difficult and even deceptive to identify an autonomous culture of the poor, in the sense of their acceptance of the values of the dominant society. It is anachronistic to assume that the tradition of proud independence of working-class families, so characteristic of the late nineteenth century, existed in earlier periods, given the almost symbolic relationship of this tradition with Victorian values: the social functions of charity. There is no reason to believe that the shame associated with recourse to charity dates back earlier than the mid-nineteenth century, when public opinion decried public charity except as a corrective and humiliating mechanism. In earlier centuries the social functions of charitable institutions argue in favour of a different attitude on the part of the poor, legitimated by the expectations of the donors. In this context charity formed part of the moral economy, something to be expected as of right by the poor, in times of difficulty or phases of the life-cycle – as with the reluctant deposit of babies and even small children in foundling hospitals, or the assumption that in old age one is entitled to relief.[77] Indeed, charity could become an important or even regular source of income for the poor, not just the fraudulent beggars of picaresque or Dickensian memory, but of respectable families cornering the market of wet nursing or artisan bachelors passing the test to marry a well-endowed, physically attractive and institutionally protected girl.[78] But if recourse to charity could be regarded as a legitimate and normal activity by the poor, access to its resources remained limited to those with the requisite knowledge and contacts; the webs of mediation that enveloped all charitable activities operated effective social discrimination within the protean world of the poor.

Poverty should thus be understood not only as a stark reality, but as a social construct. Because poverty formed an intrinsic part of the daily experience of labouring families, in the sense of a constant awareness of the possibility of a decline from being poor to indigence, it was inextricably linked to a sense of insecurity. As a social construct, poverty was dependent on this insecurity, in the sense that benefactors and philanthropists structured and mediated their assistance to the poor through an implicit identification of insecurity with the means to ensure appropriate comportment on the part of the poor. For charity, while always regarded as necessary, never gave the recipient an automatic right. Over the centuries, the methods adopted to assist the poor varied – from indiscriminate almsgiving to *renfermement* to face-to-face relationships – but the finality remained the same: to ensure deferential acceptance of the existing social order.

Notes

I wish to think Paul Ginsborg, Daniela Lombardi, Alan Milward and John Walter for their valuable comments on an earlier draft of this chapter.

1 A. Sinfield, *The Long-Term Unemployed. A Comparative Survey*, Paris, 1968.

2 R.M. Titmuss, 'The social division of welfare', in his *Essays on the Welfare State*, London, 1958; B. Abel-Smith and P. Townsend, *The Poor and the Poorest*, London, 1965; A.B. Atkinson, *Poverty in Britain and the Reform of Social Security*, Cambridge 1969; A.B. Atkinson, *The Economics of Inequality*, Cambridge, 1983; P. Townsend (ed.), *The Concept of Poerty*, London, 1970; R. Walker, R. Lawson and P. Townsend (eds), *Responses to Poverty: Lessons from Europe*, London, 1984.

3 R.M. Smith, 'The structured dependence of the elderly as a recent development: some sceptical historical thoughts', *Ageing and Society*, 4 (1984), pp. 415, 422–3.

4 L. Syson and M. Young, 'Poverty in Bethnal Green', in M. Young (ed.), *Poverty Report 1974*, London, 1974; J. Higgins, *The Poverty Business. Britain and America*, Oxford and London, 1978, p. 104; M. Orshansky, *Counting the Poor: Another Look at the Poverty Profile*, Washington, n.d. (*c.* 1966).

5 See, for example, the reports of Shelter; or, for Paris – a striking instance in recent years – *Le Monde*, 23 and 25–6 November 1984; 'Comment identifier un peuple sans connaître son histoire', *Quart monde igloos* (1978), pp. 99–100; *Primo rapporto alla Presidenza del Consiglio dei Ministri*, Rome, 1985.

6 O. Lewis, *Five Families; Mexican Case Studies in the Culture of Poverty*, New York, 1959; P. Camporesi (ed.), *Il libro dei vagabondi*, Turin, 1973.

7 B. Jordan, *Poor Parents. Social Policy and the 'Cycle of Deprivation'*, London, 1974, pp. 38–42, for examples of refusal of benefits through judgements of 'voluntary unemployment' or cohabitation out of marriage.

8 A. Sen, 'Issues in the measurement of poverty', *Scandinavian Journal*

of Economics, 81 (1979), pp. 285–307; W. Beckerman, 'The measurement of poverty', in T. Riis (ed.), *Aspects of Poverty in Early Modern Europe*, Florence, 1981, pp. 47–63.

9 A.B. Atkinson, A.K. Maynard and C.G. Trinder, *Parents and Children: Incomes in Two Generations*, London, 1983.

10 P. Slack, 'Poverty and politics in Salisbury 1597–1666', in P. Clarke and P. Slack (eds), *Crisis and Order in English Towns 1500–1700*, London, 1972, pp. 166, 176.

11 See Chapter 4 in this volume, 'The reliability of Napoleonic statistics'; D. Maldini, 'Pauperismo e mendicità a Torino nel periodo napoleonico', *Studi Piemontesi*, 8 (1979).

12 J.P. Gutton, *La Société et les pauvres. L'exemple de la généralité de Lyon 1534–1789*, Lyons, 1971, p. 53; B.S. Pullan, 'Poveri, mendicanti e vagabondi (secoli XIV–XVII)', *Storia d'Italia. Annali I, Dal feudalesimo al capitalismo*, Turin, 1978, pp. 988–97; S. Russo, 'Potere pubblico e carità privata. L'assistenza ai poveri a Lucca tra XVI e XVII secolo', *Società e storia*, 23 (1984), pp. 67–8.

13 B.H. Slicher van Bath, *The Agrarian History of Western Europe*, London, 1963; W. Abel, *Agricultural Fluctuations in Europe from the Thirteenth to the Twentieth Centuries*, London, 1980; G. Giorgetti, *Contadini e proprietari nell'Italia moderna. Rapporti di produzione e contratti agrari dal secolo XVI a oggi*, Turin, 1974, chs 1–6; C. Lis and H. Soly, *Poverty and Capitalism in Pre-Industrial Europe*, Hassocks, 1979, pp. 54–63, 97–104, 131–44; O.H. Hufton, *The Poor of Eighteenth-Century France, 1750–1789*, Oxford, 1974, pp. 21–4.

14 Gutton, *La Société et les pauvres*, p. 335.

15 Pullan, *Poveri, mendicanti e vagabondi*, p. 994.

16 J. Bentham, unpublished 'Essays on the Poor Laws', 1796, cited in J.R. Poynter, *Society and Pauperism. English Ideas on Poor Relief, 1795–1834*, London, 1969, p. 119. The distinction was a common one by the end of the eighteenth century, adopted by Patrick Colquhoun and again by the Royal Commissioners on the Poor Laws in 1832–4.

17 For a stong statement of this relationship, see Lis and Soly, *Poverty and Capitalism*; also R.G. Wilkinson, *Progress and Poverty*, London, 1973.

18 B. Geremek, *Le Salariat dans l'artisanat parisien aux XIIIe–XVe siècles*, The Hague and Paris, 1968, pp. 83–90; Gutton, *La Société et les pauvres*, p. 73; D. Sella, *Salari e lavoro nell'edilizia lombarda durante il secolo XVII*, Pavia, 1968, pp. 19–20; Pullan, *Poveri, mendicanti e vagabondi*, pp. 1027–8. A useful summary on wages and consumption, and especially on the processes of pauperization as a direct consequence of the capitalist economy can be found in Lis and Soly, *Poverty and Capitalism*.

19 Hufton, *The Poor of Eighteenth-Century France*, p. 76.

20 N. McKendrick, 'Home demand and economic growth: a new view of the role of women and children in the industrial revolution', in N. McKendrick (ed.), *Historical Perspectives: Studies in English Thought and Society*, London, 1974, p. 186, cited in D. Levine, 'Industrialization and the proletarian family in England', *Past and Present*, 107 (1985), p. 184. The enquiries of the 1830s and 1840s into child employment in England, Lombardy and elsewhere confirm the general character of the phenomenon in the early phases of mechanized production. One of the basic arguments of the proto-industrial 'school', advanced by F. Mendels and H. Medick, is the self-conscious organization of all members of the family as an economic unit.

21 R.T. Rapp, *Industry and Economic Decline in Seventeenth-Century Venice*, Cambridge, Mass., 1976.

22 Hufton, *The Poor of Eighteenth-Century France*, pp. 91, 105.

23 Gutton, *La Société et les pauvres*, p. 79; Gutton, *Domestiques et serviteurs dans la France de l'ancien régime*, Paris, 1981; Hufton, *The Poor of Eighteenth-Century France*, pp. 28–33.

24 Gutton, *La Société et les pauvres*, pp. 66–9; Hufton, *The Poor of Eighteenth-Century France*, pp. 19, 58–62.

25 C.M. Cipolla, *Before the Industrial Revolution*, London, 1976, pp. 35–6; Gutton, *La Société et les pauvres*, pp. 73–5.

26 R.M. Smith, 'Transfer incomes, risk and security: the roles of the family and the collectivity in recent theories of fertility changes', in *Forward from Malthus; the State of Population Theory in 1984*, Conference of the British Society for Population Studies, Cambridge, 1984; C.M. Cipolla, 'The plague and the pre-Malthus Malthusians', *Journal of European Economic History*, 3 (1974).

27 E.A. Wrigley and R.S. Schofield, *The Population History of England, 1541–1871*, London, 1981; T.P.R. Laslett and R. Wall (eds.), *Household and Family in Past Times*, Cambridge, 1972; L.K. Berkner, 'The use and misuse of census data for the historical analysis of family structure', *Journal of Interdisciplinary History*, 5 (1975); J. Goody, J. Thirsk and E.P. Thompson (eds), *Family and Inheritance: Rural Society in Western Europe 1200–1800*, Cambridge, 1976.

28 C.A. Corsini, 'Materiali per lo studio della famiglia in Toscana nei secoli XVII–XIX: gli esposti', *Quaderni storici*, 33 (1976); L. Dodi Osnaghi, 'Ruota e infanzia abbandonata a Milano nella prima metà dell'Ottocento', in G. Politi, M. Rosa and F. Della Peruta (eds), *Timore e carità. I poveri nell'Italia moderna*, Cremona, 1982; R.K. McClure, *Coram's Children: the London Foundlings Hospital in the Eighteenth Century*, New Haven, 1981; Hufton, *The Poor of Eighteenth-Century France*, pp. 26–36; Gutton, *Domestiques*; A.S. Kussmaul, *Servants in Husbandry in Early Modern England*, Cambridge, 1981; F. Doriguzzi, 'I messaggi dell'abbandono: bambini esposti a Torino nel '700', *Quaderni storici*, 53 (1983), pp. 445–66.

29 C. Klapisch, 'Household and family in Tuscany in 1427', in Laslett and Wall, *Household and Family in Past Times*; Gutton, *La Société et les pauvres*, p. 55; Slack, 'Poverty and politics'; Chapter 7 in this volume, 'Charity, poverty and household structure'; B.S. Rowntree, *Poverty: a Study of Town Life*, London, 1901.

30 R.M. Smith, 'Some issues concerning family and property', in R.M. Smith (ed.), *Land, Kinship and Life Cycle*, Cambridge, 1984; Smith, 'Transfer income'; Smith, 'Structured dependence'.

31 K. Wrightson and D. Levine, *Poverty and Piety in an English Village: Terling, 1525–1700*, London, 1979; Wrightson, *English Society 1580–1680*, London, 1982, pp. 44–57; A. Macfarlane, *The Origins of English Individualism: the Family, Property and Social Transition*, Oxford, 1978.

32 I wish to thank Professor H.C. Johansen for this information, resulting from enquiries by the Odense probate and Poor Law authorities. All following references to Denmark are also based on seminars given by Prof. Johansen at the European University Institute in October 1985; some comments on the Hamburg and Danish Poor Law philosophies in H.C. Johansen, 'J.G. Büsch's economic theory and his influence on the Danish economic and social debate', *Scandinavian Economic History Review*, 14 (1966), pp. 25–5, 36–7.

33 G. Politi, 'Introduzione' to M. Fantarelli, *L' Istituzione dell' Ospedale di S. Alessio dei poveri mendicanti in Cremona (1569–1600)*, Cremona, 1981, pp. xiii–xvi.

34 L. Fontaine, *Le Voyage et la mémoire. Colporteurs de l' Oisans au XIXe siècle*, Lyons, 1984; see chapter 7 in this volume, 'Charity, poverty and household structure', p. 166.

35 M. Mollat, *Etudes sur l' histoire de la pauvreté*, Paris, 1974; M. Mollat, *Les Pauvres au moyen âge*, Paris, 1978.

36 B. Geremek, 'Il pauperismo nell'età preindustriale (secoli XIV–XVIII)', *Storia d'Italia*, vol. 5:1, *I Documenti*, Turin, 1973, pp. 673–84. L. Febvre saw intolerance of the mendicant orders and the cult of work in capitalist-minded merchants as a cause of the Reformation: 'Une question mal posée: les origines de la Réforme française et le problème général des causes de la Réforme', *Revue historique*, 161 (1929).

37 T. Pini, *De Cerretanorum origine eorumque fallaciis* (1485), partly published about 1585, now in Camporesi, *Libro dei vagabondi*; B. Geremek, *Truands et misérables dans l'Europe moderne, 1350–1600*, Paris, 1980.

38 B.S. Pullan, *Rich and Poor in Renaissance Venice. The Social Institutions of a Catholic State, to 1620*, Oxford, 1971, pp. 197–215; W.K. Jordan, *Philanthropy in England, 1480–1660*, London, 1959; Gutton, *La Société et les pauvres*, pp. 257–61; M. Dubini, '"Padroni di niente". Povertà e assistenza a Como tra medioevo e età moderna', in

Politi, Rosa and Della Peruta (eds), *Timore e carità*; J. Imbert, *Les Hôpitaux en France*, Paris, 1958.

39 Hufton, *The Poor in Eighteenth-Century France*, pp. 226–30; Gutton, *La Société et les pauvres*, pp. 120, 285, 359.

40 G. Ricci, 'Povertà, vergogna e povertà vergognosa', *Società e storia*, 5 (1979), pp. 333–5.

41 For an important set of studies in this direction, see the special number of *Quaderni storici*, 53 (1983): 'Sistemi di carità: esposti e internati nella società di antico regime', edited by E. Grendi.

42 B.S. Pullan, 'Catholics and the poor in early modern Europe', *Transactions of the Royal Historical Society*, 26 (1976); M. Fatica, 'Il "De subventione pauperum" di J.L. Vives: suggestioni luterane o mutamento di una mentalità collettiva?', *Società e Storia*, 15 (1982); Gutton, *La Société et les pauvres*, pp. 231–51.

43 Pullan, *Rich and Poor*; F. Meneghetti Casarin, 'La repressione dei vagabondi alla fine del XVIII secolo: il caso della Repubblica di Venezia', *Società e storia*, 18 (1982).

44 V. Pearl, 'Social policy in early modern London', in H. Lloyd Jones, V. Pearl and B. Worden (eds), *History and Imagination. Essays in Honour of H.R. Trevor-Roper*, London, 1981; V. Pearl, 'Change and stability in seventeenth-century London', *London Journal*, 5 (1979); M. Van Leeuwen and F. Smits, 'Steunverlening en steuntrekkers in Amsterdam, ca. 1770–1800', *Skript*, 4 (1982).

45 Gutton, *La Société et les pauvres*, pp. 256–77, 275–84; Pullan, *Rich and Poor*, pp. 362–3; Slack, 'Poverty and politics', p. 22.

46 Pullan, 'The Old Catholicism, the new Catholicism and the poor', in Politi, Rosa and Della Peruta (eds), *Timore e carità*; Pullan, 'Catholics and the poor'.

47 D. Lombardi, 'L'Ospedale dei Mendicanti nella Firenze del Seicento. "Da inutile serraglio dei mendici a conservatorio e casa di forza per le donne"', *Società e storia*, 24 (1948), pp. 293–30; S. Cavallo, 'Strategie politiche e familiari intorno al baliatico. Il monopolio dei bambini abbandonati nel Canavese tra Sei e Settecento', *Quaderni storici*, 53 (1983); L. Ciammitti, 'Quanto costa essere normali. La dote nel conservatorio femminile di Santa Maria del Barraccano (1630–1680)', *Quaderni storici*, 53 (1983); L. Ferrante, 'L'onore ritrovato. Donne nella Casa del Soccorso di San Paolo a Bologna (sec. XVI–XVII)', *Quaderni storici*, 53 (1983).

48 Pearl, 'Change and stability', p. 25.

49 J. De Vries, *European Urbanization 1500–1800*, London, 1984, Appendix 1. Urbanization was a complex and contradictory process, which witnessed a drastic shift away from the Mediterranean to north-west Europe in the first half of the seventeenth century. The figures I have chosen somewhat arbitrarily are merely intended to highlight infrastructural problems where urban populations increased rapidly.

50 Gutton, *La Société et les pauvres*, pp. 275–84.
51 M. Rosa, 'Chiesa, idee sui poveri e assistenza in Italia dal cinque al settecento', *Società e storia*, 10 (1980), p. 782; E. Grendi, 'Ideologia della carità e società indisciplinata: la costruzione del sistema assistenziale genovese (1470–1670)', in Politi, Rosa and Della Peruta (eds), *Timore e carità*, *passim*.
52 Gutton, *La Société et les pauvres*, pp. 256–7, 275–9, 388–93; T. Wales, 'Poverty, poor relief and the life cycle', in Smith (ed.), *Land, Kinship and Life Cycle*, p. 376; D. Lombardi, 'L'Ospedale dei Mendicanti'.
53 G. Biagioli, 'Analisi di alcune fonti toscane: catasti, statistiche, censimenti', forthcoming in *Mélanges de l'Ecole Française de Rome*; G. Delille, 'Un esempio di assistenza privata: i monti di maritaggio nel Regno di Napoli (secoli XVI–XVIII)', in Politi, Rosa and Della Peruta (eds), *Timore e carità*; Ferrante, 'L'onore ritrovato', pp. 504–5.
54 Lombardi, 'Ospedale dei Mendicanti', pp. 296–7, 300; Ciammitti, 'Quanto costa essere normali', pp. 469–70; for the shamefaced, see n. 36 to this chapter.
55 L. Cajani, 'Gli statuti della Compagnia dei ciechi, zoppi e stroppiati della Visitazione (1698)', *Richerche per la storia religiosa di Roma*, 3 (1979).
56 D. Lombardi, 'Poveri a Firenze. Programmi e realizzazioni della politica assistenziale dei Medici tra cinque e seicento', in Politi, Rosa and Della Peruta (eds), *Timore e carità*, pp. 177–8; G. Assereto, 'Aspetti dell'assistenza pubblica a Genova nei primi anni dell'ottocento', in Politi, Rosa and Della Peruta (eds), *Timore e carità*, p. 355.
57 Gutton, *La Société et les pauvres*, pp. 343–9; Russo, 'Potere pubblico e carità privata', p. 47.
58 G.F. Riva de San Nazario, *De peste libri tres* (1522), cited in Fatica, 'Il "De subventione pauperum"', pp. 18–19.
59 Grendi, 'Ideologia della carità, pp. 73–4; M.A. Crowther, *The Workhouse System*, London, 1981.
60 Gutton, *La Société et les pauvres*, pp. 458–9; M. Marcolin, *The 'Casa d'Industria' in Bologna During the Napoleonic Period: Public Relief and Subsistence Strategies*, E.U.I. Working Paper no. 85/132, Florence, 1985.
61 D. Defoe, *Giving alms no charity and employing the poor a grievance to the nation . . .*, London, 1704.
62 See, for example, Gutton, *La Société et les pauvres*, p. 38.
63 Grendi, 'Ideologia della carità', p. 73.
64 Gutton, *La Société et les pauvres*, pp. 25–6.
65 Information on the Copenhagen Poor Law of 1799 (extended to other Danish cities in 1802–3) from Prof. J.C. Johansen; for the Napoleonic *bureau de bienfaisance*, see chapter 3 in this volume, 'The treatment of the poor', pp. 86–93.

66 Pearl, 'Social policy'; Pearl, 'Change and stability'; Slack, Poverty and politics'; Wales, 'Poverty, poor relief'; W. Newman Brown, 'The receipt of poor relief and family situation in Aldenham, Hertfordshire 1630–1690', in Smith (ed.), *Land, Kinship, Life Cycle*.

67 Pearl, 'Change and stability', pp. 7–8, 15–16.

68 Van Leeuwen and Smits, 'Steunverlening'.

69 Grendi, 'Ideologia della carità', p. 68.

70 Smith, 'Some issues', p. 75; Pearl, 'Social policy', p. 131; Wales, 'Poverty, poor relief', p. 176; Van Leeuwen and Smits, 'Steunverlening', pp. 48–51.

71 Hufton, *The Poor of Eighteenth-Century France*, pp. 2–3, 6–7; A. Forrest, *The French Revolution and the Poor*, Oxford, 1981, pp. 23–7; Poynter, *Society and Pauperism*, pp. 129–30.

72 M. Piccialuti Caprioli, 'Il "sistema della beneficenza pubblica" nel Piemonte preunitario', in Politi, Rosa and Della Peruta (eds), *Timore e carità*.

73 Poynter, *Society and Pauperism*, pp. 87–98; J.B. De Gérando, *Le Visiteur du pauvre*, Paris, 1820, especially the third edition of 1826; J.B. de Gérando, *De la bienfaisance publique*, Brussels, 1839.

74 C. Hall, 'The active age of charity: men, women and philanthropy, 1780–1850', unpublished working paper, University of Essex, October 1980.

75 L Passerini, *Storia degli stabilimenti di beneficenza e d'istruzione elementare gratuita della città di Firenze*, Florence, 1853, pp. 91–2.

76 K. Williams, *From Pauperism to Poverty*, London, 1981, pp. 41–2, 71, 75–6, 96–7, 102–3.

77 Doriguzzi, 'I messaggi dell'abbandono', *passim*; Wales, 'Poverty, poor relief', p. 388.

78 Cavallo, 'Strategie politiche', pp. 403–17; Ciammitti, 'Quanto costa essere normali', pp. 482–8.

2

The poor, proto-industrialization and the working class: Italy (sixteenth to nineteenth centuries)

Research on the history of social classes has tended increasingly to 'disaggregate', as it were, the broad categories defined by Marx by concentrating on specific groups or levels. The most obvious example is that of the 'bourgeoisie', whose comprehensive but sometimes elusive and often ambiguous character has been reduced to handier categories of historical analysis by study, in limited periods, of some of its component albeit overlapping elements, such as (for example) the skilled artisans, petty bourgeoisie, merchant capitalists or industrial entrepreneurs. Within the broad ranks of the subordinate classes, a conventional distinction, usually employed chronologically as marking the advent and diffusion of industrial capitalism, is that between the 'labouring classes' and the 'working class'. Indeed, the relationship between the two and the transformation of the former into the latter has offered (naturally enough in contemporary industrial society) an apparently inexhaustible goldseam to the historical profession. I would suggest that such studies can be misleading and are sometimes distorting, because of the anachronistic presuppositions that derive from a teleological vision of the formation of the working class, which risks reading history backwards from the age of industrial capitalism (the chronology and physiognomy of which in any case varies considerably in each nation-state).

In this so-called post-industrial age of unemployment and the hidden economy, it is perhaps not surprising that a unilinear process of affirmation of a self-conscious antagonistic working class should no longer be accepted so unquestioningly. The historiographical shift from the institutional structures to the social composition of the working class, from the factory to the residential community of the worker, is indicative of a different, deeper and perhaps less confident approach. In like manner, to study the history of the poor over a period of some centuries, from the early modern era into the age of industrialization, even in the context of a single country, inevitably offers a different perspective and provokes a range of doubts, questions and hypotheses. Who were the poor, did their composition change over the long period and, if so, in what ways? What were their relationships with, and influence upon, the 'labouring classes' and, later, the 'working class'?

At the risk of offering not one but several hostages to fortune, I wish to argue various propositions which (hopefully) may at least arouse discussion of some current orthodoxies. To state them baldly, there are three such propositions, of which one at least does not seem to me very controversial: there was a long-term increase in the scale of poverty and numbers of poor in Italy, directly connected to (although not exclusively the consequence of) structural changes in the Italian economy. My second proposition is that the permanence and ubiquity of the presence of the poor, and above the range of their responses to their condition – before, during and after the formation of an industrial proletariat – throw doubt on any simplistic identification between the poor and the modern working class or assumption of a linear passage from the former to the latter. Finally, I wish to argue that the reality of the presence of the poor and the awareness of their presence on the part of both élites and the poor themselves, make it possible and useful to consider and study the poor in their own right as a distinguishable if fluctuating social category.

Before embarking on so foolhardy an enterprise, it may be useful to clear the ground by a brief look at Marx's position *vis-à-vis* the poor. Marx did not deny their existence. In fact, in one section of *Capital*, he analysed their composition, breaking them down into four categories, one belonging to 'the sphere of pauperism' and three to that of 'relative surplus population'.[1] In a characteristically telling phrase, he summed up pauperism as 'the hospital of the active labour-army and the dead weight of the industrial reserve army'.[2] Following many economists of the later Enlightenment and turn of the century, Marx also stressed the integral link between increase of wealth and growth of pauperism, defining the latter as 'the absolute general law of capitalist accumulation':[3] the poor existed and their numbers swelled or diminished because of their relationship with the modes of production through the division of labour. Arguably, it was the process of pauperization, more than the fact of the existence of the poor, that interested Marx, a process that resulted not only from separation of economically vulnerable groups from their means of production, but also from their own biological reproduction. But because his concern was with the analysis of capitalism and the formation of the working class, Marx generally tended to obscure any distinction between the poor and the working class, subsuming the former under the latter, as the rearguard of its 'industrial reserve army'. The poor, part of the overall surplus population, pressed upon the industrial reserve army, just as the latter constrained the active vanguard of workers. And as Marx elaborated, with teleological undertones, upon the process of formation of the class-conscious working class out of the ranks of these active and reserve armies, the rearguard of the poor receded until it had all but vanished from sight.

How to define the poor is a necessary departure point. The enquiries into poverty or living standards (and the latter always finished up with the former) that appeared at various moments over the past century in most western European countries all led to the same conclusion: because poverty is a condition experienced by individuals and families for different periods (from a single occasion to indefinitely) no single definition or measuring rod is adequate. As the most recent report on poverty in Italy reaffirms, there are various thresholds and bands of poverty, which involve not just dropouts from society, but substantial strata of people leading 'normal' lives. Conventionally such thresholds are measured by income or consumption estimates (in themselves imprecise indicators at these lower levels).[4] In the pre-statistical *ancien régime*, the same primarily economic determination of poverty was conveyed by the employment of the term 'poor' as synonymous, in its broadest sense, with the 'labouring classes', while 'indigent' was used more restrictively to describe those unable to earn enough for consumption. At this lowest level, there has never been any ambiguity about who are the poor, although there has usually been much debate over what to do about them. At the successively higher bands, identification has always been more difficult, partly because all definitions of social groups become peculiarly elusive at the edges (is an eighteenth-century cobbler, a cabinet maker or a petty shopkeeper a member of the 'bourgeoisie'?), partly because the condition of poverty was so common an experience and universal an expectation in the individual life-course and family cycle of those dependent on their labour.

To be poor was more than simply an economic condition. In societies characterized by an ideal of an established social order, but also in the commercialized capitalist and industrial societies of more recent times, with greater social mobility, to be poor or to risk becoming poor was a condition relative to one's social status (however defined). Poverty has always been a relative concept, not only in the material sense, but as a state of mind, a mentality, characterizing the attitudes and comportment both of those who have lost their economic independence or social status and of the other more fortunate members of society. It is this ideological construct of a sense of 'otherness' about poverty, shared by both parties and rendered most explicit in the act of charity, that seems to me to enable us to speak of the poor as a social category.

The crisis of proto-industrialization

The decline of Italy from the sixteenth century is well known. Politically, the Italian states were conquered by, or gravitated around, the Spanish Habsburgs; economically, the peninsula lost its central location as the axis of European trade shifted from the Mediterranean to the Atlantic. The economic leadership of the north-central Italian cities in the fifteenth century, importing raw materials and exporting manufactures and services, was lost in the course of the following centuries. The traditional industries declined, most spectacularly that of woollen textiles – in Florence and Milan already from the 1560s, in Venice by the 1620s. New luxury industries developed in the seventeenth and eighteenth centuries as a result of this structural crisis – above all silk, but many others such as crystal glass, printing, soap, sweetmeats – but they only inadequately compensated for the former levels of urban production. Urban employment dropped, the traditional control of the cities over the countryside grew weaker. The guilds were unable to prevent the merchant entrepreneurs expanding their activities outside the city walls, supplying the raw materials and marketing the (semi-finished) silk products by a variety of organizational techniques that ranged from domestic putting-out to mechanical production and genuine factories, as Carlo Poni has documented.[5] Whether the inadequacies lay with the guilds or the governments, the major cities of northern and central Italy proved unable effectively to resist English, French and Dutch competition. Industrial production within the cities, previously centred on cheap cloths for both foreign and domestic markets, no longer provided for the surrounding countryside, but was now directed predominantly towards the wealthy, mostly foreign, purchasers of silk and other luxury products. The cities were no longer able to control the manufacturing activities of the countryside; the rural production of silk-spinning developed, and even the urban monopoly of silk-weaving became less significant with the shift from finished cloths to the export of silk thread and organzines.

Traditionally Italian cities had exerted a rigid control over the countryside. With the spread of proto-industrialization the relationship between city and countryside was profoundly modified: the urban monopoly (though not the control) of manufacturing was irreparably impaired, but fiscal and food provisioning privileges were imposed ever more heavily. Already by the end of the sixteenth century, the hugely populated capitals of the South – Palermo (100,000), Naples (250,000), Rome (100,000) – depended on the privileges accorded them by their governments to obtain adequate food supplies at controlled prices. If silk production developed at Naples, Messina, Catania, and a woollen industry in some of the smaller towns of the interior of the kingdom of Naples, the major cities of the South had become parasites, with little or no industrial production and enormous consumption requirements extracted from the countryside. The guilds, jealous of their privileges, offered protection to only a small minority of the population, artisans and petty traders. The great mass of the plebs, swollen during building booms and at times of bad harvest by migration from the countryside, employed irregularly or not at all, formed a sullen, threatening crowd, to be placated by the adequate functioning of the provisioning administration and institutions of charity.[6] In the northern and central Italian cities, employment shifted towards building, food-processing, domestic services and retail trade – sectors directly dependent on the fluctuating demands of the wealthy and the governments.

The effects of this transformation of the role of the cities on the countryside were extremely negative. Even after Italy ceased to provide the battleground for the European powers (from the 1630s), the repeated wars led to requisitions and heavy taxation on the peasantry. The later sixteenth and seventeenth centuries witnessed a major increase in aristocratic and urban landowning privileges, which accompanied a growing commercialization of agriculture for urban and export markets, achieved through intensification of demands on peasant labour.[7] The population increase of the sixteenth century resulted not only in recurrent subsistence crises, but also in the erosion of the traditional peasant family economy, concerned to balance the demands of subsistence against the expenditue of labour. Epidemics,[8] which occurred with increasing virulence culminating in the 1630 plague (immortalized by Manzoni and only less catastrophic than the fourteenth-century Black Death), while in general relieving the demographic pressure, destroyed the self-sufficiency of huge numbers of peasant families in northern and central Italy by scything through the labour force. The population, afflicted by natural catastrophes as well as epidemics, was to take a century to regain its former level; the renewed growth in the eighteenth century was to reveal the fragility of subsistence structures in both city and countryside.

This secular crisis of the Italian economy was fundamentally attributable to the transformation from its substantial base of manufactured products, supported by a not inconsiderable level of internal trade between north and south, to a rural-based export trade of agricultural produce and semi-finished goods. Wars, until the mid-eighteenth century, whether or not on Italian soil, raised the burden of taxation, whose weight was increasingly shifted onto the peasantry with the extension of aristocratic, urban and ecclesiastical privilege. Because of the devastating effects of plague, the effects of the process of proto-industrialization on demographic growth remain unclear in the seventeenth century; but through the eighteenth and nineteenth centuries population continued to accelerate.

Table 1   Population levels in Italy, 1550–1861

Population (in thousands)[9]						
1550	1600	1650	1700	1750	1800	1861
11,591	13,272	11,543	13,373	15,484	18,091	26,100

The consequence of these structural changes in the economy was a prolonged increase in the scale of poverty. In the short term, of course, the numbers and composition of the poor had always fluctuated, often very substantially, in immediate correspondence to temporary conjunctures such as harvest shortages or trade crises. It is arguable that the effects of such negative conjunctures in this period were the more severe as the urban economies were less able to cushion the sudden increases in the numbers of those requiring assistance. But over the long term, the study of the poor, as well as of the defensive mechanisms they developed, offers, as it were, a mirror image of these structural changes. In Italy, between the Counter-Reformation and the end of the nineteenth century, evidence of pauperism is multiple, even if it rarely emerges directly through the voices of the poor: the evidence ranges from declining levels of consumption to the organization of institutional charity, from the crisis of the guild employment to the growing exploitation of female and child labour, from enforced migration to the final, slow formation of workers' organizations and the emergence of a class-conscious proletariat. Such information is rarely quantifiable, at least over time, and hence remains impressionistic; but cumulatively it is substantial.

In the countryside, by the last quarter of the sixteenth century, there were growing signs of crisis in the peasant world, from the abandonment of cultivation by indebted peasants to the slowing of the rate of growth of the rural population. The succession of famines, culminating in the years 1590–1, destroyed, however selectively, the subsistence economy of a vast number of peasant families, and finally checked the rate of growth of the urban populations. The introduction and diffusion of maize cultivation in the seventeenth century, like the growth of peasant indebtedness (so great in Piedmont as to force the government to cancel the backlog of unpaid debts) are sure indicators of increasing pauperization in the countryside. Studies of production, productivity, consumption or peasant landholdings in seventeenth-century Italy are still too few[10] to draw any firm conclusions. But in the light of later eighteenth-century sources and such fragmentary evidence as we possess for the seventeenth century, it is possible to hypothesize that the stabilization of the population in the later seventeenth century, following upon the strong increase of the previous century, operated selectively within the peasant world: smallholders and better-off sharecroppers may have consolidated the balance of their family economies, but the margins of subsistence of the landless and near-landless became more precarious. In northern and central Italy, throughout the former area of the medieval communes, the rapidly developing silk industry offered supplementary or substitute employment to hundreds of thousands of rural inhabitants no longer able to sustain themselves off the land.

In the cities, the guilds proved unable even to guarantee employment to their own members. In Venice, where the powerful *arti* represented two-thirds of the workforce, employment in the traditional exporting industries declined during the seventeenth century and a new phenomenon emerged, of contemporaneous membership of three, four, even five guilds.[11] As the possibilities of employment, particularly of continuous employment declined, the margins of subsistence grew narrower for significant sectors of the urban populations.

The eighteenth century can be regarded as marking the end of the long-term restructuring of the Italian economy. The fragility of subsistence structures in both city and countryside emerged with increasing clarity with the renewed population growth, for the most part in the countryside. The major cities either ceased to grow, like Genoa, Venice and Florence, or increased minimally, like Milan or Rome; Naples and Turin alone grew rapidly. But although the rate of growth of the Italian population was slower than in other regions of Europe, it compressed yet further the margins of subsistence, disrupting, often definitively, the equilibrium of the family economy. Although demographically the cities dropped in importance, their consumption demands, reinforced by government legislation, determined the patterns of agricultural production and were indirectly responsible for a probable decline in productivity over the century.

The evidence of increasing pauperization in the eighteenth century is abundant. The most dramatic testimony is that revealed during the terrible famine years of 1764–7, which affected the greater part of Italy. The provisioning systems merely worsened the situation, as attempts to placate the threatening urban poor by enforced extraction of cereals from the countryside rendered the desperate position of the peasantry untenable. 'The inhabitants of the provinces are following the grain which has been seized from them and are entering Naples with it', wrote the French ambassador in 1764. The Neapolitan doctor Tommaso Fasano observed: 'thousands of poor came from the provinces in a sorry plight. . . . They were so haggard and thin that they hardly appeared human; and they stank so badly that they made the citizens feel dizzy and sick as they approached them or wandered around the streets, churches and public places.'[12] The estimated 40,000 who flooded into Naples in 1764 were equivalent to one-tenth of its normal population; at Rome 14,000 peasant immigrants, a similar proportion of the Holy City's resident population, were forced into compounds.[13]

At such moments the scale of the problem of poverty became apparent, because the sketchy borderline between subsistence and dependence on charity disappeared for vast sectors of the population. In more normal times it is far more difficult to identify this borderline. One approach is to enquire what means were employed by labouring families to ensure their independent subsistence. In both city and countryside, it is only possible to glimpse or presume the hazy contours of family, associative and community structures, whose protective cohesiveness could increase the possibilities of independent survival for its members. The welfare, judicial and festive functions of the urban guilds and confraternities acted in this way. It is easier to find evidence about their participation in processions and the subsequent drinking bouts than about their assistance to members in sickness and death or in the provision of dowries.[14] But both the former and the latter played their role in assisting these artisans to retain their independence. In the countryside, Giovanni Levi has argued, even in an area of highly commercialized agriculture of the Piedmontese plain, the behaviour of peasant families in the deployment of their small-holdings, accumulation of dowries and choice of godparents was indicative – at least in the village of Felizzano – of a complex structure at the limits of subsistence.[15]

Domestic industry, particularly silk-, wool-, hemp- and flax-spinning and weaving, which developed on a major scale through the eighteenth and nineteenth centuries to supplement ever less adequate family production of crops, was another means of retaining independence. But here too there were limits to the possibilities of such alternative earnings, not just in terms of the classic consequences of Mendels's proto-industrial model (rapidly growing population and fragmentation of property), but because of the immediate effects of technical improvements and mechaniz-ation. At Racconigi in Piedmont, the family economy and social relations were upturned at the end of the seventeenth century by the concentration of production in a few households through the introduction of silk spinning frames '*alla bolognese*'. Previously, as the inhabitants protested,[16]

the people employed ordinary silks and used hand spinning wheels to produce yarn, webs and muslins, and trade in these goods gave rise to very considerable profits to the benefit of one and all in this place; for there were many such wheels, whose use enabled a great number of families in the town to support themselves decently.

The wool-spinners and weavers of the Biellese (also in Piedmont) were to undergo the same experience during the nineteenth century.[17]

Regular migration in search of work, but equally to reduce the consumption of the family, represented another such mechanism in defence of subsistence. In Piedmont alone, according to the Napoleonic prefects, over 20,000 peasants left their mountain villages each year for periods of six to nine months in search of employment elsewhere in Italy or France as miners, masons, roof-layers, carpenters, plasterers, tin- and copper-smiths, barrel-makers, scythers, gleaners, weavers, unskilled casual labourers. As the prefect of the department of the Stura (Cuneese) noted: 'These poor people only return home with very small sums and many with nothing at all, but they are content to have lived off their work for many months.'[18] Throughout the mountainous regions of Italy, in the Apennines as much as in the Alps, migration offered the only possibility of survival. In the Tuscan Apennines, as the mayor of a mountain village reported: 'The village of Verghereto is full of poor families; because of the scarce yield of its soil, two thirds of the population is forced to expatriate in the autumn and go to the Maremma; there they stay until the end of May in order to find the wherewithal to live.'[19] In the Roman Campagna, at the time of the wheat harvest, in the words of the prefect of the department of Rome, 'legions of peasants arrive, coming down from the mountains of the Abruzzi, Terra di Lavoro, the Ancona Marches, Tuscany and Umbria. There cannot be less than 32,000 of them, without even counting those that the department itself provides.'[20]

The regular agricultural cycle, with the sowing and cropping of cereals, rice, vines, and the lengthy transhumance of vast sheep flocks from the Alps to the Po plain and the Abruzzi to Apulia, represented an essential support to the survival of the subsistence peasant economy. Less regular, but equally essential, was the employment offered by the urban building industries, which depended on immigrant artisans and especially on unskilled labourers. Sometimes moving in groups, based on profession and place of origin, like the scythers of the Campagna or the hemp-combers of the Canavese, we know nothing as yet about whether they developed more sophisticated structures, like the English 'tramping artisans' or the French *compagnonnages*.[21] But even if the more skilled, such as the tin-smiths or plasterers, possessed such organizations, they certainly never formed more than a minority of the migrants. For the majority, any form of labour was essential if the economic independence of the family was to be preserved. And, as the prefect of the Stura noted, 'in bad years the number of emigrants increases by a very sizeable proportion, in some places often even doubling or tripling'.[22] In such years, the subsistence economy was threatened by both the poor harvest and the increased difficulties of finding employment.

Despite these defensive mechanisms, there can be no doubt that during the eighteenth century the frontier between subsistence and poverty was shifting, in both city and countryside, to the detriment of the former. The evidence would seem to indicate that the effects on the labouring poor of the prolonged structural changes within the economy culminated in the half-century from the 1770s to the 1820s, when the numbers of urban unemployed and rural day-labourers increased significantly. A substantial part of the Italian Enlightenment debate can properly be read as testimony to the scale of pauperism, not just the essays dedicated explicitly to the poor and their proper treatment, but the far wider-ranging discussion on the nature of Italian economic backwardness.[23] The notable increase in the activities of urban charitable institutions, especially foundling hospitals, throughout Italy argues for an awareness of the growth in the level of poverty. Alongside the communal pawnshops (*monti di pietà*), which often dated back to the fifteenth century in central and northern Italy, by the late eighteenth century rural communes in southern Italy were setting up equivalent institutions, *monti frumentari*, which loaned grain rather than cash in order to free the peasants from the endemic practice of usurious loans.

In the countryside, the most telling evidence is the fall in nutritional levels that occurred during the eighteenth century. Maize cultivation, already quite widespread in Venetia, spread west and south, into Lombardy, Piedmont and the Apennines, in the latter part of the century. The reports of the Napoleonic prefects are unanimous. At least as far south as Tuscany, maize had become the basic food of 'the agricultural mass of the inhabitants, that is, nine-tenths of the population'.[24] *Polenta* (a maize-flour porridge) in Piedmont 'forms the basis of the normal diet of the indigent class and . . . replaces bread in the countryside'.[25]

In short, a labourer [*manoeuvrier*], a countryman who only ate two pounds of bread during the day would still need a soup in the evening: whereas, for the same price as two pounds of bread, he could buy at least six to seven pounds of polenta, which takes the place of both soup and bread and is more than enough for a man's sustenance.[26]

'Real' famines, explained the prefect of the department of the Sesia, did not result from a poor wheat crop; 'the department suffers from such famines when the maize harvest fails'.[27] Where maize did not grow well, as in the Ligurian or Pistoiese Apennines, chestnuts acted as a proxy. When the chestnut crop failed, as the sub-prefect of Novi observed, the entire population of 40,000 would abandon its villages to seek survival in the ricefields of Piedmont and Lombardy.[28] In the former duchy of Parma-Piacenza, pigs were raised everywhere, by 'agriculturists, proprietors, merchants, day labourers', but were sold by the peasants unfattened, as a supplementary form of income. Meat had vanished from the peasant diet, while consumption of wine increased. With rare exceptions such as the fertile valleys of Tuscany, from the 1770s to the 1820s, from Venetia, Lombardy and Piedmont to Liguria, the Modenese, Umbria and the kingdom of Naples, contemporaries offer uniformly grim descriptions of these relatively recent dietary habits of the peasantry.[29] The pressure of population required higher yields from the land, such as those provided by maize. The growing commercialization of agriculture reduced the margins of subsistence. In the cities, where bread retained its primacy, the quality and quantity available to the *popolo minuto* fell by the end of the eighteenth century.[30]

The authorities were aware of and alarmed by the increasing numbers abandoning the land. Some, indeed, identified the cause in the commercialization of agriculture. As a late eighteenth-century government report of the duchy of Modena explained:[31]

it is as well to reflect that the greater the improvements in agriculture – such as all agree have occurred here in the past twenty years – the greater the growth of the population, but equally the greater the privations of the peasantry. Because they compete against each other for contracts as cowherds and sharecroppers, and force themselves to subsist on a smaller proportion of the crop, they press down on their own wages until they have pushed them too low. Thus their labours, their very parsimony and in many instances their virtue become the reasons why they emigrate.

Absolute physiological limits existed to the 'self-exploitation' of peasant families. In the course of the eighteenth century, the number of abandoned children rose, sufficiently to force the foundling hospitals of Milan and Florence to restrict their traditional willingness also to act as a deposit for legitimate infants.[32] As families finally collapsed under the weight of debt, they took to the road and became beggars. Denunciations of petty thefts of crops, accusations against these vagrants, became commonplace by the end of the century. But as a Mantuan doctor pointed out, this rural proletariat had little option:[33]

> Without even a plot of land, without a hearth, lacking everything bar an abundance of children, they are obliged to camp here and there, like Tartar vagabonds, to change home almost every year . . . to move about followed by a humble retinue of a few sheep and luggage consisting of a tattered mattress, a mouldy wine cask, a few rustic tools and a little crockery.

As the frontiers of subsistence contracted, the low nutritional level imposed by the struggle for survival took its toll. It proved difficult to enrol recruits in Tuscany for Napoleon's Imperial Guard, 'because of their physical weakness'.[34] In Restoration Lombardy, as Franco Della Peruta has illustrated, the degradation of dietary and hygienic standards was to have similar prolonged effects.[35]

The poor and the working class in the later nineteenth century

The contrast is striking (and not just in Italy) between studies of the labouring poor and those of the working class. Italian historiography, indeed, has tended to isolate the two almost as if they were different worlds. Yet the continuities and links between the former and the latter are undeniable. On the one hand, a large proportion of the class-conscious proletariat, involved in strikes and trade union activities from the 1880s, was engaged in occupations characteristic of the poor – textile production, railways, building, mining and metalworking industries, and (with the turn of the century) casual labour in areas of capitalist agriculture in the Po valley.[36] On the other hand, the labouring poor, without any apparent sense of class-consciousness, did not cease to exist after the formation of an organized working class; indeed, its condition worsened.

In part, the difficulty of relating the study of the poor to that of the proletariat is one of perspective. The poor were and are seen as struggling with problems of consumption. The formation of a class-conscious proletariat is viewed within the context of capitalist production. It is the distinction, made by the social historian, between riots against increases in food prices and strikes to improve wages or working conditions. To understand the passage from the former to the latter is crucial, precisely because it was neither comprehensive nor linear.

The study of the relationship between the world of the poor and the formation of the proletariat has also suffered because of the concern of labour historians with the later developments of the working-class movement. The problem of the origins of a 'modern' working class in Italy has tended to be subsumed into a debate about the spontaneity or otherwise of the formation of its class-consciousness and organizations, in which judgements about the positive or negative role of the trade unions play a predominant part. For Stefano Merli, declining living standards and social uprooting of large masses of workers, with the introduction of the factory system, created the basis for labour militancy and a spontaneous drive towards organization.[37] For Giuliano Procacci, the role of socialist organizers, within trades and regionally, was crucial.[38] This is not the place for a discussion of these conflicting interpretations. It is enough to note that both assume the 'availability' of large numbers of families on the margins of subsistence for recruitment into class organizations. There is a tendency – not just in Italian historiography, but more generally – to assume a unilinear transformation of the pre-industrial work-force into a primarily factory-system proletariat; implicit in this is the assumption of an inevitable and general spread of class-consciousness. In line with this, artisan organizations and now (following the interest in popular culture) less politically oriented associations, such as working men's clubs, have often been studied as if their very existence was sufficient explanation of how class-consciousness was acquired, as if they were automatic transmission belts of class culture to a passive audience.[39]

To state that the working class grew out of the world of poverty is a truism. But to concentrate exclusively on the formation of 'modern' working-class consciousness is to risk ignoring the equally important problem of why by far the greatest part of the Italian working population for so long apparently failed to be affected by it. Strikes are properly used as an indicator of class-consciousness, whether they are understood as a form of expression of the subculture of the subordinate classes or as a means of exerting pressure on employers. By 1901, a year when the number of strikes and strikers shot up under Giolitti's new policy of government neutrality in industrial disputes, on the most optimistic estimate under 8 per cent of the industrial wage-earning workforce (itself only about 10 per cent of the population aged over nine) was affected.[40] The overwhelming majority of the labouring poor remained apparently untouched by 'modern' working-class consciousness, responding to the changed (and worsening) conditions imposed by mechanization and industrialization through traditional or adapted strategies of subsistence. It is important to identify these strategies as they place in perspective the process of formation of the class-conscious proletariat and offer an explanation of the particular constraints that conditioned its development.

I would argue that underpinning the various responses and strategies of subsistence, which I discuss below, were long-established values and attitudes of the poor towards society, which make it possible to consider them as a social category. In material terms, even if only a small proportion of the population found itself for lengthy periods or permanently below the level of subsistence, the likelihood of experiencing such a condition at one or more phases in the life-course and family cycle was always extremely widespread among the labouring classes. There was a constant movement back and forth from the labouring classes to the ranks of the poor, an omnipresent awareness of the condition of poverty into which economically independent families could fall. This seems to me to explain both the extreme concern of labouring families (particularly those just on the right sidé of subsistence) to distinguish themselves from the poor, and the occasional appartently contradictory gestures of solidarity with the poor, such as the spontaneous protection of beggars against arrest.

At the same time, the poor were not purely the product of socioeconomic change, but were 'constituted' through social attitudes: the poor were poor because they were so judged by the élites. The essence of this construct was the acceptance by the poor themselves of a condition of dependence on others, which implied a cluster of 'proper' values of comportment, such as public display of deference, against which individuals were judged as meritorious or otherwise. I would not argue for an autonomous culture of poverty, but rather for the appropriation by the poor of values deemed by the élites to be central to the orderly functioning of society; among these, independence of the family, social position and influence (a weaker version of patronage) were the most important. To be poor was to be wanting in all these qualities, which deficiency needed to be recognized and compensated for by appropriate behaviour (meekness, gratitude, or deference). To be poor was to identify oneself as separate from all other members of society, most publicly by dependence on charity, more generally by efforts to reincorporate these values, to rejoin the moral economy in common with the more 'fortunate' (because economically independent) subordinate strata of society. It is the deferential mentality that seems to me to allow one to distinguish the poor as a social category. The values from which the poor were excluded, or which most working people risked losing at moments in their life-course, were to be regained or retained, not by the concept (hardly new, but novel in its organizational structuring) of a continuous challenge based on class, but by the deployment of well-tested, usually family-oriented strategies. In this sense, proto-industrialization, emigration, part-time urban employment, reliance on remittances from emigrant relatives, charity, were all alternatives to strikes, which – although they did not permanently exclude the possibility of a spread of class-consciousness – in practice permitted the poor to survive materially and mentally as a numerically large category outside the ranks of the 'modern' working class.

Characteristic of industrialization and the formation of an industrial workforce in Italy was the absence of sudden ruptures with the past. Mechanization and the factory system were not responsible for the (tardy) process of urbanization, as they were mainly located in the countryside, in areas with strong proto-industrial traditions. Crucial and complementary consequences of the Italian path to industrialization were a labour-intensive form of industrialization and the tenacious survival of peasant family structures.[41]

Until the 1880s and later, Italian industrialization was characterized by the predominance of small and medium workshops, and by the expansion of hand skills and domestic manufacturing contemporaneously with the introduction of factory mechanization. Employment in silk-, woollen-, cotton-weaving, in hat-making and generally in clothing grew in absolute numbers between unification and the end of the century.[42] Silk was the leading sector, whose productive process, even when concentrated in manufactures, precisely because it was so closely related to agriculture and located in the countryside, was particularly adapted to what Alain Dewerpe has recently analysed as a prolonged form of proto-industrialization.[43] The phenomenon was not novel in Italy, even if it appears striking because of its apparent chronological 'tardiness', during decades of capital-intensive mechanization in such leading industrial countries as England, the United States, Germany, Belgium or France. It dates back to the later eighteenth and early nineteenth centuries and is new only in its scale – and then only in a restricted geographical area of northern Italy.

It is equally significant that the phenomenon was not unique to Italy. In England, during the first half-century of the Industrial Revolution, the number of handloom weavers continued to rise. Indeed, as Clapham and more recently R. Samuel have pointed out, non-mechanized forms of production remained fundamental to the British economy, in scale, size and dynamism, until at least the 1840s. Employment, not just in agriculture, but in coal-mining, building, and even in skilled trades, continued to grow. For Raphael Samuel, it is the over-supply of labour in all sectors that explains the development of 'sweating' and outwork, as well as disinclination to invest in capital-saving machinery.[44] Stefano Merli has argued that Italian capitalism was unique in the later nineteenth century in its total freedom to exploit labour and hence in its reluctance to mechanize because of the existence of an unlimited reserve army of labour. Without pushing the parallel too far, the English example, at least until the 1840s and in some respects considerably later, would seem to indicate the contrary. The degradation of skills, the mass employment of women and children, the exploitation of labour by extension of working hours (as well as intensification of labour through piece-rates) were phenomena typical of a particular form of manufacturing capitalism, neither unique nor new to Italy, stretching back to the eighteenth and early nineteenth centuries. What was new was the scale; and the massive diffusion of such forms of employment helps to explain that peculiar characteristic of Italian economic development – the long-term survival of minute, small and medium-sized enterprises, increasingly dependent on mechanized large industry, but viable primarily because of the supply of cheap labour.

The composition of the labour force in this first phase of Italian industrialization (until the 1880s and later) displays equally striking continuities with the earlier period. Population growth and the increasing pressures on the margins of subsistence with the commercialization of agriculture lay at the base of the spread of manufacturing and especially outwork employment. What was new was, on the one hand, the structural crisis that affected all Italian agriculture in the late nineteenth century, and, on the other, the rapid growth of the northern cities. Between 1881 and 1901 the active population engaged in agriculture rose from 9.4 millions to 10.7 millions, an increase proportional to that of the overall population of Italy (from 29.3 to 33.4 millions); these were decades of heavy emigration, exclusively from the poorest rural populations (Venetia, Piedmont and the South).[45] From the 1850s, diseases (of silk cocoons and then of vines) deprived many peasant families of their primary source of monetary income; following unification, heavy taxation and large-scale capital investment in the agriculture of the Po plain combined with the European agricultural depression (which affected Italy from the later 1870s) to destroy the independence of ever larger sectors of the rural population.

In northern and central Italy, the primary and predominant response to this accelerating process of proletarization was not to abandon the countryside, but to find alternative means of remaining there. The recent exemplary researches of Franco Ramella, Alain Dewerpe and Marzio Barbagli confirm the resistance of the peasant family to its expulsion through the adoption of a wide range of expedients, some well-established forms of casual employment, others new variants of proto-industrial work generated by the very process of mechanization in the textile industries. The vast programme of railway-building and public works, together with urban expansion, offered employment in the construction industries, which confirmed the traditional practice of temporary migration for some male members of the family. Contemporaries were acutely conscious of this pressure of the rural poor on urban employment and hence wage rates. A police report of 1867 on unrest among unemployed Milanese building labourers noted:[46]

Because there are no jobs in other places, everybody pours into Milan, with the result that jobs become inadequate here as well. The competition among workers is food to the well-known greed of the master-builders and contractors, who try to pay the lowest possible wages to those who work: hence protests and discontent.

But from the point of view of these rural-based casual labourers, earnings on building sites were an additional, and not a substitute source of income for the family economy. In the countryside, the rapid growth of the garment-making sector, particularly suited to the sweating system, especially with the diffusion of sewing machines, served the same function.[47] Textile factories, more rural than urban, whether for silk- or wool-manufacturing, necessitated restructuring the work roles of the individual members of the family. But it was the male head of the household, acting on behalf of the family as a single unit, who negotiated with the employers about which members should work in the factory, and searched for the means (absenteeism in the first instance) to reconcile manufacturing production with the requirements of the agricultural cycle. Textile, especially silk, mechanization, far from signifying expulsion from the countryside, represented the last means of surviving there. The success was visible in the remarkable degree of impermeability of peasant household structures to both industrialization and urbanization, with the prolonged survival of extended and multiple families, even among day-labourers.[48]

In southern Italy, rural domestic industry was destroyed by the dogmatic adherence to free trade of the victorious moderate politicians and the consequential imports of English and French textile manufactures, more than by the direct results of unification (which only took effect relatively slowly after the completion of the main railway network in 1877). The relative backwardness of the southern textile industry offered little possibility of alternative employment. The poor of the Mezzogiorno, where the rate of population growth was highest, exploited the only possibility open to them – emigration. The levels of emigration reflected both the scale of the agricultural crisis and the new alternatives opened up by cheap transport across the Atlantic and prospects of employment in the two Americas. Migration figures, net of emigrants who returned, show an increase from 378,000 in the decade 1872–81 to 845,000 in 1882–91 and 1,378,000 in 1892–1901; total departures from Italy were three times as high.[49] The history of the Italian poor from the later nineteenth century until the First World War is, for the greater part, the history of Italian emigration. But it is important to note that remittances from emigrants were on so large a scale that they covered the balance of payments deficit in the Giolittian years. It is possible that the emigrants consisted more of owners of minute plots of land than of landless labourers.[50] In part at least, their remittances were used to purchase small plots of land or to repay debt.[51] In this sense, it can be argued that, like emigration itself, remittances acted as a safety-valve and eased the pressure for some families on the subsistence borderline, enabling them to prolong their existing condition.

In northern Italy, where emigration from the agricultural regions (Venetia, Piedmont) was also high, the rural poor would seem to have turned in two mutually exclusive directions: towards Catholic charity, or towards employment in industry. Although the creation of a Catholic lay organization, the *Opera dei Congressi*, dates from 1874, the effective structure of assistance – through Marian congregations in the cities and parish, diocesan and regional committees in the countryside – only developed in the 1880s, in conscious opposition to the spread of socialism. The 'real' Italy, which the *Opera dei Congressi* claimed to defend against the 'legal' Italy, was a rural, opposed to an urban, Italy, exalting the virtues of the countryside against the corruption of the cities. Temporary emigration, particularly to foreign Protestant urban centres, could have corrosive consequences. As the curate of Mestrino stated in 1875:[52]

> Unless religious instruction precedes temporary migration, the places to which great masses of workers go are morally dangerous for both the emigrants and their villages, where they will sow the evil maxims they have imbibed in these foreign parts. Far less in danger is the faith of rural cultivators who emigrate, for example, to South America, without the certainty of ever returning.

But the network of rural savings banks and co-operatives, which saturated unindustrialized Venetia and spread on a far smaller scale in Lombardy, Piedmont and Tuscany, were of assistance primarily to the smallholders, petty tenants and sharecroppers, not to the agricultural day-labourers or part-employees of industry.[53]

The role of these Catholic organizations in assisting the poor, a traditional role, remains to be studied in its various forms, effectiveness and limits. One basic limit, in this period of industrialization, was constituted by the insistence on charity and class collaboration, as can be seen in the definition of the purpose of the rural savings banks:[54]

> to redeem the farmer from usury; to give him the means by which to cultivate his land rationally, to offer him capital at reasonable conditions, to enable him to avoid selling his crops precipitately; and at the same time to draw him out of his isolation, bring him closer to the proprietors and persuade him to improve himself morally.

These aims, which could have been voiced by the Enlightenment reformers a century earlier, however valid in themselves, sounded anachronistic by the 1880s, and above all applicable to only small segments of a crisis-ridden agricultural sector.

The Italian class-conscious proletariat was to emerge from the northern urban and rural poor. But, as we have seen, the particular form of industrialization permitted, even encouraged, the maintenance of strong links with the soil. The effect of such ties was to render the more difficult the spread of class-consciousness, at least as embodied in working-class organizational forms. Perhaps the most revealing indicator of the gap that separated the embryonic industrial proletariat from the labouring poor was the major phenomenon of urban part-employment of members of rural families, particularly in the major textile and building industries, commuting from the countryside or residing temporarily within the cities.[55] It was the difference between regular employment and casual or intermittent labour, which Charles Booth saw as the fundamental distinction in his analysis of London workers in these same years.[56] In general, temporary migration accentuated the personalistic physiognomy of recruitment and employment. Acquaintance or friendship, family relationship or favours, necessarily played a disproportionate role in the hiring of workers, whether in the small textile workshops that trained new female operatives or in the daily selection of building labourers and apprentices at the Milan 'Ponte'. After they had been hired, the large numbers of intermittent or casual workers, who constituted by far the greatest proportion of the labouring poor, remained highly dependent on the regular workers, whether masons, textile foremen or chief compositors in the printing industry.[57]

Migration, especially if temporary, acted as a divisive factor not only in employment, but in living conditions. Immigrants to the city of Milan averaged annually nearly 7500 (or 26.8 per 1000 of the population) in the 1870s and 11,900 (or 33.6 per 1000) in the 1880s. Emigrants out of the city averaged between one-half and two-thirds of the immigrants, and at least half of these only left the metropolis to go to the same or neighbouring provinces,[58] indicating the high level of temporary migration. In 1878 a former police official affirmed that some 8000 homeless lived in Milan.[59] The degradation of living conditions in a rapidly expanding city such as Milan was symptomatic not only of desperately low wages and of the lethargy of the municipal authorities in areas such as housing, but most probably of a hostility of the resident working class towards the immigrants, such as Louis Chevalier has shown in nineteenth-century Paris.[60] The compilers of the 1881 census pointed to instances in Milan where one or two rooms housed ten or more, 'a collection of individuals linked not by family ties, but by the identity of the trade they practise – as chimney sweeps, porters and fruitsellers'.[61] It is a revealing comment about the hierarchy of poverty.

This hierarchy offers a crucial clue towards understanding the processes of formation of the Italian proletariat from the ranks of the poor. Studies of the formation of the working class in England and France, such as the classic works of Thompson, Hobsbawm and Agulhon, or the more recent contributions of Stedman Jones, Foster, Lequin, Sewell or Scott,[62] have stressed the essential role of artisans and craft workers, resisting the loss of independence by the creation of labour organizations, ranging from mutual aid and friendly societies to trades unions. Both the early organizations – the mutual aid societies that spread, with unification, from Piedmont into Lombardy and central Italy – and the early strikes in Italy would seem to offer such examples. The strikes of the typographers at Milan in 1860 or of the silk-weavers at Como, the woollen-weavers of the Biellese and the hatters at Monza in the 1870s were typically in defence of wages or job control against the downgrading effects of mechanization.[63] The union structures, involving hardly more than a minimal proportion of the industrially employed, only turned into organizations of class resistance in the 1880s. But even then, they developed primarily (although not exclusively) among craft or skilled workers, as can be seen from an 1885 listing of societies:[64]

workers in textile industries; mechanics, turners, foundrymen, blacksmiths, etc.; carpenters, caulkers, cabinet-makers and woodworkers; typographers, lithographers and similar; engine-drivers, stokers, and lower railway personnel; rail and steam-tram personnel; tanners, furriers, glovers; tobacco workers; shoemakers, hatters, tailors, saddlers, trunkmakers, upholsterers, umbrella-makers, etc.; builders and similar; varnishers, painters, plasterers; potters of crockery, earthenware, vases; glassworkers; kilnmen.

It is possible, as Andreina De Clementi has argued, that the contribution of the artisans towards the formation of a class-conscious proletariat was much less significant in Italy than in England.[65] But if this is true of the decades when the widespread existence of a working-class movement is easily visible, and a higher level and diffusion of mechanization had weakened the centrality of the role of skilled workers, it is far from clear for the 'pre-history' of this proletariat in the preceding decades. What remains equally unclear is the relationship between the skilled and the unskilled labourers.

The process of formation of this first phase of industrialization in Italy, precisely because of its strong rural physiognomy, points towards structural limitations to the diffusion of class-consciousness among the labouring poor, who – within the limits of their possibilities (and overseas emigration marks these limits) – exploited the expanding opportunities offered by industrialization to retain at least a simulacre of their established way of life. For this reason, it may well prove that the history of the formation of the industrial proletariat may be explored most fruitfully through the study of the labouring poor. It required the successive phase of industrialization, based on iron and steel, chemical and engineering industries, which developed rapidly with the new century, for a class-conscious proletariat to expand its base.

Notes

I wish to thank Geoff Crossick, Steve Smith and Harry Lubasz for their valuable and critical comments on an earlier version of this chapter.

1 Vol. 1, ch. 24, para. 4 (Penguin edition, Harmondsworth, 1976), pp. 794–8. The four categories of pauperism were: vagabonds and worse, the 'actual lumpenproletariat'; those able to work, but unable to find employment through trade crises; orphans and abandoned children; and those unable to work. The three permanent categories of the relative surplus population were the floating (rejects of industrial centres); the latent (expelled from the countryside); and the stagnant (mostly from declining handicraft industries). The distinction Marx makes between the second pauper category (those suffering from trade crises) and the floating category of the surplus population appears to be one between artisans, on the one hand, and workers in modern industry, on the other.

2 ibid., p. 797.

3 ibid., pp. 799–802.

4 Commissione di Indagine sulla Povertà, *Primo rapporto alla Presidenza del Consiglio dei Ministri*, Rome, 1985.

5 C. Poni, 'All'origine del sistema di fabbrica: tecnologia e organizzazione produttiva dei mulini da seta nell'Italia settentrionale (sec. XVII–XVIII)', *Rivista storica italiana*, 88 (1976).

6 M. Aymard, 'Villes laborieuses, villes oisives: l'Italie à l'époque moderne', in *La Force du travail dans les cités méditerranéennes du milieu du XVIIIe au milieu du XIXe siècle*, Université de Nice, Publication des Cahiers de la Méditerranée, ser. spéc., 3, 1974; J. Revel, 'Le grain de Rome et la crise de l'annone dans la seconde moitié du XVIIIe siècle', *Mélanges de l'Ecole Française de Rome*, 84 (1972); R. Villari, *La rivolta antispagnola a Napoli. Le origini (1585–1647)*, Bari, 1967.

7 S.J. Woolf, 'Sviluppo economico e struttura sociale in Piemonte da Emanuele Filiberto a Carlo Emanuele III', *Nuova Rivista Storica*, 46 (1962); F. McArdle, *Altopascio. A Study in Tuscan Rural Society, 1587–1784*, Cambridge, 1978; M. Aymard, 'La trasizione dal feudalesimo al capitalismo', in *Storia d'Italia. Annali I, Dal feudalesimo al capitalismo*, Turin, 1978; T.B. Davies, *Famiglie feudali siciliane. Patrimoni redditi investimenti tra '500 e '600*, Caltanissetta – Rome, 1985.

8 L. Del Panta, *Le epidemie nella storia demografica italiana (secoli XIV–XIX)*, Turin, 1980.

9 A. Bellettini, 'La popolazione italiana dall'inizio dell'era volgare ai giorni nostri. Valutazioni e tendenze', in *Storia d'Italia*, vol. 5: 1, *I Documenti*, Turin, 1973, pp. 509–21.

10 Davies, *Famiglia feudali*; G. Delille, 'Aziende e produzione agraria nel Mezzogiorno', *Quaderni storici*, 43 (1980); *Ricerche di storia moderna*, I and II, Pisa, 1976, 1979; G. Delille, *Croissance d'une société rurale. Montesarchio et la vallée Caudine aux XVIIe et XVIIIe siècles*, Naples, 1973.

11 R.T. Rapp, *Industry and Economic Decline in Seventeenth-Century Venice*, Cambridge, Mass., 1976, p. 21 and *passim*.

12 F. Venturi, '1764: Napoli nell'anno della fame', *Revista storica italiana*, 85 (1973), pp. 405–6 and *passim*.

13 F. Venturi, '1764–1767: Roma negli anni della fame', *Rivista storica italiana*, 85 (1973), pp. 530–1.

14 E. Grendi, 'Confraternite e mestieri nella Genova settecentesca', *Miscellanea di Storia Ligùre*, 4, Genoa, 1966; E. Grendi, 'Le confraternite ligùre in età moderna', in *La Ligùria della casacce*, Genoa, 1982.

15 G. Levi, 'Terra e structure familiari in una comunità piemontese del "700"', *Quaderni storici*, 33 (1976).

16 Poni, 'All'origine del sistema', p. 470.
17 F. Ramella, *Terra e telai. Sistemi di parentela e manifattura nel Biellese dell'Ottocento*, Turin, 1984.
18 ANP, F20.435, Pô, Doire, Marengo, Sésia, Stura, 1810–11; C. Corsini, 'Le migrazioni stagionali di lavoratori nei dipartimenti italiani nel periodo napoleonico (1810–12)', in Dipartimento Statistico Matematico, Università di Firenze, *Saggi di demografia storica*, Florence, 1969.
19 ASF, Arno, 485, 20 October 1809.
20 ANP, F20.435, Rome, 7 January 1813.
21 E.J. Hobsbawm, *Labouring Men*, London, 1964; E. Coornaert, *Les Compagnonnages en France*, Paris, 1966.
22 ANP, F20.435, Stura, 20 June 1811.
23 F. Venturi, *Settecento riformatore*, 4 vols, Turin, 1969–84.
24 ANP, F11.474–5, Sésia, 19 thermidor an 13 (7 August 1805).
25 ANP, F11.472–3, Pô, 30 September 1812.
26 ANP, F10.430, Gênes, 26 June 1812.
27 ANP, F10.474–5, Sésia, 19 thermidor an 13 (7 August 1805).
28 ANP, F10.429, Gênes, 9 October 1811.
29 Some examples for the later eighteenth century in S.J. Woolf, *A History of Italy 1700–1861. The Social Constraints of Political Change*, London, 1979; for the nineteenth century, in F. Della Peruta, 'Per la storia della società lombarda nella età del Risorgimento', *Studi storici*, 16 (1875); M. Aymard and H. Bresc, 'Nourritures et consommation en Sicile entre XIVe et XVIIIe siècles', and J. Revel, 'Les privilèges d'une capitale: l'approvisionnement de Rome à l'époque moderne', both in *Mélanges de l'Ecole Française de Rome*, 87 (1975).
30 Revel, 'Les privilèges'; Aymard and Bresc, 'Nourritures et consommation'.
31 G. Orlandi, *Le campagne modenesi fra rivoluzione e restaurazione (1790–1815)*, Modena, 1967, p. 54.
32 C. Corsini, 'Materiali per lo studio della famiglia in Toscana nei secoli XVII–XIX: gli esposti', *Quaderni storici*, 33 (1976).
33 C. Vivanti, *Le campagne del Mantovano nell'età delle riforme*, Milan, 1959, pp. 224–5.
34 ANP, F15.508, Arno, 17 December 1811.
35 Della Peruta, 'Per la storia'.
36 A. Lay, D. Marucco and M.L. Pesante, 'Classe operaia e scioperi: ipotesi per il periodo 1880–1923', *Quaderni storici*, 22 (1973), pp. 95, 145–7 and *passim*. Of these sectors, metalworking is perhaps the only non-traditional one for the poor.
37 S. Merli, *Proletariato di fabbrica e capitalismo industriale. Il caso italiano: 1880–1900*, Florence, 1972.
38 G. Procacci, *La lotta di classe in Italia agli inizi del secolo XIX*, Rome, 1970.

39 More recent work has certainly shown greater sensitivity towards the complexity of the issues involved, particularly to the often ambivalent relationships between family, community and work or working-class culture and political activism. For example, M. Perrot, *Les Ouvriers en grève. France 1871–1890*, Paris – The Hague, 1974; G. Stedman Jones, 'Working-class culture and working-class politics in London, 1870–1900: notes on the remaking of a working class', in his *Languages of Class. Studies in English Working-Class History 1832–1982*, Cambridge, 1983; V. Lidtke, *The Alternative Culture. Socialist Labor in Imperial Germany*, Oxford and New York, 1985.

40 Procacci, *La lotta di classe*, p. 4, estimates the wage-earning industrial workforce at 2,593,000, excluding artisans, workshop and factory owners, independent textile-weavers and spinners and white-collar workers. There were 196,542 strikers (in 1900 only 80,858) involved in 1042 strikes (in 1900 only 383): Lay, Marucco and Pesante, 'Classe operaia', p. 145.

41 A. Dewerpe, *L'Industrie aux champs. Essai sur la proto-industrialisation en Italie du Nord (1800–1880)*, Rome, 1985; M. Barbagli, *Sotto lo stesso tetto. Mutamenti della famiglia in Italia dal XV al XX secolo*, Bologna, 1984.

42 Merli, *Proletariato di fabbrica*, especially pp. 38–42.

43 Dewerpe, *L'Industrie aux champs*.

44 R. Samuel, 'The workshop of the world: steam power and hand technology in mid-Victorian Britain', *History Workshop*, 1 (1976), 3 (1977).

45 O. Vitali, 'Popolazione attiva in agricoltura attraverso i censimenti in Italia: nuove valutazioni', *Quaderni storici*, 14 (1970), pp. 573–4 for these figures and *passim* for significant underestimates of female employment. In 1901 the official figure for population engaged in agriculture represented 588 per 1000 employed, compared to 116 per 1000 in England.

46 M.T. Mereu, 'Origine e primi sviluppi dell'organizzazione di classe dei muratori milanesi', *Classe*, 5 (1972), p. 282.

47 A. De Clementi, 'Appunti sulla formazione della classe operaia in Italia', *Quaderni storici*, 32 (1976), pp. 694–5.

48 Ramella, *Terra e telai*; Dewerpe, *L'Industrie aux champs*; Barbagli, *Sotto lo stesso tetto*.

49 M. Livi-Bacci, *A History of Italian Fertility During the Last Two Centuries*, Princeton, 1977, pp. 53, 270; R.F. Foerster, *The Italian Emigration of Our Times*, Boston, 1919, New York, 1968 edn, pp. 42–3, gives slightly different figures. For a quantitative study of emigration, E. Sori, *L'emigrazione italiana dall'Unità alla seconda guerra mondiale*, Bologna, 1979.

50 Vitali, 'Popolazione attiva', p. 55 asserts this, but gives no source.

51 Foerster, *The Italian Emigration*, pp. 447–52.

52 A. Gambasin, *Gerarchia e laicato in Italia nel secondo Ottocento*, Padua, 1969, p. 241.

53 ibid., pp. 100–29, 266–7.

54 G. De Rosa, *Storia del movimento cattolico in Italia. Dalla restaurazione all'età giolittiana*, Bari, 1966, p. 188.

55 L. Osnaghi Dodi, 'Sfruttamento del lavoro nell'industria tessile comasca e prime esperienze di organizzazione operaia', *Classe*, 5 (1972), p. 101; Mereu, 'Origine e primi sviluppi', pp. 256–8; Merli, *Proletariato di fabbrica*, pp. 80–1, 127, 441, 450; De Clementi, 'Appunti sulla formazione', pp. 710–1; G. Berta, 'Dalla manifattura al sistema di fabbrica: razionalizzazione e conflitti di lavoro', *Storia d'Italia, annali I, Dal feudalesimo al capitalismo*, Turin, 1978, p. 1090.

56 C. Booth, *Life and Labour of the People of London*, London, 1889.

57 Berta, 'Dalla manifattura', pp. 1088–91 and generally pp. 1087–106; Ramella, *Terra e telai* pp. 190–2, 211–17.

58 A. De Maddalena, 'Rilievi sull'esperienza demografica ed economica milanese dal 1861 al 1961', in *L'economia italiana dal 1861 al 1961*, Milan, pp. 104–5.

59 P. Locatelli, *Miseria e beneficenza. Ricordi di un funzionario di P.S.*, cited in V. Hunecke, 'Comune e classe operaia in Milano (1859–1898)', *Studi storici*, 17 (1976), p. 91.

60 L. Chevalier, *Labouring Classes and Dangerous Classes in Paris During the First Half of the Nineteenth Century*, New York, 1973.

61 Hunecke, 'Comune e classe operaia', p. 92.

62 E.P. Thompson, *The Making of the English Working Class*, London, 1963; E.J. Hobsbawm, *Labouring Men. Studies in the History of Labour*, London, 1964; M. Agulhon, *Une Ville ouvrière au temps du socialisme utopique. Toulon de 1815 à 1851*, Paris, 1970; G. Stedman Jones, *Outcast London: a Study in the Relationship Between Classes in Victorian Society*, Oxford, 1971; J. Foster, *Class Struggle and the Industrial Revolution: Early Industrial Capitalism in Three English Towns*, London, 1974; Y. Lequin, *Les Ouvriers de la région lyonnaise (1848–1914)*, Lyons, 1977; W.H. Sewell, *Work and Revolution in France. The Language of Labor from the Old Regime to 1848*, Cambridge, 1980; J.W. Scott, *Glassworkers of Carmaux: French Craftsmen and Political Action in a Nineteenth-Century City*, Cambridge, Mass., 1974.

63 A. Gigli Marchetti, 'Gli operai tipografici milanesi all'avanguardia della organizzazione di classe in Italia', *Classe*, 5 (1972), pp. 26–7; Osnaghi Dodi, 'Sfruttamento del lavoro', pp. 121–2; A. Cocucci Deretta, 'I cappellai monzesi dall'avvento della grande industria meccanica alla costituzione della Federazione Nazionale', *Classe*, 5 (1972), p. 192; De Clementi, 'Appunti sulla formazione', p. 713; Berta, 'Dalla manifattura', pp. 1088–91; Ramella, *Terra e telai*, chs 1, 9, 10.

64 Merli, *Proletariato di fabbrica*, pp. 583–4.

65 De Clementi, 'Appunti sulla formazione', p. 709.

3

❧❦❧

The treatment of the poor in Napoleonic Tuscany. 1808–14

What to do with the poor was a problem that had afflicted European societies for many centuries and had forced itself uncomfortably upon the attention of church, administrations and public-minded individuals increasingly from the sixteenth century. The presence of poverty, in town and countryside, was always visible and periodically – in times of pestilence, economic crisis or war – drew unpleasantly close for the comfort of the more fortunate members of society. In the later sixteenth and early seventeenth centuries religious scruples and concern about public hygiene had led to the foundation of numerous hospitals, congregations, charitable institutions, poorhouses, official pawnshops, in the Italian states, as in France, Spain and England. Private charity, in life or (more substantially) at the point of death, accompanied and usually surpassed public assistance in the endowment of these institutions. Their wealth, dependent upon the vagaries of human whim and the economic resources of local administrations, thus varied enormously, and tended to be concentrated within the larger cities. As eighteenth-century critics were quick to point out, inefficient organization and deliberate fraud deflected a substantial part of these funds from the purposes for which they had been donated. But, irrespective of maladministration, by the eighteenth century it was evident that the poor-relief system, massive, uncoordinated and ultimately uncontrolled, was failing even as a palliative.

Rising population, inadequate employment opportunities and relative scarcity of food supplies can now be seen as longer-term structural causes of the increase of poverty by the later eighteenth century. But for the Enlightenment reformers the charitable institutions were themselves in fair part responsible for the growth in the numbers of the poor. It was necessary, as Muratori pointed out already in 1723, to distinguish between those deserving of assistance and the able-bodied poor and beggars who exploited charity in order to avoid work.[1] Charity was due to those categories of unfortunate individuals traditionally identified as genuinely destitute and incapable of aiding themselves – the aged, infirm, orphans, widows, girls in danger of losing their virtue, deserving poor. The able-bodied – the professional beggars, the vagabonds, the fraudulent cripples and blind, the swarms of children exploiting the compassion of respectable citizens and the resources of charitable institutions – should be cured of their idleness and forced to work. In perhaps the most extensive analysis of the structure of poor relief produced by the Enlightenment, the Modenese minister Lodovico Ricci offered a detailed description of the existing institutions in the capital of the duchy and outlined his blueprint for their reform:[2] the numbers and incomes of the institutions were to be severely reduced, their administration was to be rigidly controlled by honest, frugal citizens under the supervision of the state, education and technical training was to be provided in order to produce useful citizens.

Ricci's basic principle was as simple as it was rigid: 'charity merely facilitates subsistence, and hence is the main reason for the constant hordes of poor'; in consequence, if charitable funds were reduced and kept at a fixed level, the numbers of poor able to benefit from them would be similarly fixed, and the remainder would be forced to look for other means of survival.[3] Even in Ricci's own terms of reference, at least one major question was begged: what to do with the deserving poor, the *pauvres honteux*, the *poveri vergognosi*? For these were meritorious members of society, often former owners of minute plots of land or craft tools, struck down by misfortune or illness and reduced to destitution. The line between self-subsistence and dependence upon public aid was thin and easily disappeared in times of stress. It was awareness of this that underlay the Robespierrist declaration that society owed subsistence and employment to its less fortunate citizens (*Déclaration des Droits*, article 21).

This was the most radical formulation on poverty of the Revolutionary years. Revolutionary legislation of the years II and III, while maintaining the right to public assistance of parents unable to earn enough to sustain their families, otherwise tended to follow the main distinctions of Enlightenment ideas: the able-bodied did not deserve help and should be forced to work in *maisons de répression*; begging and vagabondage were to be suppressed; the deserving poor merited assistance at home, to be given in a discreet manner so as to avoid shaming them before the community; hospitals and other charitable institutions were to be removed from the hands of the religious and placed under secular control. But far from solving the problem of poverty, the effect of these laws – particularly the sale of the lands of the hospitals and charitable institutions (law of 23 messidor an II (11 July 1794), revoked – too late – on 9 fructidor an III (26 August 1795)) – was to worsen the situation. Successive laws of the directory, consulate and empire bore witness to the permanent presence of large numbers of poor and the necessity of meeting their needs by a system of poor relief based upon the traditional structures, reorganized under increasingly centralized control. By the heyday of the empire, despite the rigid supervision exercised by the prefects and Ministry of the Interior, responsibility for the poor had once more been placed upon the local communes. As before the Revolution, the adequacy of local poor relief depended upon the resources of the commune and the proportion of the population classified as poor. Private charity had re-emerged, with imperial encouragement, as a necessary support to the official institutions of public assistance.

The immediate consequence of the annexation of Tuscany to the French empire (8 January 1808) was the adoption of French legislation and administration in the three departments of the Arno, Ombrone and Méditerranée. As in the departments annexed in earlier years, the introduction of the new administrative structure and practices took a varying period of time. Despite the orders and chiding of the Junta (responsible for the transition to the new regime) and then of the prefects, the restructuring of the Tuscan system of poor relief only became an administrative reality during 1809. The purpose of the present study is to examine the nature and degree of success of the new French system of public charity.

Tuscany differed from the other regions of western Europe annexed to the empire in one fundamental respect: it possessed a proud tradition of reforming activity, still fresh in the minds of the numerous administrators who had assisted or witnessed the transformations of the years of the grand-duke Leopold and were now willing to collaborate with the French. Charitable institutions had been subjected to a series of reforms, according to the most modern theories of the Enlightenment. Hospitals had been removed from diocesan control and reordered under the supervision of local communes or the government; in the cities, particularly Florence, the different hospitals had been brought together under a single administration. With the suppression of most confraternities, their possessions had been given to diocesan ecclesiastical commissions, with responsibility for paying stipends to parish priests and alms and dowries to the poor. The suppression of many religious orders had, in some instances, benefited the patrimonies of hospitals and charitable institutions. But these same institutions had been affected negatively by Leopold's attempts to reduce the public debt and by his abolition of mortmain, as (like the local communes) they had been obliged to sell many of their lands and invest the proceeds in the public debt.[4] It was argued at the time that these enforced sales were beneficial to the institutions, as the inefficiency of their administrations meant that they received extremely low returns from their lands (or none at all), whereas they were guaranteed a regular income through interest on their loans to the state. Whatever the validity of this claim at the time, the charitable institutions soon found that they had lost a substantial portion of their patrimonies with the suspension of interest payments on these *luoghi di monte* (state bonds) during the political upheavals following the Revolution.

This deterioration in the financial situation of the hospitals and other charitable institutions reflected the sharp decline from the venerated years of Leopoldine reformism to the unsettled and financially disastrous governments that followed. Even after

Leopold's reforms the thirty-seven hospitals of the grand-duchy continued to show substantial annual deficits.[5] Ferdinand's military preparations in the 1790s, the French occupation of 1799, the Lorraine restoration and renewed French occupation, the creation of the improvident kingdom of Etruria, all repercussed negatively on the resources of the charitable institutions, incapable of resisting demands for further loans to the state. By 1804 the Etrurian administration had reached a point of near-bankruptcy; poor relief had been reduced to a pale shadow of earlier decades. In 1808 the French were to find themselves confronted by a structure of public charity that had been severely weakened during a decade when the rising prices and economic stringencies that accompanied the political disturbances had unquestionably increased the number of those in need of public assistance.

How many poor existed in Tuscany is, of course, impossible to calculate with any accuracy. In 1809 the prefect of the Arno department was asked to prepare a table of the total population and poor in each commune; the figures, which were sent to Paris in 1812, amounted to 580,157 for the total population of the department and 97,497 (equal to 17 per cent) for the poor. There is incontrovertible evidence that the figures for the poor were reduced by 11,000 at least before their despatch to Paris, which would raise the proportion of the poor to 19 per cent.[6] There is a strong element of ambiguity about the criteria used by the mayors of the communes to enumerate the poor. In general it would appear that they included not only beggars, residents dependent upon alms, and the deserving poor, but also labourers on the border-line of poverty, unable to earn enough to sustain their families without assistance. Vagabonds and itinerant beggars were definitely excluded, as – almost certainly – were those kept in hospitals. Of the former we know nothing, except that they were sufficiently numerous to be regarded as a perpetual worry. Statistics exist for the latter, who numbered 18,252 in all the hospitals of the Arno during 1809.[7] Even if one assumes that over half this number had already been included in the census of the poor, the proportion still rises to over 20 per cent. However cautiously one wishes to treat such statistics, it is clear that not less than one in every five or six persons was regarded officially as belonging to the category of the poor. As is to be expected, the proportion of the poor rose steeply in the remote sterile villages in the Apennines and in the major cities. In some villages, like Badia Tedalda or Verghereto, some two-thirds of the population migrated to the Maremma for half the year or more. Florence, with a population of 75,758, admitted to the presence of 23,455 poor; Prato, with 24,377 population, to 8215 poor; and Pistoia, with 9217 population, to 3418 poor. A proportion of one-third poor was thus acknowledged by these cities, although some others, such as Cortona or Arezzo, claimed surprisingly that only one-sixth or one-eighth of their population was poor. It is worth recalling that estimates of the poor in late eighteenth-century France amount to between one-fifth and one-tenth of the population, with higher concentrations in the cities.[8] The problem was of formidable proportions, with pockets of accentuated pauperism both in communes with meagre physical resources and in the cities, with their more sophisticated structures of poor relief.

It is not inappropriate, for an enquiry into the treatment of the poor, to adopt the major categories employed by the institutions founded for their assistance. For poverty, like so much else in western societies, was regarded as separable into tidy compartments, often with hierarchical labels. For those at the receiving end, the poor, the categories could prove frustrating and were frequently unreal: even if a family in the city of Florence could prove that none of its members begged, and that they were not of 'a birth and condition to be day-labourers', it was not always so easy to demonstrate that they were 'to be noted as possessing the characteristics of shamefaced poor by birth'.[9] But for the donors, to divide the poor by categories was traditional (reaching back into the Middle Ages), rational – and necessary, if their offerings were to make any visible impact on the ubiquitous, proteiform world of poverty. It is not surprising that Napoleonic administrators, with their passion for uniformity, rationalization and order, should have regarded the institutions of public charity as needing co-ordination, economies and control rather than any drastic reshaping of their structures.

Where subsistence at the lowest level ended and destitution began was difficult to mark, as the paths that descended from the former to the latter were so varied, each masking its private tale of human misery. But in the lengthy descent (for destitution rarely occurred overnight), one crucial point was institutionally identifiable – recourse to the *monti di pietà*. These communal pawnshops had been set up for the most part in the later sixteenth century in an attempt by the church to free the poorer sectors of society from usury and the Jews.[10] The *monti di pietà* represented a fragile, but essential barrier against destitution. They advanced small sums of money against household objects, however petty, at low rates of interest (4 to 6 per cent). They were almost the only safeguard against eviction or starvation for the small peasant in the months before the new crops, for the craftsman or petty trader in moments of industrial stagnation, for the widow awaiting the next instalment of a pension, for the family with one more mouth to feed. The *monti di pietà*, still at the end of the eighteenth century, offered the only means for a vast number of people without reserves, reliant solely upon their manual labour, to maintain their independence and avoid the humiliations of public or private alms.

There were some in official circles whose attitude towards the *monti* remained ambivalent, through fear lest they encourage improvidence. Lodovico Ricci, while convinced of their utility, had expressed this reservation:[11] 'If the pawnshops correct the greed of usurers, if on occasion the tearful complaints and direct sufferings of families cease, it remains true that such pawnshops also ease the lot of the dissolute.' For an anonymous Parisian bureaucrat, arguing the case for a high rate of interest to be exacted by the Florence *monte di pietà*, a valid point to bear in mind was that 'to lower the rate of interest and of tax on pledges would unfortunately be likely to encourage improvidence and that only too common desire to satisfy needs which are more artificial than real'.[12] In the big cities there was an element of truth in these allegations: the prefect and the mayor of Florence fought a losing battle against husbands who pawned or sold the bed or bedclothing they had successfully importuned from the local charitable institution.[13] But in the smaller towns and communes the *monti* served an essential function, as Fauchet, the Arno prefect, was quick to recognize:[14]

The Montevarchi *monte di pietà* only has limited resources and its needs are great, as the commune has a large number of distressed persons who lack work for part of the year. Their means of getting through the bad season is to pawn their personal effects temporarily, at an interest of 4 per cent, which enables them to keep going until the time of year when what they earn from their work and their economies allow them to redeem the articles which they had deprived themselves of.

The *monti di pietà* were relatively numerous. There were at least eleven in the department of the Arno, some in small communes like Anghiari, Castiglion Fiorentino, Laterina, Modigliana. Although their prime function was to lend to the needy, they were regarded as an integral part of the structure of poor relief and were sometimes required institutionally to offer assistance to other sectors of the system. The Florence *monte* loaned money to a local congregation, the Borgo San Sepolcro *monte* had given money to the foundling hospital since the seventeenth century, the Montevarchi *monte* was obliged to give dowries to poor girls, the *monte dei paschi* of Siena paid half the commune's expenditure for the upkeep of the insane in hospital and subsidized the education of poor girls, the *monte di pietà* of the small village of Laterina had completely changed its functions and used its resources to provide meals for beggars.[15] But these obligations remained marginal to the pawnshops' main activities. The accounts demanded by the prefects, and even more the inspections carried out in 1810, revealed the enormous scale of their loans. At Montevarchi, with a population of 6520, the *monte di pietà* accepted 9467 pledges for pawns in 1810; at Monte San Savino (population 5450), 9831 pledges were accepted in 14 months (1808–9); at Pistoia (population 9217) in 1810 21,318 pledges were received; at Prato (population 24,377) 16,434 pledges were held in eighteen months; at Florence (population 75,753) there were 66,337 pledges held in December 1808.[16] The small sums loaned (from 1 to 14 lire) and the interminable inventories of pledged objects are clear indicators of the class of borrowers: from the unusually valuable 'silver box' to the more common 'tattered and mended sheet', the 'piece of hemp' or the 'two copper bedpans with brass handles, and pair of scales, all much worn'.[17]

The documentation on the *monti di pietà* leaves little doubt that the demands made upon them increased during the years of French rule. By 1812 the number of pledges received by the Florence *monte* (certainly the largest in Tuscany) had risen to 142,477.[18] The *monti* were under serious pressure and private usury, although illegal, had become a significant problem at Florence by 1813.[19] But the difficulties of the *monti* derived not only from the increase in demand upon them which accompanied the rising prices and general economic difficulties of these years, but from the sharp fall in their funds. The capital employed by the *monti* had been provided by religious foundations, civic authorities and private individuals. Sometimes the money had been loaned without interest, but in most instances a low rate of interest was charged, between 3 and 5 per cent. The *monti*, in turn, loaned to the needy at 4 to 6 per cent, but calculated that, because of the continuous circulation, their capital yielded between 5 and 7 per cent annually. In normal times they were thus able to cover their administrative expenses and add some profit annually to the capital. The danger lay if their capital fell to a point where it was no longer adequate to cover both the demands of their clients and their administrative expenses.

Maladministration and deliberate fraud were obviously widespread. When the prefect of the Méditerranée department enquired into the bankruptcy of the *monti di pietà* of Portoferraio on the isle of Elba, he discovered that the larger part of its funds had been taken over by the communal administration or was owed by the last cashier of the *monte* who had died insolvent.[20] A common source of fraud was the sale of unredeemed pledges at prices calculated by valuers 'which they could do at their fancy, looking to their own interests and always at the expense of the owners'.[21] But abuses occurred in the payment of salaries to employees of the commune who had nothing to do with the *monte*, in maintaining an excessively large staff, in paying pensions to former employees, or – quite simply – in manipulating the accounts.

Nevertheless, such malpractices – widespread in all administrations of the period – were not the real cause of the crisis of the *monti di pietà*. The origins of their difficulties were to be found in the utilization of their capital by the government in the previous years.

Most of the *monti* had been obliged to place part of their resources, often on more than one occasion, in the public debt, and had then seen the interest due to them withheld and added to the capital already immobilized in state bonds. Even when interest was received on the public debt, it only yielded 3 per cent, compared to the 5 to 7 per cent of loans on pledges. At Florence, the *monte di pietà* possessed a capital in 1782 of 1,176,000 francs (according to French calculations), which yielded annually 58,000–60,000 francs and allowed a small surplus to be added to the capital. In 1783, and then on a far larger scale between 1800 and 1807, the *monte* was obliged to purchase bonds for a total of 895,671 francs, or over three-quarters of its capital.[22] The accounts of the other *monti* reveal a similar story. At Portoferraio, the French consul removed 9000 lire in 1799 to meet the needs of the French garrison; at Prato in 1799, general Gaultier ordered the free restitution of all pledges valued at less than 10 lire, which caused a loss of over 75,000 lire, or over 20 per cent of the capital in the *monte*. At Montevarchi the *monte* was forced to give the commune over 15,000 lire to pay for the expenses of troops in the troubled years 1799–1801; this represented nearly 15 per cent of its capital in 1810. In all the *monti* by 1808 a varying but always sizeable portion of their capital had been withdrawn from circulation by obligatory investment in the public debt.[23] The already shaky finances of the *monti* received the *coup de grâce* with Napoleon's liquidation of the public debt (imperial decree, 9 April 1809). With the exception of the Florence *monte* the pawnshops lost their capital without compensation.

The consequences were felt immediately. The *monti di pietà* of all the major cities – Prato, Pistoia, Pisa, Siena, Florence – and many minor ones were on the point of collapse, unable to pay interest to their creditors, or meet their administrative costs without drawing heavily on their capital. The prefects appealed for reimbursement, even if (as in Florence's case) it was in the form of State *rentes*, calculated on a far smaller capital than that originally loaned. In some instances, such as Leghorn, they were successful. Elsewhere – at Florence, Pisa, Siena – by 1812–13 they were obliged to excogitate methods of closing the *monti*, partially reimbursing creditors and reopening them on a much reduced basis.[24] In the very years when the pressures of war and economic crisis were felt so acutely, the most effective defence for the poorer wage-earners was drastically lowered.

Aid for the deserving poor had always been provided in many different forms. The basic distinction was between assistance, outdoor, *a domicilio*, and that offered in hospitals. The Directory had maintained this distinction in its reorganization of public assistance. By the law of 7 frimaire an V (27 November 1796), confirmed by the imperial decree of 2 February 1810, *bureaux de bienfaisance* were to be created in every commune, with responsibility for organizing *secours à domicile*. In theory, the separation of responsibilities between hospitals and *bureaux* seemed clear and simple. In practice, it could lead to uncertainty and dispute: as late as 1812 the administration of the Florence hospitals wanted to make the Florence *bureau* pay for the bandages used on hernia patients formerly treated by the *bureau* at home, but subsequently removed to hospital.[25]

Apart from such demarcation disputes, a serious difficulty was that of finding an adequate number of respectable citizens to form the administrative commissions of the *bureaux*. As the sub-prefect of Arezzo pointed out, it was often impossible to provide a full list of names from which to choose the commissions 'because there are no more individuals living in the communes really suitable for public office';[26] inevitably, in the smaller communes (and many did not possess *bureaux*) the mayor and the parish priest tended to dominate.

Even more serious than lack of personnel (always lamented by Napoleonic administrators) was lack of funds. When the statistic of the poor and beggars was compiled in the Arno department in 1809 only 18 of the 114 communes acknowledged possessing any income set aside for assisting the poor.[27] According to the laws, the funds of the *bureau* were made up of the incomes from the patrimonies of charitable bodies formerly responsible for *secours à domicile*, from part of the *droit des pauvres* exactable on theatre tickets, and from legacies or donations. As the mayor of Greve pointed out to the prefect, there was little reason to create a *bureau* there, as no charitable institutions had existed previously, nor was there ever any theatre, and[28] thirdly, because it seems to me extremely unlikely that any donations will be made to the *bureau de bienfaisance*, as most property in the commune is owned by the royal demesne or by Florentine gentlemen who will be indifferent to the *bureau*, given their absenteeism; while the other proprietors all have family charges, such as not to be able to make donations or legacies.

The commune only has rateable properties for 1200 *fiorini*, or thereabouts, split up into lots of small farms and houses, and the peasants are almost all poor and so heavily indebted that one cannot hope for more than very meagre alms from collections.

If we want charity, *bienfaisance*, that spirit of charity capable of making everyone happy, then let us unite to ensure the triumph of the Christian religion which is the basis and overflowing source of true fraternal charity; then we shall most surely see the prodigious and useful results.

Certainly there was little to hope from alms, however strong the spirit of Christian charity, according to the mayor of Fiorenzuola, for the total figure collected in the churches amounted to 56 centimes: 'Popular ignorance is such that the villagers adapt badly to the new systems, however praiseworthy they are; so not much is to be hoped for in future, at least for some time.'[29]

The mayor of Lastra, as late as 1813, could complain that the commune had no funds for its own needy, let alone for 'foreigners', and ask plaintively how he was expected to pay beggars passing through the village the allowance to which they had legal claim.[30]

Naturally not all country villages were so destitute of resources. Some possessed legacies, occasionally even substantial ones. The commune of Vernio won a long and bitter struggle against its former feudatories, the Bardi, for possession of various legacies left by earlier members of the family for charitable purposes. It found itself in possession of a vast income of over 40,000 francs – far too much, according to the sub-prefect: 'It is rationally impossible to abandon the administration of a revenue of 40,000 francs to a commission of joiners and small peasants.'[31] In the minute commune of Laterina, the resources of the former *monte di pietà* were turned over to the *bureau de bienfaisance*.[32] But in the countryside, in general, particularly in the poorer regions of

Tuscany, where *bureaux* existed their resources were so limited as to be of little assistance to the deserving poor. Even in some of the cities the amount distributed was negligible. At Arezzo in the first quarter of 1811 subsidies (for the most part ranging between 1.68 and 5.04 francs) were given to only thirty-six poor.[33] As in all other respects, the major cities alone – Florence, Prato, Pisa, Leghorn – already possessed sufficient resources and institutions to make the *bureau de bienfaisance* a meaningful reality.

The variety and complexity of assistance to the deserving poor can best be illustrated by the example of Florence. During the preparatory discussions for the creation of the *bureau* a list was compiled of the existing charitable institutions in the city: there were twenty-one, with some additional legacies administered either through confraternities or by private families.[34] Most confraternities were suppressed and the *bureau* was formed with responsibilities for supervising and co-ordinating the activities of the surviving eight institutions. According to the imperial decree of 2 February 1810, the assistance offered by the *bureau à domicile* to the indigent and poor could assume many forms, from food (bread, meat, soup) to clothing and medical aid.[35] In practice the Florence *bureau* and the prefect maintained the considerably wider patterns of aid given traditionally by the eight institutions. Each charitable body had a clearly defined function. The *Conservatorio della SS Annunziata 'detto di Orbetello'* offered lodging to unmarried pregnant girls during childbirth; the *Casa di educazione di Fuligno* educated and gave dowries to poor girls; the *Casa Pia di San Filippo Neri* educated poor orphan boys; the *Spedale di San Onofrio* gave lodging to the poor without a roof over their head; the *Compagnia della Misericordia* transported the poor ill to hospital and the poor dead to the cemetery; the *Compagnia per i Catecumeni* provided for the poor converted to Catholicism; the *Congregazione di San Martino 'detta dei Buonomini'* gave subsidies to 'those poor families of civil condition, by birth or employment or the exercise of noble arts, laid down by some misfortune, who languish, neglected and shamefaced, in their misery'; the *Congregazione di San Giovanni Battista* also gave aid to 'indigent families of our city who, despite applying themselves to work, do not earn enough for their entire subsistence, because of those critical circumstances which often accompany the misery of the poor.'[36]

The patterns emerge clearly. Children were a central concern: besides the various institutions for which it was responsible, the *bureau* also gave subsidies to the Bigallo hospital for abandoned children. Respectable families who found themselves in a state of indigence through no fault of their own formed the other main category. While assistance was the most immediate need, attempts were also made to re-establish the independence of the needy by offering the possibility of work. A significant part of the funds of the major institution – the Congregation of San Giovanni Battista – was employed in the production of woollen, linen and cotton cloths and in providing tools to poor families to enable them to become self-sufficient. The children at San Filippo Neri, Fuligno and Bigallo were taught a range of trades, from spinning and weaving for girls to tailoring, umbrella- and furniture-making, even market gardening for the boys. But whatever the funds employed to train or offer the tools of their trade to the poor, the numbers assisted in this manner represented only a minute proportion of those in need of daily aid.

In the early 1790s a count was made of those requiring bread subsidies every day, excluding the poor already looked after by other congregations or possessing permission to beg: according to the officials of San Giovanni Battista, who had stationed themselves at the entrance of every church in Florence on Easter Sunday, they amounted to 56,918.[37] Many of these may have been included in the interminable lists of supplications for aid made to this congregation by the poor. The criteria for receiving aid were strict: the recipient had to be a Florentine citizen, a 'shamefaced poor' by birth, former trade or employment, of good character, and in a state of total destitution, without the possibility of assistance from relatives or other sources; support from the parish priest, corroborated by a deputy of the congregation, was essential for an application to be successful. In twelve months from January 1811 to January 1812, 1854 applications were received.[38]

The institutional structure of relief for the needy and deserving poor in Florence was thus both extensive and varied, as was to be expected of a relatively wealthy capital city. But it was far from comprehensive. Indeed, the multiplicity of institutions, as much as the partly illusory expectation of opportunities offered by a city, attracted the rural poor to Florence, as it did to all large cities like Prato, Pisa, Siena or Leghorn. The insistence on residence or lengthy domicile in Florence as a qualification for assistance reflected the attempts by the Congregation of San Giovanni Battista and the smaller charitable bodies to limit their responsibilities and exclude the floating population of vagrants and beggars. Even so, the institutions found themselves unable to meet the rising demands made upon them from the later eighteenth century. Peter Leopold, in his reform of the Congregation of San Giovanni Battista in 1767, had endeavoured to increase its resources by a systematic collection of alms in the churches, 'which', commented the town councillor F.A. Corsi Salviati in 1809, 'is still practiced today with little success.'[39] The enforced conversion into state bonds of much of the property of the institutions had led to the same negative consequences experienced by the *monti di pietà*. But, quite apart from this dependence upon the regularity of interest payments on the state debt, Leopold had been obliged to subsidize the institutions in order to maintain the level of assistance. As conditions worsened, after Leopold's departure for Vienna, resources diminished. Between 1777 and 1790 the Congregation of San Giovanni Battista had received from the Depositeria Generale a figure varying from 15,120 to 22,480 francs every six months (according to 1809 calculations); under Ferdinand III this had risen to amounts of between 17,640 and 30,240 francs; under the kingdom of Etruria, it had fallen to between 7560 and 10,080 francs.[40] By the time of the French annexation charitable institutions for the deserving poor were in considerable difficulties.

Primary responsibility for these institutions was now placed upon the local authorities. The main source of finance for the *bureau* and its dependent bodies in the capital city came from the civic administration of Florence (from 54 per cent rising to 64 per cent). Income from legacies and inheritances fell from 33 per cent to 27 per cent, while the tax on theatrical performances never yielded more than 8 to 14 per cent. The rising proportion of income provided by the local administration is the more significant in that its initial generous annual subsidy of 50,000 francs was reduced by the French authorities to 30,000 by 1811.[41] The figure proved inadequate and the prefect was soon forced to search for additional sources of income. As always, the rigid system of financial control – requiring authorization from Paris – hampered his efforts. Departmental revenues in Tuscany were less well endowed than some communal revenues,[42] so limiting the possibility for the prefect of distributing the resources available for the poor according to the needs of the different areas. Increasingly the prefects in all three departments were obliged to turn to private charity.

Despite the inadequacy of resources, the functions of the *bureau* were gradually extended. Responsibility for the distribution of financial subsidies to poor noble families, initiated by Napoleon as a facet of his policy of *ralliement*, was vested in the *bureaux*.[43] The mayor of Florence handed over to the *bureau* the administration of the civic cemetery at Trespiano and the exaction of funeral taxes.[44] The *bureaux* could even be employed to assist the enforcement of public hygiene regulations, precisely because they were in direct contact with so wide a section of the poor urban population. In 1811, and again in 1812, the prefect Fauchet turned to the *bureau* for lists of all mothers with infant children, and ordered that their subsidies be stopped unless their children had been vaccinated against smallpox:[45]

> Undoubtedly it is regrettable that one should be obliged to employ such measures, but they are legitimated by the duty of preserving for society and their families infants who would soon become victims, if the authorities did not use all means in their power to save them.

The winter months always dilated the problem of poor relief. In an effort to relieve the pressure on the *bureaux*, the prefects regularly ordered the civic authorities to extend their programme of public works. Building and road works were the obvious solution, as the mayor of Florence stated in a public notice in December 1810: 'The Town Council has been invited to open up various works. It believes that it should choose something capable of employing a large number of persons, whatever their age or sex.' As always, the civic administration tried to limit its responsibilities to its own citizens:[46]

The only persons accepted for work will be the real poor, of both sexes, recognized as such by certificates from their appropriate police commissioner; and anybody of their class found idle and wandering about the city will be obliged by the police to present himself for the above work.

As it is a question of providing subsistence for the poor inhabitants of this city, all the poor from the communes outside its walls will be excluded.

A police guard will be permanently on duty at the place of work to control that public decency is maintained, given the promiscuity of the sexes.

But by 1812 the entire system of assistance for the needy and poor was in danger of breaking down because of the sharp rise in grain prices. The normal forms of aid – bread, money and employment – were proving inadequate. The prefects were instructed to make the *bureaux* in the cities provide soup kitchens. All other forms of aid in kind were to be substituted by a twice-daily distribution of 'an extremely nourishing soup to which no bread needs to be added'; private individuals who gave charity regularly were to be encouraged to change their alms from cash to coupons for soup; detailed enquiries were carried out into the suitability of the cheaper grains and vegetables, such as maize, sugar-beet flour, leeks, carrots, potatoes, etc., as ingredients for the soups. A tone of unusual urgency pervaded the prefect's instructions to the Florence *bureau's* administrative commission:[47]

In difficult circumstances, particularly when the extreme scarcity of food makes itself felt, the primary concern of an administration must be for the indigent class; it must excogitate the means to procure the sustenance required for survival itself. . . . You are undoubtedly aware, gentlemen, that the shortage of cereals makes our situation extremely ticklish. Despite the provident measures just taken by the government, it is only too likely that this department will find itself extremely embarrassed over its food supplies and that all the care and vigilance of the authorities may not succeed in thwarting the manoeuvres of speculators.

What can we do to succour the indigent when the only cereals still in the department will be in the hands of well-to-do persons who bought them in advance or reserved their supplies out of the harvests they sold? Charitable institutions will no longer be able to distribute assistance in kind and the money that they will give the poor will be no more than a useless gesture to buy bread, or a dangerous expedient which may lead them to excesses, the consequences of which will inevitably trouble public tranquillity . . .

I repeat, gentlemen, that we are hard pressed for time, the demands are unremitting. Take care that there is not too much talk, and above all ensure that not a word escapes from your *bureaux* about this problem until it can definitely be carried through.

For a brief moment the prefect hoped to create a continuous, generalized system of free soups, explaining that it had already been successfully undertaken in past years in some departments of the interior. The *bureau* was thus to organize soup kitchens on the assumption of a distribution 'in all the large towns, not only in times of dearth or when cereal prices are high, but in all circumstances and throughout the seasons of the year'.[48] But inevitably this scheme proved too grandiose. By December 1812 over 22,000 soups had been distributed in Florence; in January 1813 the daily distribution was raised from 400 to 600 soups daily, and the prefect was taking advantage of its organization to feed prisoners as well. During the winter of 1813–14 it proved necessary to adopt the same system.[49] Humanity and public order equally demanded that means be found to feed the urban poor.

Lodging the poor was also a matter of humanity and utility (if not of public order), for which responsibility lay with the hospitals. By tradition hospitals served a dual function: they looked after the ill who could not be kept at home, and acted as poorhouses for the aged and orphans. Both categories of inmates belonged exclusively to the poor, as no family with resources would risk endangering the life of a relative by sending him to hospital. Prolonged illness and frequent death in hospitals resulted from multiple causes, nearly all attributable to unhygienic conditions. Inadequate warmth or inappropriate sustenance for newborn babies abandoned in winter on the steps of hospitals, spoilt food provided by dishonest almoners who sold the hospital's fresh produce for private profit, unclean food and fruit brought in by relatives to supplement the inadequate diet, the putridity of decomposing bodies in the professor of anatomy's mortuary chamber, woollen mattresses soiled by human excreta, open gutters of blood flowing out of the hospital slaughter-house, were symptomatic – for the horrified French administrators – of a general state of affairs in which human carelessness accentuated the dangers engendered by the climatic extremes of central Italy.[50] In the words of Luca Donati, surgeon of Orbetello hospital:[51]

> One sees so many unfortunates go to hospital with a tertian fever and then fall into a typhus fever; or others who go there clean in body, who catch scabies and lots of other maladies. In most cases, so as not to indict the hospital beds as the source of a thousand herpetic, malignant and tabetic infections, everything is explained in terms of the predisposition of the patient who became the victim of these acquired diseases, and without further thought the matter is spun out and humanity sacrificed against those very principles for which hospitals were originally created. . . . Besides the damage which society suffers through the loss of so many individuals, the hospitals themselves are ruined, as hundreds of sick settle in and, becoming incurable, never leave the hospitals except at death.

The statistics of Tuscan hospitals bear out this appalling picture. An annual average of 13,985 patients entered the seventeen hospitals of the department of the Arno during the years 1809 to 1812. Of these, an average 2577, or 18 per cent, died annually. Infant mortality was always very high and inflated the overall figure (average annual adult deaths amounted to 15 per cent).[52] In the decade 1774–83 an annual average of 872 infants were accepted at the Innocenti hospital at Florence, of whom 707 or 81 per cent died every year. In 1810, out of a total of 17,962 deaths in the department of the Arno, 3444 or 19 per cent died under the age of three months and 7773 or 43 per cent under the age of 2 years.[53]

Inadequate hygienic measures evidently acted as a prime agent of mortality in the hospitals. Nevertheless, the hospitals' role as poorhouses tended to accentuate the proportion of deaths, since infants and the aged constituted the most vulnerable segments of the population. This social role of the hospitals – offering lodgings to those lacking, or abandoned by, their families – was particularly marked in the smaller centres, where legacies and endowments had been given to the hospitals over the centuries precisely for these purposes. The description of the duties of the Cortona hospital can be regarded as typical of most:[54]

> Maintenance and care of the sick poor; reception, custody and maintenance of foundlings, wet-nursing for them and for the legitimate children of the poor; fulfilment of many obligations, legacies, dowries (these last for an annual sum of 185 scudi), dowries for female orphans to marry, benefices for parish priests, life annuities and 149 scudi in dowries received by contract from the Ecclesiastical Patrimony in exchange for corresponding properties.

The social role of the hospitals, in fact, overlapped with that of the charitable institutions grouped by the French in the *bureaux de bienfaisance*. The Montevarchi hospital, for example, gave clothes to fourteen poor children each year, as well as providing help for the ill and poor and bread for the 'wretched'.[55] The Volterra hospital traditionally gave dowries of 147 francs to the girls in its care, 'who otherwise would lack all means of establishing themselves', especially given 'common prejudice about their birth'.[56] Responsibility for children, in particular, remained without clear division between hospitals and *bureaux*, despite official French regulations that children passed under the auspices of the *bureaux* once they reached the age of 12.[57]

Concern for the lives of infants and children had always been widespread, for religious, humanitarian and utilitarian reasons: 'the loss of these infants creates a gap in society, damages the ruler's greatness by reducing the number of his subjects, and leads all honest men to careful reflection', wrote an anonymous critic of the Innocenti hospital at Florence.[58] Illegitimacy was widespread, an inevitable consequence of the promiscuity in which the poor lived. Fear of incest underlay the readiness with which the Congregation of San Giovanni Battista gave beds to poor families, to separate parents from children, brothers from sisters. Dowries were given in an endeavour to conserve virtue and canalize into marriage youthful inclinations, constantly subject to dangers 'which wretchedness accentuates'.[59] Infanticide was indirectly encouraged by the reprobation in which unmarried mothers were held: 'In a general hospital, the honest but poor woman, the girl victim of a momentary error or seduction, are subject to glances from the public and the gossip of the trainees or staff responsible for providing them with medicaments and meals.'[60] The attitude towards unmarried mothers remained ambivalent, oscillating between a desire to protect the innocent offspring and a moral righteousness expressed in the harsh treatment of expectant mothers, only received into hospitals in the final stages of their pregnancy.

But the high level of infant mortality was attributable less to social ostracism of unmarried expectant women than to lack of care of infants. Too many died as they were brought after birth from the countryside to a hospital. Two special 'deposit houses' had been opened in the Tuscan Romagna in Leopold's years because 'the commissioners of those years had shown that many creatures died, above all in the winter season, because they were brought to the nearest hospital over great distances, along difficult paths, and so suffered hunger and cold'.[61] Tuscany was well endowed (excessively so, according to French administrators in 1812) with hospitals for children: there were seven in the department of the Arno, at Florence, Arezzo, Cortona, Castiglion Fiorentino, Borgo San Sepolcro, Pistoia and Prato, to which new-born babies were brought directly (often abandoned on the steps) or sent from other hospitals. In the years 1809–12 an annual average of 1971 infants were received into these hospitals, of whom 821 or 42 per cent died. Most of the deaths did not occur within the hospital walls. The vast majority of infants were sent out to wet-nurses in the countryside – an average of 84 per cent from the Arno hospitals. A more detailed analysis of the foundling hospitals of Florence, Borgo San Sepolcro and Cortona in 1810 showed that 65 per cent of the deaths occurred in the countryside.[62] As the anonymous critic of the Florence Innocenti hospital commented: 'The death of infants of the Innocenti hospital occurs because of the lack of care and of wet-nurses. There are few wet-nurses, mostly overburdened with infants; with the aid of a number of goats and lots of gruel, they nourish these unhappy infants. . . . These infants die of hunger.'[63]

That the wet-nurses should have proved so unsatisfactory is hardly surprising, given the extremely low salaries they received. Already in 1805 the Regent Maria Luisa had increased payments.[64] The state of near-crisis grew worse after the French took over. Each commune was financially responsible for the infants it placed in hospital. But the communes were frequently unable to pay, while the tariffs fixed by the government were inadequate. The immediate consequence was that the hospitals began to resist accepting infants from outside their communal boundaries: in 1809 the Arezzo hospital was seeking to exact payment from seventeen communes for its foundlings; by 1811 the prefect was seriously worried lest it collapse through debt.[65] Inadequate wages for wet-nurses, combined with delays in payments to hospitals, threatened the breakdown of the entire system. The administrative committee of the Borgo San Sepolcro hospitals made a final desperate appeal to the prefect in July 1810 for an immediate subsidy from the Treasury or permission to send the infants back to their respective communes:[66]

The instructions we requested from the higher authorities, which should have served as a thermometer for us, have never been given. . . . These hapless victims of weakness or vice, who should find in us the succour and protection of natural paternity, only experience misery and neglect, against our wishes. Complaints are reaching us on all sides from wet-nurses and custodians, who have not been paid for months now and threaten to bring back the foundlings entrusted to them to nurture and lodge. Already we find ourselves personally responsible for sucklings without finding women willing to feed them. We cannot even offer our protection to those unfortunate children who appeal to us because they are badly treated by their custodians. For how can we reprove the latter if their services are without reward? How can we withdraw their charges, if everybody rejects them? This weighs heavily on our heart, our humanity and sensibility. But what will happen when confidence has died out completely? We will no longer be able to uphold the life of unfortunate foundlings and ensure useful hands to society.

The situation lamented by these Tuscan hospital administrators was common to all the Empire. In July 1811 the government finally acknowledged that the funds for abandoned infants were inadequate and assigned a further four million francs. At the same time the hospitals were reorganized and wages increased for wet-nurses; in the Arno department, the seven hospitals were reduced to three (at Florence, Arezzo and Pistoia).[67] There is little evidence about the effects of these changes, but the reduction in the number of hospitals in a mountainous region such as Tuscany almost certainly increased the incidence of mortality among the newly born: at the Florence Innocenti hospital, the number of deaths rose from 578 in 1811 to 737 in 1812.[68]

Attempting, as always, to fit social realities into neat administrative categories, the French had distinguished between different classes of infants: abandoned children (*trovatelli* and *esposti*) and orphans and children of poor families. The distinctions were traditional, but their application appears to have become more rigid during the years of French rule. The vast majority of children under hospital control belonged to the category of abandoned infants: they averaged 1606 annually between 1809 and 1812 in the Arno department, compared to 337 orphans and children of poor families.[69] The disproportion was revealing of the inadequacies of the structure of poor relief, as it was generally recognized that a major cause and symptom of the descent from poverty to indigence was the addition of new mouths to feed. The reluctance to accept infants from poor families was based upon the fear that the children would subsequently be reclaimed, so transforming the hospitals into temporary deposits during periods of family crisis. Instructions were strict about not allowing parents to reclaim their children unless they paid for their expenditure. Hospital administrators were warned against accepting infants with markings which would enable their parents to identify them later.[70] Worry lest the hospitals be flooded with such temporary inmates was obviously one practical reason for such restrictions. But another, more 'ideological' reason was the belief that since society bore the expense of raising these infants and children, it had the right to exact repayment from them once they had grown up. As the 1811 regulations stated, all children raised by the state were 'at its disposal'; if not employed in some other manner, they could be taken over by the military marine once they reached the age of twelve.[71]

The desire to create 'useful' citizens coloured the discussions of what to do with these vast numbers of abandoned children. They were to be trained in some trade and placed in workshops. Even if the ministry of the Marine had the legal right to take over male boys, in practice most were passed over to the *bureaux de bienfaisance*. The girls were also to be given a professional training, or at least taught some domestic arts. Their utility to society, however, ultimately lay in their ability to procreate after marriage. In consequence, high priority was given to dowries, without which at best they would remain spinsters, at worst they would become unmarried mothers. As the Volterra hospital administrators explained, spinsterdom was dangerous given the 'fervid inclinations' of youth, while reasonable dowries ensured marriage to young peasants, so making an important contribution to this class of the population, which represented the very basis of agriculture.[72] Dowries were the pilaster of the family structure, a defence against illegitimacy, a precondition for increase of the population. All hospitals offered dowries to the girls in their care; they had always constituted a major object of religious legacies; communal administrations, such as those at Poppi, Bibbiena, Borgo San Sepolcro, had set aside part of the revenue from the salt *gabelle* to fund dowries for girls from deserving poor families or in hospitals; the grand-ducal family had endowed a steady flow of such dowries for the same categories, amounting to 508 annually by the time of the French annexation.[73] It was hardly surprising that imperial occasions, such as the victory of Austerlitz or the birth of the king of Rome, should be marked by the distribution of dowries in preference to all other forms of charity.[74] As always, the cities were given preference over the countryside, both in numbers and size of dowries.

But the problem remained of what to do with the children, if employment or marriage could not be found for them. Once more the evidence is slight. Schemes were constantly devised to create workshops under the control of the *bureaux de bienfaisance* or within the *dépôts de mendicité*. But these could only have had a marginal effect in resolving the problem. The hospitals, especially in the rural areas, continued abusively to maintain their charges, once they had passed the legal age of minority. The only alternative was to throw them on the streets.

Of all groups looked after by the hospitals, children received the greatest attention. In part this was because of their numbers – an average of 14 per cent of total admissions to Arno hospitals between 1809 and 1812[75] – but even more because neglect comparable to that endured by other inmates would have led to a sharp and unacceptable rise in the already high rate of mortality. There was less concern for the aged, the incurables, the cripples, the blind, the maimed, precisely because they were a burden upon society. But, inevitably, mortality was lower among these groups; between 1788 and 1812 mortality among the infirm and aged averaged nearly 16 per cent in the Santa Maria Nuova hospital at Florence.[76]

The hospitals, like the other institutions for the poor, had been restructured by Leopold. They had been removed from episcopal jurisdiction and administratively unified within the single cities under the control of the civic administrations, except for the major cities, where government supervision was maintained. A special hospital had been created for the insane at Florence, which gathered together patients from all Tuscany. Hospital resources had been considerably increased by the assignation to them of parts of the ecclesiastical patrimony, whose revenues far exceeded their obligations to pay pensions to the ex-monks and -nuns and parish priests. Despite these reforms, the hospitals remained consistently in deficit.[77] As with the *monti di pietà* and the other charitable institutions, they had suffered from the enforced conversion of part of their patrimony into public debt bonds (sometimes passed on to them in this form with the suppression of convents). But undoubtedly more significant reasons for their financial difficulties were maladministration of their large, scattered estates and peculation. In the troubled years after Leopold's departure the condition of the hospitals worsened as the government tapped institutional funds and defaulted on the public debt. From 1791 there was a sharp rise in debts owed to private lenders.[78] By 1805 the regent of Etruria had to take emergency measures and assign sums from the salt *gabelle* and other revenues to relieve the crisis of the

Florence hospitals.[79] But these payments, like interest on the public debt, were stopped with the new French regime.

Despite the very considerable efforts of the prefects, the situation worsened during the years of French rule. Although they had never been despoiled of their land like the French hospitals, the complicated inheritance of the previous decades had left the Tuscan hospitals with a mass of debts and an imposing body of non-exactable credits. Only in 1810 did it prove possible to draw up budgets, which merely confirmed the disastrous financial situation. Theft of foodstuffs, of bedclothing, of medicines, abusive admittance to the hospitals of healthy poor, an excessive number of staff who sometimes offered their families board and lodging in the hospitals, illegal maintenance of now unemployed secularized priests, were a few of the many faults identified by the French as responsible for the deficits. As the Arno prefect wrote to the administrative commission of the Florence hospitals:[80]

> In no way do I wish to accuse your zeal; indeed, I pay tribute to the personal sacrifices of each administrator in trying to make up, as far as possible, for the confusion of the accounts and for everything which is perverse in the ordering of the hospitals. But I think I have noticed that you are too considerate and hence that one abuse soon replaces the other you have just destroyed. It is incredible, in fact, that with an enormous endowment in rents, properties, house rentals and income from the city's revenues, one cannot pay for about 1500 sick or aged and 1500 to 1600 infants almost all suckled in the countryside.

Ruthless pruning of surplus staff and pensions, together with a close check over every detail of expenditure, were certainly responsible for the notable reduction in the deficit of the Florence hospitals in 1811. But from this year until the collapse of French rule the deficit rose again. This was in part attributable to the rigidity of the French system of administration.

The drastic reorganization of state finances affected all institutional lenders negatively because of the delays and suspension of interest during the lengthy liquidation of the public debt (only finally decreed on 18 February 1812). Even though the debts owed by hospitals for loans from suppressed monasteries and annuities to ex-monks and -nuns were cancelled at the same time (so freeing the Florence hospitals of annual payments of over 355,000 francs, besides an accumulated debt of 295,000 francs),[81] the hospitals lost heavily with the liquidation. Equally serious were the strict administrative limitations on the use of communal revenues, which impeded the hospitals from exacting from the communes their previous liabilities for placing children and the insane in hospitals. By 1812 the communes of the three Tuscan departments had an accumulated debt of 264,000 francs solely with the Bonifazio hospital for the insane.[82] Inevitably the Florence hospitals (responsible for over three-fifths of all patients in the department), like those throughout Tuscany, tried to avoid taking in patients from outside the communal boundaries. By December 1813, as the French combed the country to raise new troops, the prefect of the Arno was forced to send a sharp reminder to all hospitals that it was their obligation to take in conscripts who fell ill during their long trudge towards assembly points.[83] Unable to exact their credits, obstructed in the sale of their possessions or acceptance of legacies by the need for the permission of the minister of the interior and the emperor, the hospitals found that even the prefect could not protect them against the demands of the minister of war, who forced the Florence hospitals to accept all ill soldiers, offering them a lower daily tariff than that for civilian patients, which in any case was usually paid only after protest and considerable delay, sometimes in the form of coupons which could not be exacted in Tuscany. The minister of war, when prevailed upon by his colleague the minister of the interior to order part payment in 1813, was unable to raise the daily tariff as it had been fixed by Napoleon.[84] The apparent simplicity and clarity of imperial administration, when put to the test at the local level, revealed a rigid lack of communication between the different sectors – communal, departmental, military, hospital financing – that led to a bureaucratic nightmare for those unable (legally or otherwise) to meet their costs. The sharp rise in food prices from 1811 dealt a final blow to hospital finances, as the administrative commissions were forced to keep within a fixed daily tariff that no longer covered the costs of feeding the patients. The only solution, as the Arno prefect insisted, was to allow them to sell part of their patrimony. By January 1814, when Napoleon finally signed the decree allowing the Florence hospitals to sell 120 houses, they appeared to be on the point of collapse.[85] The ability of the hospitals to continue to function in these disastrous conditions can only really be explained in terms of a credit system that permitted at least institutions with official backing to accumulate debt indefinitely.

The structure of poor relief had always been based on the assumption that certain categories – children, the aged, the infirm, the deserving and needy poor – merited aid from society. There were other categories, however, who were unworthy of such assistance – the able-bodied beggars and the vagabonds. Their numbers had grown, their presence was ubiquitous. Inevitably, the Napoleonic administrators who reorganized the system of poor relief endeavoured to devise an institutional solution for the problem of the beggars. Even if they retained their optimism, against mounting evidence, about their success in meeting society's obligations towards the deserving poor, their experience with the *dépôts de mendicité* in Tuscany must have led to moments of doubt.

Dépôts de mendicité, or houses of correction, were no novelty: they had existed, under that name, in pre-Revolutionary France and, under various titles, in most states, often tracing their origin back to the sixteenth or seventeenth centuries. The aims were always the same: to remove mendicants and vagrants from public view and make them work. As in many other spheres, the imperial administrators were merely reconstituting earlier institutions in a more systematic and apparently efficient manner. A decree of 5 July 1808 and administrative circulars of 28 October and 19 December 1808 ordered the formation of a *dépôt* in every department. Begging became a criminal act according to the penal code (articles 274–82). Vagrant beggars were to be subjected to the full rigour of the law, imprisoned and despatched to their place of origin. Resident beggars were to be sent to the *dépôt*; the circular specified that this latter category was to include women and children under the age of 16, whatever their place of domicile, the infirm and sexagenarians incapable of working, and the able-bodied poor.[86] To assess the number who would need to be accommodated, a census was made of the poor and beggars. The ministry of the interior also proposed the creation of 'free charitable workshops' in every *arrondissement* lacking in industry or manufactures in order to offer employment during the slack periods of the agricultural year. These *ateliers* were to be kept quite distinct from the houses of correction and were to be voluntary; only in the subsequent development of the *dépôts* did the two merge.

The wheels of bureaucracy ground slowly and in this instance not very thoroughly. The Méditerranée *dépôt* was opened at San Gimignano in August 1811, the Arno and Ombrone *dépôts* only in December 1813.[87] The census of poor and beggars drawn up for at least the Arno *dépôt* dated back to 1809, but it was being employed as a basis in 1812 discussions.[88] By then it had become clear that it was not going to prove possible to shut all beggars in a *dépôt*, as there were over 6400 in the Arno department and 2500 to 3000 in the Méditerranée.[89] The capacity of the Arno *dépôt* was calculated at 535 and that of the Méditerranée at about 300.[90] Stress was now being placed on the possibility for relatives and communes to reclaim mendicants placed in the *dépôt* so long as they were kept from begging.[91]

The basic ambiguity, which reappeared in a variety of contexts, derived from the fusion of the concept of the *dépôt* – repression of begging – with that of the *atelier* – offering beggars work. It was easy to see how the two aspects had merged: reprobation of idleness was an integral part of the ethic of work, that tended to gloss over the scarcity of employment opportunities as a (though not the only) cause of begging. In the scandalized words of an anonymous French bureaucrat:[92]

> The appalling quantity of poor who inundate the cities and countryside offer less of an idea about public destitution than of the propensity for sloth of a particular class of individuals who have turned their state of mendicity into a profession. The tolerance of this shameful vice is such that in most towns of this department [Arno] the poor have managed to negotiate with the well-to-do citizens a sort of subscription, by which they receive an agreed wage each week.

The difficulty about making beggars work was that the category, as defined in the circular of 19 December 1808, included many who were incapable of working. The full significance of this contradiction only emerged when the mayors and sub-prefects were ordered to send those found begging to the *dépôts*. The prefect of the Méditerranée department was conscious of the problem, but optimistically shifted the burden of finding employment onto the *bureaux de bienfaisance*:[93]

> All those able to work will surely not ask to be admitted to the *dépôt*. Where no work exists, the committee of charity is committed to finding some. Private individuals, relieved of the importuning of alms, will not refuse this sort of succour, which reconciles their interests with their most sacred duties. Those who do not wish to work will be abandoned to the vigour of the laws and police. . . . Able-bodied beggars, even if they are without work, will not be able to claim that because of this they are deprived of all means of subsistence.

Implicit in this view was the belief that the *dépôt* should act as an uncomfortable poorhouse, supplementary to the hospitals and charitable institutions, rather than as a house of correction. It was a view clearly shared by the mayors, who could see no other reason why the local landowners should be asked to contribute to the cost of maintaining the *dépôt*. The mayor of Greve protested that the director of the Arno *dépôt* had sent away a widow and her three children, whom she was incapable of looking after:[94]

> I only want the condition of this family to be taken into account – without home, bed or food. The smallholders of our commune know that 500 francs a year are paid for this reformatory; they are displeased by this and refuse to give alms as well. So how can this family live?

Of the first seventy-two who requested admission to the Arno *dépôt*, thirty-eight were over 60 years old (five over 80), ten were wholly or nearly blind, eight were crippled, three suffered from physical defects and one was mad.[95]

Faced with this situation, the Arno prefect placed his full authority behind a restrictive interpretation of who should be admitted:[96]

Hence, as I have stated, the *dépôt de mendicité* should only accept able-bodied individuals who are able to work. The others – that is, the aged over 65, the maimed, the infirm, the blind, etc. – must be maintained by the hospitals or the *bureaux de bienfaisance*.

If the hospitals or *bureaux* of charity do not have adequate resources for this expense, then supplementary funds must be raised for them, either by collections in the villages, or by tax rolls for an amount calculated according to needs and specially designated either to relieve the hospitals where the sick are assisted and cured or to reinforce the *bureaux de bienfaisance* so that they will be able to distribute outdoor relief.

The prefect's insistence was understandable in view of the immense effort and expense in organizing the *dépôt* as a manufactory. In discussions as early as 1809 the proposal had been made to model the industrial activities of the workhouse on those of the Congregation of San Giovanni Battista: the inmates could produce textiles, shoes, marble and similar products, to supply both 'the different *ateliers* and shops of private individuals' and the hospitals and charitable institutions.[97] Above all, there was to be no competition with private industry, and indeed the suggestion was made that private individuals could set up their own machines in the *dépót*;[98]

> The government's intention is that luxury works will be avoided by the *dépôt de mendicité*, so that they cannot harm factories and manufacturers in the department nor check their operations. As far as possible the work will be limited to the production of ordinary goods, suitable for use by the community itself within the establishment, in hospitals and prisons; it is a matter of deciding the types of goods which these individuals will produce. . . . These different workshops will be independent of those which the market will want to set up inside the building, and in distinct, separate locations.

In logical manner, supervision of the *dépôt* should be in the hands of merchants: 'It seems appropriate to choose the members of this council in the chamber of commerce and among the worthiest merchants.'[99]

The *dépôts* could thus prove their worth to society by increasing production in a non-competitive manner; and at the same time pay for themselves.

The difficulties began once the choice had been made of what goods to produce. The proposals for the Arno *dépôt* had included, for the women, hemp, flax- and woollen-spinning, stockings, bonnets and vests; for the men, woollen and linen cloth-weaving and shoes; for the children, the production of small nails and pins; straw hats were to be made by the women, children and the infirm; joinery and metalwork were also considered for the internal use of the *dépôt*.[100] Similar lines of production were suggested for the Méditerranée *dépôt*: straw hats, wool-carding and spinning, hemp cloths, carpentry and perhaps an iron forge to utilize the local ore deposits.[101] In the event, probably only a restricted number of goods were produced. The accounts of the Ombrone and Méditerranée *dépôts* only mention woollen and linen cloths, carpentry and shoes.[102] Part of the reason must have been the difficulty of procuring the necessary raw materials and machinery. The director of the Florence *dépôt* proposed approaching Bolognese merchants for hemp, merchants at Florence, Crema, Cremona and Milan for flax, others at Leghorn, Montagone, Montalcino and Civitavecchia for wool, and yet others at Carmignano and Prato for straw; some of the machines were bought second-hand, others were constructed within the *dépôt*.[103] It is perhaps hardly surprising that these manufactures, once they had started after many teething problems, failed to pay for themselves.

By the time the *dépôts* opened, they had aroused notable resentment among the local communes, who had been forced to pay considerable sums for their equipment and running expenses. Indeed, as costs rose, even some *bureaux de bienfaisance* and charitable institutions were forced to contribute. The Florence *bureau* complained bitterly that it was already over-committed, particularly with the silk crisis in 1811, which had increased the number of needy poor. The Bigallo hospital for orphans protested that the girls who had been placed in the silk industry were being sent back: 'If the hospitals are exempted from this tax, perhaps because their finances are in disastrous state, why make their institute for orphans pay, in order to subject it to the same disaster?'[104]

In fact it proved necessary to reduce the original estimate for local contributions in the Arno department from 82,000 francs to 61,880 francs by 1814, of which 14,650 remained unpaid; the Méditerranée communes offered similar resistance.[105] The bureaucratic rigidities of the system could be seen in the obligation on the Florence *bureau* to pay 6000 francs for the *dépôt* on 10 December 1813, only to receive back the same sum on 15 December as a subsidy for the economic soups.

If the local tax-payers felt aggrieved at the need to subsidize the *dépôts*, those meant to populate them felt terrified. The similarity to a prison was hard to deny, and indeed was commented upon by the mayor of S. Gimignano. Within days of the opening of the Arno *dépôt*, the mayors were asking for the release of beggars, nearly always in response to appeals from their families: between 11 December 1813 and 27 June 1814 eighty-six beggars were released, nearly all from the city of Florence; at San Gimignano the inmates sent out desperate letters searching for a relative to act as guarantor; twenty-four escaped from the *dépôt*, some more than once, openly declaring that they preferred prison.[106] In the summer they were forced to rise at 4.30 a.m. (in the winter at 6.30), attend a service and exercise themselves until 9 a.m., after which they worked until 6 p.m. with only a brief interval for a meal; in the evening they were allowed one hour's recreation. The Ombrone prefect hardly needed to insist in his definition of the purpose of the *dépôt*: 'The prime aim is to force work upon individuals who dedicate themselves to begging through idleness.'[107]

The *dépôts de mendicité* failed wholly to solve the problem of begging. When they were first opened their directors soon found themselves obliged to refuse entry, as there was inadequate space. Once the beggars were enclosed, if they did not die, they endeavoured to obtain their rapid release. But at this point they discovered that the directors refused to free them, even at the request of the mayor, as once trained to work their employment was regarded as obligatory for at least a year. Small wonder that they sought to escape, or that the directors requested military guards to keep order. Whatever the other reasons, the *dépôts* ultimately failed because of this confusion of purpose. At the moment of the French collapse, the conflict was summed up by one of the Arno sub-prefects, Luigi Pratesi, in a very Tuscan manner as a clash between the rationalizing, utilitarian, bureaucratic mentality of Napoleonic administrators and the humanitarianism of Leopoldine reformism:[108]

> When an impounded beggar is claimed by his family, which is ready to give the appropriate guarantee that the former beggar, once freed, will no longer be found begging, the establishment has obtained its effect with respect to that individual, and it would be a violence and cruelty if he were not returned to the family which asks for him. . . . By adoption of this method, from the moment of the creation of the *dépôt*, it has been possible to reconcile the rigour of French regulations with the mildness of Tuscan customs. . . . Only now, with the idea of extracting a profit from these unfortunates, is that a proposal to deprive the sub-prefects of this praiseworthy faculty, and oblige those impounded, even if reclaimed, to stay in the *dépôt* for a year or more at the discretion of the director. If he is anxious to make economies in the institution, I know that there are various sectors he can take into consideration, leaving aside this particular one which clashes with the principles of civil liberty.

Poor relief, in a technical sense, ended with the *dépôts de mendicité*. But poverty went deeper and those poor unable to take advantage of any of the institutions set up for their assistance had to improvise ways of resisting hunger and cold. Some tried to solve their problems by theft or assault. The prisons represented the last link in the long thin chain of institutional reactions to the world of poverty. Only because their inmates were poor do they enter marginally into the present discussion.

In the lists of crimes drawn up at Paris, with the customary Napoleonic passion for statistics, the Italian departments always tended to figure near the top. Although the Piedmontese departments produced more criminals, the Tuscan departments were not far behind: in 1809 and 1810 the Arno department came fourth in the list for the whole empire and the Méditerranée sixth.[109] In a single month of 1808 (May or June) there were 223 inmates of the prisons of the Arno department, of whom 173 were at Florence.[110]

All, except one bankrupt, were without private resources to make their stay more tolerable. Their crimes were those of the unemployed poor, rarely meriting more than three months in prison, for the most part only two to twenty-five days: theft, sometimes with violence, fraud, receipt of stolen goods, vagabondage, brawls, resistance or lack of respect towards public officials, seditious talk.[111] Their crimes reflected the petty underworld of poverty, where enforced leisure and hunger could lead only too easily to clashes with the forces of order.

That their periods of imprisonment were so brief may have been due, at least in part, to the terrifying conditions of the prisons. At Florence, according to Aldobrandini, deputy mayor, overcrowding produced the absurd situation of thirty-seven prisoners in one cell.[112] The prisons were only fumigated after contagious outbreaks, and lack of the most elementary sanitary services meant a permanently foul air. In many cities the prisons and tribunals were located in the same building, with the result that the judges too began to complain about conditions. The president of the court of first instance of Arezzo made a public protest against delays in moving the tribunal to a separate building: 'As far as possible, we must avoid staying in this old building in contact with the cramped and overpopulated prisons in the most dangerous season for unhealthy exhalations.'[113] Fear of infection was well founded. In February 1809 an outbreak of fever rapidly spread to seventy-six prisoners in the Florence life-time penitentiary, creating fears that it could spread beyond the prison walls: 'The result for those who have been attacked by this sort of fever up to now could not have been graver, as for the most part they have unhappily died. . . . It would be no novelty should such fevers, called prison fevers, spread to the inhabitants of the city and degenerate into a deathly contagion.'[114] Contact between the prisons and the civilian population of the towns was not infrequent, with supplies of food brought in daily, supplemented by an abusive traffic in tobacco sold by prison guards.[115]

Prolonged periods of imprisonment, in fact, implied a high risk of illness, to which inmates succumbed the more easily because of their state of physical debility. As the supervisor of the Florence prisons commented in 1808, over fifty young men who had attempted to evade military conscription had been held for so long on bread and water that they were rapidly becoming 'unfit for military service'.[116] But if in this instance the prisons were directly responsible for the destruction of health, the severity of their regime only proved so disastrous because of the low physical resistance of the poor in general, even of those in the care of charitable institutions. When the Arno prefect tried to send a contingent of adolescents from the hospitals to the Imperial Guard, of 220 only 78 could be sent 'because of their great weakness'.[117] For the poor, the institutions for their relief or correction hardly offered an encouragement to idleness.

Poverty, when so endemic as in the early nineteenth century, could not be eliminated by institutions of poor relief. Nor indeed was this the purpose of these institutions. The aim was to provide that minimum of assistance which would keep the deserving poor from death by starvation or cold, while making conditions so uncomfortable for the able-bodied poor that they would be induced to work. The provision of work for the unemployed remained a secondary consideration. The philosophy underlying poor relief contained a confused mixture of religious, humanitarian, utilitarian (and hypocritical) beliefs. There was a Christian and moral obligation to help one's less fortunate neighbour; society owed assistance to those unable to help themselves; children, the innocent products of vice and poverty, could be trained to be of use to society; the poor, especially the beggars, should be removed from the streets and public view. But, whatever the intent, the structure of poor relief probably rarely proved adequate to meet the need. Because so sizeable a proportion of pre-industrial societies lived at or near the level of subsistence, only minor and temporary setbacks could occasion a vast increase in the number of the destitute. These setbacks could be personal – illness, an accident, imprisonment, conscription – or of an impersonal nature – a bad harvest, industrial recession, war. When they occurred, their pressure on the structure of poor relief revealed the fragility of the institutional response. The only solution society could offer was to extend the traditional methods of charity and, at moments of emergency, reinforce the ranks of the custodians of law and order.

The French administrators in Tuscany found themselves confronted by a large, probably a growing, number of poor and indigent, and a structure of poor relief that had been weakened in the previous two decades by government borrowing. Their response was to adopt the structure – similar in all essentials to that of pre-revolutionary France – while endeavouring to improve it by rationalization, co-ordination and close supervision. If utilitarian reasons underlay this response – the maintenance of public order, hopes of a more productive population – so did humanitarian ones, such as the genuine concern for abandoned children.

But the reforms introduced by the French in some respects made the system less responsive. The reasons for this were to be found in the rigidity of the bureaucratic controls imposed upon the institution and the contradictory elements contained in the apparently simple and coherent system of administrative centralization. For example, while it is arguable that without the French reforms the communes would never have been able to pay their backlog of debt to the hospitals for the maintenance of their infants and insane, it is unquestionable that, although these debts were recognized as legitimate, they could not be paid because no entry for them existed in the communal budgets. Similarly, although the hospitals were obliged to care for the military ill, the maximum daily allowance that the ministry of war was allowed to pay was substantially less than that permitted for civilian patients. On a broader scale, almost all the institutions of poor relief found their resources significantly curtailed by the liquidation of the public debt. The close attention paid to the day-to-day running of the institutions, while beneficial in checking maladministration and peculation, led to long, sometimes almost interminable delays in adopting solutions (such as the sale of property) that were no longer adequate by the time they were put into effect. Such bureaucratic rigidities also masked rivalries between different sectors of the administration: the prefect of the Arno department was never able to persuade the ministry of war to authorize the removal of the military ill from the Bonifazio hospital for the insane to other quarters.[118] Nor was he often able to win the struggle against the ministry of war or the Domaine for the utilization of former convents for institutions of poor relief.[119]

Nevertheless, these negative direct effects of French administration were less significant than the indirect effects of the Napoleonic wars. From 1811 the evidence of increasing pressure on the structure of poor relief is unmistakable. This pressure was the consequence of the sharp price rise for foodstuffs, the fall in employment in the silk industry, the increasing weight of taxation. The liquidation of the public debt in 1812 in one way only served to bring into the open the crisis of the institutions for the poor. By 1814, when French power collapsed, the institutions were clearly unable to cope. The wars that accompanied the final breakdown of French dominance affected the greater part of Tuscany and further increased the numbers of the destitute. The pitiful inadequacy of the institutions for their relief was to be revealed, in tragic manner, during the terrible famine of 1816–17.

Notes

1 L.A. Muratori, *Della carità cristiana in quanto essa è amore del prossimo*, Modena, 1723, especially chapters 31–5.
2 L. Ricci, *Riforma degli istituti pii della città di Modena*, Modena, 1787.
3 ibid., p. 27 and *passim*.
4 A. Zobi, *Storia civile della Toscana dal MDCCXXXVII al MDCCCXLVIII*, Florence, 2 (1850), pp. 106–7, 173, 352 n. 2, 443.
5 Zobi, *Storia civile della Toscana*, vol. 2, pp. 477–80.
6 ANP, F15.509, 4 March 1812. The original returns of 1809, which give a total larger by about 11,000, are in ASF, Arno, 485. See 'The reliability of Napoleonic statistics', chapter 4 in this volume.
7 ASF, Arno, 316, 'Stato di cambiamento . . .'.
8 O. Hufton, 'Towards an understanding of the poor of eighteenth-century France', in J.F. Bosher, *French Government and Society. Essays in Memory of Alfred Cobban*, London, 1973, p. 145 and *passim*.
9 ANP, F15.508, collection of 74 *suppliche* to the Congregation of S. Giovanni Battista, Florence.
10 B.S. Pullan, *Rich and Poor in Renaissance Venice. The Social Institutions of a Catholic State, to 1620*, Oxford, 1971, Part 3.
11 Ricci, *Riforma degli istituti*, p. 132.
12 ANP, F15.509, 20 July 1813.
13 ASF, Arno, 322, 4 August 1812; Arno, 83, 13 September 1810.
14 ANP, F15.510, 21 October 1813.
15 ASF, Arno, 314 (Florence, December 1808 capital account); Arno, 315 (Borgo San Sepolcro, 1808 account); Arno, 314 (Montevarchi, 22 May 1810 account); ANP, F15.2644 (Siena, 6 November 1813 account); ASF, Arno, 314 (Laterina, 1808 account).

16 ASF, Arno, 314 (Montevarchi, capital account, 1810); Arno, 315 (Monte San Savino, 31 August 1809 capital account); Arno, 315 (Pistoia, 7 July 1810 inventories); Arno, 315 (Prato, 1808–10 inventories); Arno, 314 (Florence, December 1808 capital account).

17 ASF, Arno, 314 and 315 contain a substantial collection of inventories. The items quoted come from the Monte San Savino *monte di pietà* (Arno, 315).

18 ASF, Arno, 314, 28 September 1813.

19 ANP, F15.2644 (Quinette to Minister), 23 February 1813.

20 ANP, F15.2644, 18 October 1812.

21 ASF, Arno, 314, Florence, report of Angiolo Mezzeri, n.d., but 1813.

22 ANP, F15.509, 20 July 1813; ASF, Arno, 314, Florence 1808 accounts.

23 ANP, F15.2644, 18 October 1812 (Portoferraio); ASF, Arno, 315, Prato, 30 November 1808; Arno, 314 Montevarchi, 13 June 1808 account and 1810 capital account.

24 Zobi, *Storia civile della Toscana*, vol. 3 (1851), Appendix, p. 333 (text of the 9 April 1809 decree, with mention of the Florence *monte di pietà*. The figure given there can be compared with those for state bonds in the accounts in ASF, Arno, 314, Florence). The Leghorn *monte* and other unspecified ones are mentioned in Fauchet's letter of 21 October 1813 on behalf of the Montevarchi *monte* in ANP, F15.510. For the bankruptcies of the Florence, Pisa and Siena *monti*, see ANP, F15.509 and F15.2644.

25 ASF, Arno, 322, 22 June 1812.

26 ASF, Arno, 403, 23 June 1809.

27 ANP, F15.509, 4 March 1812.

28 ASF, Arno, 403, 10 July 1809.

29 ASF, Arno, 508, 18 December 1810.

30 ASF, Arno, 179, 13 January 1813.

31 ASF, Arno, 504, 1 December 1812; and for the dispute that led to a revolt in 1799, cf. Zobi, *Storia civile della Toscano*, vol. 2, pp. 465–7.

32 ASF, Arno, 508, 5 May 1810.

33 ASF, Arno, 403, account of the *bureau de bienfaisance* of Arezzo, first *trimestre* 1811.

34 ASF, Arno, 508, 7 June 1808.

35 ASF, Arno, 322, 22 June 1812.

36 For lists and descriptions of the different institutions, see (e.g.) ASF, Arno, 508, 7 June 1808; Arno, 83, 3 September 1811. For the quotations, Arno, 508, 26 April 1809 (F.A. Corsi Salviati).

37 ASF, Segreteria di Gabinetto, filza 154, no. 10.

38 ASF, Congregazione di Carità di S. Giovanni Battista, Registro de' Segni dei Poveri, 70, 22 January 1811 to 21 January 1812.

39 ASF, Arno, 508, 26 April 1809.

40 ASF, Arno, 508, 4 March 1809 (Emilio Pucci, mayor, to prefect); Arno, 508, 26 April 1809 account.

41 ASF, Arno, 508, account for March–August 1810; Arno, 403, account for January–June 1812; Arno, 158, account for July–December 1812.

42 ANP, F15.509, 19 November 1812 (Corsini to Minister).

43 ASF, Arno, 508, 27 March 1810; Arno, 321, 9 August 1811, 18 August 1811, 29 November 1811; ANP, F15.315, 27 June 1812, 26 June 1813.

44 ASF, Arno, 323, 23 January 1813, 29 January 1813, 20 February 1813, 30 March 1813; Arno, 158, 8 February 1813.

45 ASF, Arno, 322, 26 June 1812; see also Arno, 321, 23 March 1811, 7 May 1811.

46 ASF, Arno, 485, 27 December 1810; see also ANP, F15.2747 'Arno', 15 September 1812, 14 December 1812, 1813 budget; F15.2757 'Méditerranée', 7 July 1812, 2 November 1813.

47 ASF, Arno, 322, 2 June 1812.

48 ASF, Arno, 322, 8 June 1812.

49 ASF, Arno, 322, 1 April 1812, 2 June 1812, 8 June 1812, 10 June 1812, 25 June 1812, 4 July 1812; Arno, 323, 26 January 1813, account 20 February 1813, 3 March 1813, 15 December 1813; ANP, F15.2747 'Arno', 14 December 1812; Archivio di Stato di Pisa (henceforth ASP), Prefettura del Mediterraneo, Sottoprefettura di Volterra (henceforth Volterra), F54, n. 46.

50 ASF, Arno, 310, anon. mémoire to Prefect (1810–11) on reform of Innocenti hospital (infants); Arno, 310, anon. mémoire on S. Maria Nuova 1810 (?) (food); Arno, 488, 19 July 1809 (anatomy chamber); Arno, 311, 'Riforma economica . . . del chirurgo Luca Donati' (mattresses); Arno, 322, 16 April 1812 (slaughterhouse).

51 ASF, Arno, 311, 'Riforma economica dei regolamenti degli spedali dell'Etruria del chirurgo Luca Donati . . . 1808'.

52 ASF, Arno, 316, 'Stato di cambiamento . . .'.

53 ANP, F20.165, table of population statistics for city of Florence; ASF, Arno, 316, 'Stato di cambiamento . . .'.

54 ASF, Arno, 317, no. 14.

55 ASF, Arno, 317, no. 13.

56 ASP, Volterra, 1, no. 11 (7 January 1810), no. 69 (5 February 1810).

57 ASF, Arno, 322, 15 October 1812.

58 ASF, Arno, 310, anon. mémoire to prefect (1810–11).

59 ASP, Volterra, 1, no. 69 (5 February 1810).

60 ASF, Arno, 486, 22 October 1813.

61 ASF, Arno, 310, 25 September 1812.

62 ASF, Arno, 316, 'Stato di cambiamento . . .'; Arno, 317, nos. 7–10.

63 ASF, Arno, 310, anon. mémoire to Prefect (1810–11).

64 ANP, F15.508, 20 October 1808.
65 ASF, Arno, 310, 23 November 1809; Arno, 321, 29 March 1811. For Volterra hospital, see also, ASP, Volterra, 1, nos. 88, 399.
66 ASF, Arno, 321, 12 July 1810.
67 ASF, Arno, 317, no. 1 (15 July 1811); ANP, F15.509, 28 July 1812, 18 August 1812.
68 ASF, Arno, 316, 'Stato di cambiamento . . .'.
69 ASF, Arno, 316, 'Stato di cambiamento . . .'.
70 ANP, F15.509, 28 July 1812; ASF, Arno, 310, anon. mémoire to prefect (1810–11). On the whole question of foundling hospitals in Tuscany and Lombardy and their growing reluctance to accept legitimate sucklings, see now C. Corsini, 'Materiali per lo studio della famiglia in Toscana nei secoli XVII–XIX: gli esposti', *Quaderni storici*, 33 (1976).
71 ASF, Arno, 317, no. 1 (15 July 1811).
72 ASP, Volterra, 1, nos. 69, 14.
73 ASF, Arno, 489, 'Note des dots . . .'; 27 October 1810; 'Prospetto delle doti . . .'; Arno, 485, November 1810 mayor of Sestino; ANP, F15.508, 14 August 1810.
74 ASF, Arno, 485, 30 November 1810; ANP, Flc. III 'Ombrone' 1, 6 May 1811.
75 ASF, Arno, 316, 'Stato di cambiamento . . .'.
76 ANP, F20.165, statistics of population, births and hospitals; ASF, Arno, 316, 'Stato di cambiamento . . .'.
77 Zobi, *Storia civile della Toscana*, vol. 2, pp. 174, 322–7, 477 n. 53, 479; ASF, Arno, 316, accounts.
78 ASF, Arno, 317, no. 2.
79 ANP, F15.510, 15 December 1813; Zobi, *Storia civile della Toscana*, vol. 3, p. 617 n. 8.
80 ASF, Arno, 321, 6 November 1811.
81 ASF, Arno, 575, 'Stato delle rendite . . .'; Arno, 313, *idem*.
82 ANP, F15.509, June 1812 report to minister.
83 ASF, Arno, 323, 18 December 1813.
84 ANP, F15.509, 29 June 1812, 19 November 1812, 9 March 1813, 5 April 1813; F15.510, 28 December 1813; ASF, Arno, 323, 12 February 1813, 12 August 1813, 16 September 1813.
85 ANP, F15.510, 14 January 1814; F15.509, June 1813.
86 ASF, Arno, 319, 19 December 1808.
87 ASP, Volterra, F54, no. 56 (18 July 1811); ASF, Arno, 319, no. 1 (5 October 1813), no. 4 (19 November 1813); ANP, F16.538, 'Ombrone', 19 January 1814.
88 ANP, F15.509, 4 March 1812.
89 ANP, F15.509, 4 March 1812; C. Ciano, 'Il problema della mendicità nella Toscana napoleonica', *Bollettino Storico Pisano*, 42 (1973) pp. 170–1.

90 ASF, Arno, 319, no. 5 (28 April 1814); Ciano, 'Il problema della mendicità', p. 186.
91 ASF, Arno, 319, decrees of 14 October 1812, 5 October 1813.
92 ASF, Arno, 508, no. 38, anon. mémoire 1810 (?).
93 ASP, Volterra, F54, no. 56 (18 July 1811). I wish to thank Professor Giuliana Biagioli for this reference.
94 ASF, Arno, 319, no. 6 (6 June 1814).
95 ASF, Arno, 319, no. 4 (19 November 1813).
96 ASF, Arno, 319, no. 2 (24 December 1813).
97 ASF, Arno, 485, 7 October 1809.
98 ASF, Arno, 504, 'Régime des malades à l'infirmerie . . .' (1810–11).
99 ASF, Arno, 504, undated mémoire for Conseil Général.
100 ASF, Arno, 504, 'Régime des malades à l'infirmerie . . .' (1810–11).
101 Ciano, 'Il problema della mendicità', p. 186.
102 ANP, F16.538, 19 January 1814; F16.540A, 28 April 1812.
103 ASF, Arno, 485, 12 May 1813, 26 May 1813, 20 August 1813, 5 September 1813; Arno, 504, 23 September 1812.
104 ASF, Arno, 319, no. 3 (11 August 1811) (*bureau*), 9 August 1811 (Bigallo).
105 ANP, F15.509, 4 March 1812; ASF, Arno, 319, nos. 3, 7, 9; Arno, 485, 18 January 1813; Ciano, 'Il problema della mendicità', pp. 188–93.
106 ASF, Arno, 319, no. 5; Ciano, 'Il problema della mendicità', p. 214 n. 20.
107 ibid., pp. 211–12; ANP, F16.538, 21 January 1814.
108 ASF, Arno, 319, no. 5 (27 May 1814).
109 ANP, AFIV.10.42.
110 ASF, Arno, 370.
111 ASF, Arno, 370, prisons at Florence, May 1808.
112 ASF, Arno, 370, 21 November 1808.
113 ASF, Arno, 512, speech of Arezzo president of tribunal, n.d. (1811?).
114 ASF, Arno, 488, 'Salubrità pubblica', 6 February 1809.
115 ANP, F15.509, 20 March 1812.
116 ASF, Arno, 370, 30 April 1808.
117 ANP, F15.508, 17 December 1811.
118 ASF, Arno, 321, 3 September 1811; Arno, 322, 10 April 1812.
119 ASF, Arno, 321, 25 November 1811.

4

❧

The reliability of Napoleonic statistics:
the 'List of the poor and beggars
in each commune'
in the department of the Arno, 1812

The statistical enquiries of the Revolutionary and Napoleonic
years, on population, agriculture, industry, commerce, etc., represent a necessary starting point for much historical investigation of
social problems in Western Europe. The methods of their
compilation, and hence their degree of reliability, often remain a
matter of dispute. The purpose of this chapter is to examine the
process of formation, and the limitations, of a little-known statistic
in a single department of the Napoleonic empire: the 'List of the
poor and beggars in each commune and of the certain revenues
assigned for their needs, drawn up by the prefect of the Arno, 4
March 1812'.[1]

Detailed enquiries into the numbers, living conditions and needs
of the poor date back, of course, to many decades before the
Revolution, and culminate in the vast enquiry of the *Comité de
Mendicité* of 1790–1.[2] It was generally recognized that the numbers
of the poor had increased during the later eighteenth century and
especially during the Revolutionary years. Whatever the deeper
structural causes – rising population and a backward economy – the
breakdown of private charity and the upheavals caused by the
Revolution were acknowledged by Napoleonic administrators as
immediately responsible for the ubiquitous presence of the needy
and the beggars. As in many other spheres of activity under the

empire, there was a return to pre-Revolutionary institutions to deal with the problem. The houses of correction, *dépôts de mendicité*, that had existed in every *généralité* of the kingdom before 1789, were to be formed in each department of the empire, according to a decree of 5 July 1808 and administrative circulars of the ministry of the interior of 28 October and 19 December 1808.[3] Begging became a criminal act, according to the provisions of the penal code (articles 274–82), and all visible evidence of vagrants and beggars was to be eliminated by their enforced despatch to the *dépôts*.

The statistic under discussion derived directly from these administrative decisions. Before suitable convents could be assigned and adapted to the purposes of a *dépôt*, it was necessary to estimate the number of inmates they would be required to receive. The circular of 19 December 1808 requested the prefects to supply such information. The prefect was required to compile a list of the communes in each *arrondissement* with their respective populations, number of the poor, number of the beggars and financial resources set aside for the assistance of the poor (excluding those of the hospices and hospitals). That more information was required than that strictly relating to the creation of the *dépôts* is not surprising. The houses of correction constituted one link in an extended chain of public institutions of poor relief. The functions and competence of each institution were precisely defined and delimited on the assumption, typical of the self-confident Napoleonic bureaucracy, that social realities could always be fitted neatly into administrative categories. Hospitals and hospices were responsible for children, the aged and infirm; the remainder of the deserving poor received assistance from a variety of institutions, grouped administratively in *bureaux de bienfaisance*; the houses of correction were intended primarily for the able-bodied poor, the professional beggars, who had no legitimate claim on society and who should be obliged to work for their keep. Apart from the desire to accumulate as much 'useful' information as possible (to be found in so many Napoleonic statistics)[4], it was relevant to acquire precise figures about the deserving poor, as well as about the able-bodied beggars.

The information requested, apparently precise, left room for considerable ambiguity. The term '*pauvre*' was in itself unclear, for it subsumed a wide vocabulary of categories of poor, from the *vrai pauvre* to the *mauvais pauvre*, from the *pauvre honteux* to the *misérable* or the *indigent*; the terminology for beggars extended as widely.[5] Thus the local officials responsible for providing the information, the mayors of the communes, defined both 'poor' and 'beggar' in varying manner. Some of the mayors when sending in their returns, explained whom they had included or excluded. For the mayor of Gaiole, a largish village in the Chianti zone (population 4252), the poor (967 in number) were those who practised an art, but were unable to earn sufficient for themselves and their dependents and hence also received alms from the proprietors.[6] The mayor of Rovezzano, on the outskirts of Florence (population 3429), regarded the poor (3302 in number) as those just above the subsistence level, whereas the 166 beggars he listed were those dependent on charity: 'The column for the poor includes all who practise an art and live of their own labour. The column for the beggars consists of the impotent, who are unemployed every day.'[7] The mayor of Capraia, in the Arno valley near Empoli (population 2200) regarded the poor (186 in number) as having at least some work ('The number of poor is great, but nobody is without some work to do'), while the reason why nine were reduced to begging was 'their advanced age, burdened with various chronic ailments'.[8] In sharp contrast, the mayor of Dovadola, in Tuscan Romagna (population 1513), excluded from the category of the poor (of whom he listed only fifteen) those who worked at all: 'The number one could regard as poor would be much higher than those listed, were it not for the fact that they live of their domestic industry and by going out to work whenever they can find it.'[9]

Even more revealing are the comments of the mayors of two mountainous, poverty-stricken villages. The mayor of Verghereto, in the upper Savio valley near Monte Fumaiolo (population 2121), gave the number of poor as 1698, of whom 1596 could be classified as beggars, as they were obliged to migrate for half the year: 'As we have reported on other occasions, the commune of Verghereto is made up of poor families. Because the produce of the soil is so scanty, two thirds of the population of the village is forced to migrate in the autumn to the Maremme and stay there until May in order to find the means to survive.'[10] The mayor of Badia Tedalda, on the Presale pass (population not given), had a similar tale to tell.

He listed only thirteen 'wretched beggars, a number you will find very small; but you would have found the number of poor very large, if I had been asked for them [but 215 poor are listed]. In fact, the population is obliged to eat flour made from acorns and maize husks by no means infrequently.' But the real reason for these small numbers, as he immediately explained, was obligatory migration: 'There are no others reduced to misery in this commune; but their number would be enormous, as a proportion of the population, if a large number of men and women, some with unweaned babies, did not migrate to the Maremme for at least six months a year in order to escape hunger.'[11]

The sharp difference between city and countryside, between mountains, hills and plains, as well as the extremely flexible connotations of the terms 'poor' and 'beggar', led to the compilation of numbers for these two categories, whose only common denominators were that the poor lived at the very edge of the subsistence level, while the beggars were dependent for the most part or wholly on charity. The range of criteria employed by the mayors meant that the figures were not strictly comparable and could only be regarded as an approximation to reality. But there is no evidence that the officials in the bureaucratic hierarchy were aware of this weakness. Indeed, as the figures were processed through successively higher levels of the administration – from sub-prefect to prefect to ministry – their very listing displays a hardening confidence in their absolute validity.

A further point to be noted is that the figures for the beggars were based upon the mayor's information about those reduced to mendicancy who were resident in his commune. In consequence, they hide a definite error of omission and a possible error of inclusion: they exclude the large, floating population of vagrant beggars, rejected by all communal officials as outside their responsibilities; and they often include – alongside able-bodied beggars – some aged or infirm residents, living with families or (more usually) alone, to whom alms were given in a spirit of communal charity. The distortions that resulted from these different interpretations of the term 'beggars' were to be revealed when the Arno house of correction was finally opened in December 1813. As the prefect Fauchet protested, in a letter printed and circulated to all mayors on 24 December, the first groups of beggars sent to the *dépôt* consisted in good part of 'old folk over seventy, paralytics, cripples, sick, blind, and children under ten years old', while able-bodied beggars (presumably vagrants) continued to circulate freely in both city and countryside.[12]

Some further comments are required. First, in many instances the figures provided by the mayors are too 'round' to be easily acceptable. Whereas the figures for overall population were based on previous enquiries and on a mechanism to update them (the *état civil*), understood and applied by local officials, those for the poor and beggars represented a response to yet one more enquiry for new information, the accuracy of which depended upon the capacity, honesty and resources of each mayor and his staff. We can use the probably unique example of the return of F.R. Fabroni, mayor of Marradi, a village deep in the Apennines (population 4558) to illustrate the contrast with the more casual methods employed by most mayors. The mayor of Marradi listed 1130 poor and 102 beggars and explained how he had arrived at these figures:[13]

> The beggars live of alms given them by residents, the other poor live of their own work and employment by the day, which they get from one or another person.
>
> I must add as a premiss to the lists which I have the honour to send you that, in order to make them as exact as possible, I requested details from the parish priests, and utilized the returns made according to the law of 19 and 22 August 1791 and the information obtained last August for the poll-tax. Besides all this, I consulted the former collectors of the grist-tax who, as a general, constant rule, classed in the eighth [lowest] category everyone who had no property, no trade, no fixed employment, and lived by offering his labour on a daily basis wherever he could find work and bread. Such people, if prevented from working by illness or any other circumstance, even only for a few days, have no means of subsistence. But I have included them in the general category of the poor, while drawing up a special category for those who live totally from begging.
>
> You will note, Sir, that the poor constitute one-quarter of the

population of this commune. I hope that you will recognize from these lists that I have never exaggerated in describing the poverty here.

It is clear that few other mayors were as conscientious as Signor Fabroni, while some discharged their duty to the sub-prefect by producing a figure rounded to the nearest ten. Examples of such suspiciously neat returns are particularly marked in the *arrondissement* of Arezzo (e.g. Anghiari, Borgo San Sepolcro, Caprese, Cavriglia, Marciano, Montemignaio, Monte San Savino, Pieve Santo Stefano, Stia, Subbiano, Talla). No attempt was made by the sub-prefects, directly responsible for the returns, to check the accuracy of the information. Indeed, it is difficult to see how they could have checked it, except through the parish priests who were already responsible in good part for providing names to the mayors. As in so many other areas of administration, a basic weakness of the Napoleonic regime – reflected in this statistic – lay in the scarcity of reliable and honest personnel.

Two final comments relate directly to the administration. First, the utility of the figures was much impaired because of the time that passed between the initial request and their compilation, and even more between their compilation and their final despatch to Paris. The ministerial circular of 19 December 1808 received no reply and a further letter was sent to the prefect of the Arno department on 30 April 1809 before any action was taken. Model forms were then sent to the sub-prefects for despatch to the mayors on 22 September 1809. The replies from the mayors were received between October and December 1809. But the final list, of which copies are to be found in both the Florence and Paris state archives, is dated 4 March 1812.[14] The figures adopted in Paris thus referred to a calculation of the numbers of poor and beggars in the department of the Arno made nearly two and a half years before – years in which military and economic measures had certainly not improved the situation. This lapse of time is almost certainly explicable in terms of the delay between the original decision and the practical measures for the creation of the *dépôts de mendicité*: the decree ordering the establishment of a *dépôt* in the department of the Arno is dated 14 November 1810 and ministerial instructions only followed on 31 March 1812 (that is, after the receipt of the 'List of the poor and beggars').[15]

Finally, it is clear that a significant discrepancy exists between many of the figures returned by the mayors and sub-prefects to the prefect and those sent to Paris by the prefecture at Florence. The archives of the prefecture at Florence contain the returns for 83 of the 114 communes in the final lists sent to Paris.[16] The figures for communal population show almost no changes: in four instances local figures exist that do not appear on the final list; in five other cases the local figures show differences (at least one of which –

Table 2   Numbers of poor and beggars

Commune	Original returns, 1809	Final list, 1812
(a) Poor		
Lastra a Signa	1560	1132
Premilcuore	167	338
Rovezzano	3302	1175
Sestino	1275	375
Verghereto	1698	698
Pieve Santo Stefano	1600	1300
Carmignano	1916	228
Marliana	2940	940
Montale	1859	185
Popiglio	1955	955
Porta Carratica	1849	1829
(b) Beggars		
Capraia	9	14
Marradi	100	103
Premilcuore	14	13
Scarperia	255	155
Verghereto	1596	15
Borgo San Sepolcro	500	100
Castiglion Fiorentino	356	156
Monte San Savino	160	60
Porta Lucchese	300	150
Sambuca	965	65
San Lorenzo d'Uzzo	270	72

Bagno – is almost certainly a transcription error); the remaining seventy-four are identical. In the case of the figures for 'poor' and 'beggars' the same four communes offer figures not included in the final list, but in eleven other cases in each column there are differences between the local returns and the final list. In a few instances it is conceivable that the final list incorporated transcription errors. But in only three cases did these possible errors increase the numbers in the final list – whereas in the other nineteen instances, the numbers of poor or beggars were reduced in the final list, often very substantially. In the list of 'poor', the figures shown in Table 2 (*a*) changed. In the list of 'beggars' the changes shown in Table 2 (*b*) occur. The number and nature of these changes would seem to point to a deliberate, if wholly arbitrary, reduction in the numbers of the poor and beggars, carried out within the Florence prefecture before transmission to Paris.

The effect of these changes was to reduce the total numbers for the eighty-three communes for which the original returns can be compared to the final list as shown in Table 3. It is at least likely that the original returns that have not been located for thirty-one communes would also show some discrepancies that cannot be accounted for by transcription errors. No evidence exists as to why such changes were made, nor about what (if any) criteria were adopted. It can only be hazarded that the numbers were too high to appear administratively realistic and so – as in the case of the revolutionary *Comité de Mendicité*[17] – were artificially reduced.

It would be excessive to deduce as a general conclusion that Napoleonic statistics are without value or cannot be relied upon. In many instances the information obtained by such lists can be regarded as reliable, because of the difficulties and dangers of evasion (e.g. the *état civil*). But this particular statistic of the poor and beggars should not be regarded as valueless. In the first place it

Table 3 Changes to the totals of poor and beggars

	Poor	*Beggars*
Original returns	61,402	8262
Final list	50,760	4767

shows clearly the concentration of poverty within the major cities. As an anonymous official in the ministry of the interior noted,[18] Florence (where one in three of the population was described as poor) accounted for one-third of the total poor of the department. The figure of 23,455 poor is probably an underestimate, if one compares it to the 56,918 in need of a daily bread subsidy within the city of Florence, according to an estimate of a charitable congregation in the early 1790s.[19] But the difference between these two figures may be explained, at least partly, by the more restrictive criteria employed (presumably with some accuracy in the capital city) by the Napoleonic officials. Secondly, despite the variety of criteria employed by the mayors, it offers some indications of the degree of poverty in the different areas of the countryside, which are frequently confirmed by other sources. In general, although the statistic cannot be utilized as an accurate enumeration, it offers a reasonable assessment of the size and location of poverty in the department of the Arno soon after its annexation to the empire.

Notes

1 'Etat des pauvres et des mendiants existant dans chaque commune': ANP, F15.509. A copy exists in ASF, Arno, 575.
2 C. Bloch and A. Tuetey, *Procès-Verbaux et rapports du Comité de Mendicité de la Constituante 1790–1* (Paris, 1911). On the whole question of *enquêtes* about the poor in France, see O. Hufton, *The Poor of Eighteenth-Century France*, Oxford, 1974. I owe thanks to Professor Hufton for allowing me to read the proofs of this book before publication.
3 D. Higgs, 'An Aspect of French poor relief in the nineteenth century: The *dépôt de mendicité* of Toulouse, 1811–1818', *Annales du Midi*, 86 (1974); C. Ciano, 'Il problema della mendicità nella Toscana napoleonica', *Bollettino Storico Pisano*, 42 (1973); D. Maldini, 'Il *dépôt de mendicité* del dipartimento del Po: analisi di una struttura assistenziale nel Piemonte', and G. Assereto, 'Aspetti dell'assistenza pubblica a Genova nei primi anni dell'Ottocento', both in G. Politi, M. Rosa and F. Della Peruta (eds), *Timore e carità. I poveri nell'Italia moderna*, Cremona, 1982.
4 Hufton, *The Poor of Eighteenth-Century France*, p. 18; O. Hufton, 'Begging, vagrancy, vagabondage and the law: an aspect of the problem of poverty in eighteenth-century France', *European Studies*

Review, II (1972), 99ff.; J.C. Perrot and S.J. Woolf, *State and Statistics in France 1789–1815*, Chur–London–Paris–New York, 1984.

5 ASF, Arno, 485, 15 December 1809.
6 ibid., 20 October 1809.
7 ibid., 23 October 1809.
8 ibid., 22 November 1809.
9 ibid., 20 October 1809.
10 ibid., 21 October 1809.
11 ASF, Arno, 319, no. 2.
12 ASF, Arno, 485, 4 November 1809.
13 The correspondence between the prefect, sub-prefects and mayors (which also refers to the ministerial letters) is to be found in ASF, Arno, 485. For the final list of 1812, see above note 1, p. 126.
14 ASF, Arno, 319, decree of prefect, 14 October 1812.
15 The returns for the *arrondissement* of Florence (32 of a total 57) are those made by the individual mayors, as they are the original returns made to the sub-prefect of Florence, whose archives are included in those of the prefecture. The returns for the *arrondissements* of Arezzo (33 of a total 38) and of Pistoia (18 of a total 19) are mostly from the sub-prefects, although some individual returns from the mayors exist (six for Arezzo and one for Pistoia *arrondissements*), usually for communes already included in the sub-prefect's lists. They are all in ASF, Arno, 485. It is probable (although I have not checked) that the original returns by the mayors for the two latter *arrondissements* are to be found in the sub-prefectural archives in the Archivio di Stato at Arezzo and Pistoia.
16 Hufton, *The Poor of Eighteenth-Century France*, pp. 22–3 and n. 1.
17 Note accompanying the table in ANP, F15.509.
18 ASF, Segreteria di Gabinetto, filza 154, no. 10. I should like to thank Giuliana Biagioli for this reference.

5

Problems in the
history of pauperism in Italy,
1800–15

I

The history of poverty, almost by definition, needs to be studied over a long time-span, the *longue durée* of French historians. Because of its near-permanent and ubiquitous presence in the western world since the early Middle Ages, poverty (more than many other social phenomena) gains in significance primarily when studied in the context of change over time. Whether approached quantitatively or qualitatively, in terms of composition or causality, the history of the poor can only be fully analysed when studied in relationship with both long-term structural and short-term conjunctural changes in the economy and in society.

Conceptually and methodologically, however, it is important to distinguish between, on the one hand, the processes of pauperization and, on the other hand, the world of the poor and society's responses to their presence. It would be superfluous to insist on the close and continuous link between the two aspects, given that the dimensions of poverty were constantly related to the processes of pauperization. But to state, for example, that poverty was the 'normal' condition of the great majority of the urban and rural population because of the economic and demographic processes of the eighteenth century,[1] is conceptually inadequate as an explanation of poverty, in that it reduces the poor to an indeterminate passive mass, denying the possibility (perhaps even the validity) of exploring the internal differentiations among the pauperized, the mechanisms of survival employed by their various segments or groups, the practical and ideological significance of the relationships between these groups and the society that enveloped them. Methodologically, the need to distinguish between the two aspects is equally important, and is reflected in the different types of sources employed in research. The study of the processes of pauperization requires, as a *sine qua non*, the analysis of the economy *à longue durée*, and hence is based on sources measuring changes in the economy. The study of the poor offers an explanation of the causes of their condition only in highly personalized or immediate terms (family or agricultural cycle, local drop in urban employment, accusations of *ozio* or idleness, etc.), and then mostly within the context of a broader investigation of social relationships. The sources for the study of the poor are necessarily of a highly localized nature, primarily based on the organization of assistance, and hence interpret the world of poverty through the subjective eye-glass of those responsible for charity or repression, according to their judgement of the legitimacy or illegitimacy of the causes of an individual's state of poverty.

My concern in this chapter is with the poor in Napoleonic Italy and hence only incidentally with the structural causes of pauperization. Even so, some justification is required for studying pauperism in Italy during so short a period as the fifteen years of French rule.

There are, I would suggest, three main reasons. Firstly, the administrative reorganization and, even more, the Napoleonic passion for the accumulation of practical knowledge, of descriptive statistics, has resulted in the survival of a remarkably rich documentation, which offers the possibility both of analysing the composition of poverty at the end of the eighteenth century and of assessing the character and effectiveness of systems of charity during the preceding period of Enlightenment criticism and reform. Secondly, the French administrative response to poverty (as to so many other aspects of the organization of society) led to a radical restructuring of the institutional framework, to what appears to be a significant shift towards state assumption of responsibility for poor relief. The nature and limits of this institutional reorganization merit study in their own right, as an important stage in the history of charity, and in their implications for the poor both during these years and over the longer term. Thirdly, the years of French rule appear to mark a transition in *mentalités*, in social attitudes towards poverty and charity, from the hostile rationality of much Enlightenment criticism to the Catholic philanthropy of the Restoration, a transition that can be traced, in part at least, through the documentation on pauperism and charity in this period. My brief comments will concentrate on problems within these three categories.

2

The abundance but apparently parochial nature of the documentation can be confusing and deceptive: confusing because it reflects the characteristically local, communally based structure of charity and usually lacks the synthesizing surveys or reports offering a *coup d'oeil* of poverty in an entire region or department; deceptive because figures were only produced in response to administrative enquiry about those regarded as deserving assistance (or discipline) and hence do not necessarily relate to the overall numbers of the poor. As the prefect of the Arno department noted during the famine crisis of 1812, the soup-kitchens he was setting up in Florence would be of use not only to the clients of the charitable institutions, but also 'to the poor who do not qualify for assistance, to families in difficult circumstances'.[2] Even when the figures claim to relate to overall numbers of categories of poor, they need to be treated with circumspection, because of the mutability of criteria adopted in definitions of poverty and the possibility of arbitrary administrative adjustment in order to reduce their magnitude.[3]

Nevertheless, during the French period the range of sources at different administrative levels (from ministerial enquiries, through prefects and sub-prefects, all providing their own comments, to communal replies) offers the possibility of constructing as full, probably a fuller analysis of poverty and its mechanisms as in earlier periods. The historian can usually expect to find ample documentation on the core of the 'structural poor' (to employ Gutton's expression) – those regularly dependent on charitable institutions or licensed to beg. But in these years the administrative reorganization and Napoleonic faith in the collection of information have also thrown up a quantity of documentation on the 'conjuncturally poor', the 'crisis poor', ranging from the lists of urban inhabitants applying for short-term assistance (which contain family and socio-professional details) to the descriptive statistics of the rural poor forced into regular migrations, from the inventories of pledges at the *monti di pietà* to the administrative accounts of the 'economic soups' provided during the famine of 1812.[4] Taken together with the statistical enquiries and sources relating directly to the economy (on agriculture, trade, manufacturing, rural industry, etc.), the Napoleonic years offer a remarkable vantage point for the study of pauperism in Italy.

It is abundantly clear that the structures of poverty revealed in these sources are not new, and hence that the relative significance of the dimensions, location and persistence of the forms of pauperism (since the crisis of the end of the sixteenth century? Or since the mid-eighteenth century?) can only be properly assessed when set against earlier and later years. Compared to the more heterogeneous sources of earlier periods, the novelty, for the historian, about the Napoleonic documentation is that it allows pauperism to be studied geographically on a new scale. The localized, often extremely idiosyncratic methods of recording the activities of charitable institutions, characteristic of the *ancien régime* states, are for the most part superseded by a relatively homogeneous – and hence internally comparable – corpus of documents, the product of the uniform systems of administrative practice which followed on Napoleon's manipulation of the political map. This applies not only to the third of Italy annexed by France, but to the kingdom of Italy, so closely allied in its administrative and statistical methods to the French model. At the present state of research (or, more accurately, lack of research) it is difficult to tell whether this also applies to the kingdom of Naples. It should be possible, on the basis of co-ordinated and systematic research, to map a geography of poverty, comparing the levels and official categories of the poor, as well as the institutional structures for their relief. To take the easier problem of the institutions, it would, for example, be possible to draw some important conclusions about the levels of support for the poor in the different regions of Italy by a simple comparison of the number of beds provided by the hospitals as a proportion of the population in different cities and towns, or of the total official charitable funds in various departments (before the Revolutionary changes) relative to the overall population.[5] In a peninsula of such profound physical, economic and historical contrasts as Italy, the importance of such a map needs little stress, offering direct or indirect answers to multiple queries about the economy: the effects of the abolition of the guilds on unemployment, the relationships between subsistence and rural domestic industry, between migration and smallholdings in mountain, hill and plain, etc.

For the moment, in the absence of such comparative research, we can only conclude in the broadest possible terms that – as in France – rising population and developing capitalism over the previous half-century, combined with military-political upheavals in the 1790s (extending beyond the immediate areas of warfare to include the secondary effects on trade and manufacturing) had led to growing pressure on institutional resources by 1800, as witnessed by contemporary evidence of, on the one hand, the inadequacy of charitable (mostly urban) funds and, on the other hand, the increased incidence of vagrancy and petty rural theft.

We still know virtually nothing about whether and in what ways the years of French rule modified this apparently longer-term trend towards increasing pauperization. The statistical enquiry into temporary migration of 1810–12 and the various *enquêtes* into agriculture during the empire would seem to argue against any significant effect in the countryside, except negatively where the new political frontiers impeded the traditional trading outlets (as, for example, for parts of the department of the Apennines, separated from the former duchy of Parma-Piacenza). The poor harvests of 1811–12 worsened the situation in some departments (Genoa, Montenotte, Taro, Appennines, Meditérranée, Arno, Trasimeno), but by no means in all. As for the towns and cities, it is necessary to distinguish between the ports (Genoa, Leghorn, etc.) – where unemployment increased rapidly from the middle years of the empire – and the inland centres, where the economic effects of French rule remain unclear, at least until the crisis of the final years.

Figures, of varying reliability, exist of those counted as poor. The numbers of infants, aged and infirm looked after by the hospitals can be regarded as reasonably accurate. As against this, the 'list of the poor and beggars' of each department, divided into *arrondisse- ments* and communes, compiled in preparation for the establishment of the *dépôts de mendicité* (1808–12), must be regarded as more problematic, offering figures for the poor that range from 17 to 19 per cent of the population for the department of the Arno to under 6 per cent for the department of Genoa.[6] The numbers contained in this list can only be regarded as extremely approximate indicators, to be compared cautiously against earlier estimates, although they can be employed with more confidence to map the geographic location of poverty within and between departments. But, in the final resort, it is from evidence about the economy, rather than from such direct statistics or documentation on poverty, that it will prove possible to assess whether French rule encouraged the trend towards pauperization.

3

Evidence about the organization of assistance to the poor is, as always, far more abundant than about the poor themselves. Given Catholic society's almost sacramental respect for testators' wishes, a respect codified through legal regulation, it is hardly surprising that charitable institutions, legacies and bequests should have survived the centuries in Italy virtually intact. *Ancien régime* governments, attempting to redirect the employment of charitable funds in order to meet the needs of the living poor, had regularly been blocked by a literal interpretation of the written words of the dead. Hence the documentation collected by the Napoleonic administrators offers what can almost be regarded as a geological cross-section of the sedimentations of successive centuries of charitable impulses – the multi-purpose medieval confraternities, the fifteenth-century Franciscan foundations, the more specialized Counter-Reformation charities, the vast urban *ospizi* and *alberghi dei poveri*, evidence of the policy of *renfermement* practised in Italy between the later sixteenth and early eighteenth centuries.

Institutional charity in Italy by the later eighteenth century, as in neighbouring France, was in financial crisis and vulnerable to criticism. Resources were increasingly inadequate, as donations diminished and pressures increased; the very structure of the seventeenth-century solution of massive poorhouses, was accused of generating rather than reducing pauperism. But, more than in France, the institutions of charity had already been subjected to drastic reorganization – at least in the Habsburg states of Lombardy and Tuscany – before the revolution.[7] The starting point of any assessment of the Napoleonic years must necessarily be this intervention by the reforming states in the 1780s, even if the reforms were only partly put into effect and then inhibited by the political and military upheavals of the 1790s. At the same time one must recognize that the structure of poverty in Italy was not faced with the same catastrophic situation that resulted in France from the revolutionary attack on the church and the destruction of the religious institutions. The relative tardiness with which the revolutionary experience reached Italy ensured that the peninsula escaped the consequences for the organization of charity of the full onslaught of Revolutionary anti-clericalism. Hence the reorganization of charity in the Napoleonic years can be viewed – at least in regions such as Tuscany or Lombardy – as a development of an existing tradition of reform, rather than in terms of an absolute rupture.

At first sight, the Napoleonic reorganization of assistance in Italy offers the image of a massive structural change, analogous to (and inevitably far more rapid than) the introduction of the specialized institutions of the sixteenth century or the all-embracing hospital-prisons of the seventeenth. These institutional innovations appear to lay the structures for the introduction of a new, public system of charity. But the image is an illusory one. As in so many other fields, neither the aims nor the instruments of Napoleonic policy were innovative. The Janus-face character of Counter-Reformation charitable practice – assistance for the meritorious, punishment or reclusion for the unworthy – was confirmed and consolidated. Charity in Italy, under French rule, was organized around three traditional structures – the *bureaux de bienfaisance*, the hospitals and the *dépôts de mendicité*. The *bureaux* were responsible for outdoor relief, the hospitals for categories of deserving poor without family support (infants, aged and infirm), the *dépôts* for the repression of able-bodied beggars and vagabonds. There was no trace here of that humanitarian assumption of responsibility for the poor by the state, voiced by the members of the 1790 revolutionary *Comité de mendicité*, at most one can pick up pale echoes ín the discussions of the Italian 'jacobins' during the triennium of 1796–9.

What was new and without precedent was the comprehensiveness and degree of centralization. Thus, for example, the institutions responsible for various forms of outdoor relief – alms given on a regular or temporary basis, lodgings, education and dowries for orphan children, temporary housing for unmarried expectant mothers, etc. – were not suppressed and substituted, but placed under the co-ordinating control of the communal *bureaux de bienfaisance*; similarly the hospitals did not change in function, but within each city were controlled by a single administrative commission. The *dépôts de mendicité* offered the major novelty for Italy (though not for France), but even they were little more than the extension and centralization, at the department level, of the *alberghi dei poveri* of the major cities of *ancien régime* Italy. Within the context of the very long-term shift in responsibility for the organization of institutional charity – from church to lay municipal authorities to the state – these years are significant because of the controls energetically exercised by the central administrators, the prefects and sub-prefects. But it would be mistaken to confuse the Napoleonic government with anything related to the modern welfare state. The role of the Napoleonic state was limited to close supervision of finances and administration, and only marginally envisaged responsibility for welfare.

Responsibility for assistance remained with the local communes and private individuals, as it had done in previous centuries. At most, the Napoleonic state accepted what were traditional responsibilities for the extremes of the charitable spectrum – for the survival of abandoned children (by exceptional financial grants from 1811) and for the repression of mendicancy (by the creation and partial funding of the *dépôts de mendicité*). In most other respects it continued to rely on the generosity of private individuals and the financial responsibility of municipalities, merely insisting on central supervision. Indeed, the Parisian administrators of the third division of the ministry of the Interior (responsible for charity) could confirm that most traditional of the forms of Catholic charity – dowries given to poor girls by small hospitals and institutions – but contemporaneously assert that even private charitable institutions 'cannot be useful and inspire well-founded confidence, however pure their original purposes, unless they are subjected to the examination of the public administration, and authorized, regulated and supervised by it'.[8]

This bureaucratic character of the Napoleonic reorganization of charity explains both its successes and its limitations. The suppression of the religious orders assisted the hospitals and similar institutions by reducing the accumulated debt and annual interest they owed; the French administration's rigid determination to balance budgets undoubtedly had a salutary effect on waste and peculation (cardinal sins of the *ancien régime* institutions); government control facilitated the allocation of buildings (usually ex-convents) for the *dépôts de mendicité*. But the conversion into state bonds of the properties owned by charitable institutions meant an effective reduction of income, worsened through the delays in payment by the state demesne and military authorities; while the rationalization of financial responsibilities between institutions and local authorities could plunge some institutions (such as hospitals for abandoned infants or the Tuscan Bonifazio hospital for the insane) into unbearable levels of debt. Given these administrative limitations, it is hardly surprising that the later Napoleonic years should have witnessed a return to official encouragement of private charity.

4

The organization of charity, over the centuries, had been based on the ideology of a well-ordered society, with established and recognizable ranks, privileges, rights and codes of conduct. Society offered a model to which individuals conformed, for the most part willingly. In this sense, the distinction between 'deserving' and 'non-deserving' poor merely signified the separation of those who accepted society's norms from those judged to display hostility to such norms. The charitable institutions, with their detailed regulations for every hour of the day, were constructed in conscious imitation of the expected or ideal behaviour patterns of the larger society which created them. The conflict between the implicitly static, or at least highly regulated, stratification of society by rank or status, and the generation of wealth, increasingly visible from the later sixteenth to the eighteenth centuries, required adaptations in the organization and ideology of charity in order to take account of and absorb the tensions and contradictions thrown up by such conflicts. Thus the definition of shamefaced poor, the *poveri vergognosi*, became increasingly restrictive through the seventeenth century (yet another facet of that more general process of withdrawal into rigid structures of Italian society), but contemporaneously the recognition of the manufacturing decline of the same period led to the extension of outdoor relief (the quintessential form of relief for *vergognosi*) to unemployed artisans. In similar fashion, resident mendicants were still regarded as 'acceptable' (at first in all cities, then for the most part in rural communes), but the categories of the 'unacceptable' grew larger, the 'stranger' or *forestiero* was equated ever more summarily with the vagabond and hence expelled. The dividing lines between the 'deserving' and 'non-deserving' poor were gouged more deeply. But the very attempt to draw such boundaries, precisely because they were conceived as bulwarks for a society of ranks, offered possibilities of deceit and dissimulation – the noble simulating poverty, the Christian pretending to be a converted Jew, in order to qualify for assistance.[9]

In France the anachronisms of the society of orders had led to, and been swept away by, the Revolution. But by the time the Revolution reached Italy, in its Napoleonic form, the concept of legal equality had been whittled down, and was to be further contained with the creation of the empire. Moreover, if the society of legally consecrated ranks was abolished with the French conquest of Italy, the social distinctions underlying the stratifications of the *ancien régime* were only marginally impaired, and the ideology of society as the ideal-type survived intact. In this sense, the documentation of the Napoleonic years is uniform in confirming a continuity of *mentalités*. For the Napoleonic administrators the distinction between deserving and undeserving poor was drawn ever more rigidly. This explains why the documentation is particularly abundant for the *bureaux de bienfaisance* and the *dépôts de mendicité*, the administrative structures responsible for giving support to the deserving but temporarily dependent poor and for punishing the undeserving mendicants.

The deserving poor needed to be assisted because they formed an integral part of society. As Giovanni Ricci has pointed out, the imperial distribution of subsidies to Tuscan and Genoese ex-nobles marked the continuation of the *ancien régime* concept of *vergognosi*, a category whose relative poverty impeded them from upholding the dignity appropriate to their rank.[10] But far more significant, in terms of numbers and resources, was the aid given to honest artisan or working families forced by economic necessity into temporary dependence on charity. At Turin the 'shamefaced poor and artists (i.e. artisans) unemployed through lack of work' formed the largest proportion of those considered to require assistance; at Florence many thousands applied for help to the Congregazione di San Giovanni Battista, compared to the 200 ex-nobles who received their subsidies through the traditional organization of the Buonomini.[11]. Assistance at this socially lower but equally meritorious level was no innovation: as Edoardo Grendi has noted, in Genoa in 1630 the *vergognosi* included numerous artisan categories; and many other examples can be found, particularly but not exclusively in times of crisis.[12] But it seems likely that the problem inherited by the Napoleonic administrators had grown in scale in the eighteenth century, as the process of pauperization forced increasing numbers of working families on the edge of subsistence into a state of indigence.

The evidence about the mendicants is to be found primarily through the documentation accompanying the creation of institutions new to Italy, although dating back to the 1760s in France – the *dépôts de mendicité*. It is already evident from the few studies of individual Italian *dépôts* that the mendicants who entered these houses of correction only represented a small fraction of this significant marginal category.[13] Nor is this surprising, given the bureaucratic concern to limit expenditure, and hence the spatial capacity of the *dépôts*. The importance assigned to these institutions, explicitly defined as houses of correction, is to be explained in terms of the by now almost total identification of able-bodied mendicants as undeserving idle vagabonds. Mendicity, 'a vice in social man',[14] was to be repressed, just as the shamefaced poor were to be assisted. Once more there was nothing new in the Napoleonic ideology, although the relative richness of documentation about these two categories may also reflect the pressures brought to bear upon these particular links in the thin chain of the institutional response to poverty.

I have referred frequently to 'categories' of poor. The term is an accurate representation of contemporary attitudes. It is revealing of western society's bureaucratic response to pauperism, in its prolonged retreat from the initial acceptance of Christ's poor, through fear of abuses, towards an ever greater discrimination among groups defined as deserving or undeserving poor. Categorization was a means of defence against the moral and physical demands of the poor. But it was also understood by contemporaries as a means of offering more effective assistance to the deserving, while repressing the undeserving. It was developed and formalized in this sense, with typical rationality, by the Napoleonic regime, which extended assistance for those it regarded as the meritorious helpless (such as abandoned infants), while enclosing and punishing those it placed into categories of undeserving poor (such as vagrants and beggars).

But to analyse the world of the poor simply through these categories of contemporaries can be misleading. The categories of poor were based on moral and juridical distinctions which did not necessarily coincide with – and even less adapted quickly to – those produced by the economy. Eighteenth-century awareness of the relationships between availability of employment, wage levels and poverty has often been noted by historians. It is confirmed in the documentation of these years. It is present in the ambivalent definition of *poveri vergognosi* – both as artisans without work and, in traditional social terms, as those who otherwise would risk losing their status. It underlies the constant stress on the need to assist large numbers of families during temporary difficulties caused by economic events beyond their control, in both city and countryside. What merit attention are the criteria employed to distinguish between the deserving and the undeserving poor, not only because of the practical consequences for the supplicants, assigned to one or the other side of this crucial boundary, but for the light they shed on social attitudes to poverty in the early nineteenth century.

Three fundamental criteria seem to me to assume the function of pledges of reliability and meritoriousness for unfortunate members of the social body. The presence of these criteria implied a readiness by society to assume responsibility, their absence aroused suspicion and often repression. The criteria were family, domicility and employment; complementary to all three was good conduct or behaviour. Where the family existed, but was incapable of ensuring the sustenance of its members (through birth, illness or death), society recognized an obligation to offer assistance. This acceptance of the implications of the life-cycle explains the presence of multiple organizations for expectant mothers, abandoned infants, children, funeral processions, etc. The assistance was regarded both as supplementary to that provided by the family and as temporary – although in the absence of family, and in defence of life and honour, the community was ready to accept the burden of the helpless individual for as long as twelve years (for a boy) or even twenty-four years (for a girl). Where the supplicant was a resident of a community, his needs could be vouched for by a parish priest or neighbour; against this, the non-resident – unless recognized through tramping his regular migratory route – was liable to be regarded as a vagrant and a threat. Where the supplicant could offer some evidence of normal or even occasional employment, society recognized a duty to provide some form of supplementary assistance in times of recession or a negative economic conjuncture. The individual with family, domicile and some evidence of past employment, provided he was also of upright behaviour, 'of good morals', was entitled to expect assistance in times of need. The degree of need was often described by a hierarchy of terms – 'lacking work', 'needy', 'poor', 'wretched', etc. But, by the eighteenth century, the entitlement to aid no longer seems to have depended on social hierarchy. Indeed, I would argue that the deserving and the undeserving poor can be represented most realistically as two parallel hierarchies, ranging from the shame-faced poor alongside the idler (*ozioso, fainéant*), down to the licensed resident beggar alongside the reprehensible vagabond.

There was nothing new in these distinctions. What was new was the profundity of the divide between the two sectors of the poor, and even more the oppressive and relatively effective manner with which the authorities applied the distinctions. In Napoleonic Italy, as elsewhere in the empire, order and hygiene were equally regarded as necessitating constant surveillance; police and public health justified constraints upon the freedom of the individual. Prisons changed in purpose from short-term detention to long-term incarceration, *dépôts de mendicité* (like hospitals) were employed to enclose those lacking the expected supports of family, domicile or work. Repression of the undeserving undoubtedly became more effective, relief of the deserving in theory more complete.

If the criteria for defining appurtenance to the sector of deserving poor were wholly traditional, those employed for justifying repression seem to me to have been changing in content during the Napoleonic years. This can be appreciated most easily by turning to the relationship between pauperism and work. *Ozio*, or idleness, in the Counter-Reformation was conceived of fundamentally as a moral sin requiring intervention in order to redeem the individual from a disordered and undisciplined life. By the mid-nineteenth century idleness had acquired the dual connotation of deliberate abstention from economic production and immoral, sinful comportment. It would be easy to conclude that social attitudes moved directly from the former to the latter position, as capitalist values permeated society. It is possible to point to the identification made by enlightened reformers such as Lodovico Ricci between poverty and idleness. This was the moral justification that underlay the Napoleonic *dépôt de mendicité*, a house of correction for able-bodied idlers, where work was assumed to possess the positive benefits of punishment for past sloth and obligations now repaid to society.

The *dépôts*, like the hospitals and charitable institutions, were also seen as possessing some economic functions, in the sense of employing as many physically able inmates as possible in the production of manufactured goods. These state manufacturies were not to compete with private enterprise; indeed private entrepreneurs were encouraged to organize and profit from their activities. The desirability of such a relationship between the organization of charity and the market economy is stated explicitly in the documentation of these years. But too much stress should not be placed on such instances of what was only subsequently to become a central pillar in social attitudes towards poverty. The ties between charitable institutions and economic production were neither new nor even conceived primarily in terms of the market. Since the seventeenth century at least, some charitable institutions had engaged in manufacturing activities in order to train the young with necessary skills to provide for themselves in later life, or to offer adult artisans employment during economically slack periods. Equally, the financial conservatism of the Napoleonic regime, the obsessive concern for balanced budgets, especially on the part of the administrators directly responsible, played a major part in elaborating the (illusory) concept of the *dépôts* as self-financing institutions. Charity in Napoleonic Italy was not yet seen as an economic support or cheap labour supply for a free market economy. Idleness was not necessarily, or even primarily, an economic sin, since it was recognized that unemployment was often the result of economic forces outside the control of the individual. The earlier Enlightenment optimism that growth in wealth would alleviate poverty was giving way to resignation that pauperism would continue, perhaps even increase, despite the pursuit of profit. In later years progress and poverty would be reconciled through the work ethic. But there is not yet, as far as I know, any idealization of work because of its therapeutic or reintegrative values, such as was to be developed initially in the schemes of Restoration philanthropists for prisons and asylums.[15]

There can be little doubt that these years witnessed a return to private charity, which can be linked directly to the humanitarian traditions of the Enlightenment, and which was to become a central part of Restoration ideology and practice. This shift in social attitudes is to be explained in terms of the reaction against the abstract rationalism and individualism of the Enlightenment and Napoleonic experiences, the religious revivalism, the return towards the values of family and community. Research is needed into the reality and nature of the structures of such private charity in these years. Alongside philanthropic organizations to assist expectant mothers, distribute bread and soup or educate children, traces can be detected through the official documentation which hint at less formal patterns of private charity, based on patron-client relationships. Within the framework of the general criteria of worthiness – family, local residence, employment, 'good conduct' – the act of charity remained personal, structured around the desirability of direct contact between donor and recipient: 'it is right that the pauper should know his benefactresses in order to pay them the proper tribute of gratitude, and that the rich, who might be unaware of the miseries of the poor, should be awakened by the touching example of ladies dedicating their finest hours to relieve unhappiness'.[16]

Behind the institutions of charity lies the world of the poor, about which – in all periods – we remain too ignorant. Research into private charity should offer some answers, although probably only about restricted groups of 'respectable', deserving poor. The sources for the study of the undeserving poor – criminal records, documentation on the *dépôts de mendicité* and similar institutions of reclusion – remain too selective, both quantitatively and qualitatively. Alongside the study of organizations *for* the poor, it is time to turn our attention to the organization *of* the poor. The guilds had been abolished by 1800, but formal and informal groupings survived, based on occupational solidarities, frequently organized in confraternities. In the department of the Apennines in 1808 there were nearly 300 confraternities, with mutual aid and processional functions. 'In Italy, almost everybody belongs to some confraternity, but these confrères have nothing in common among themselves', exclaimed the prefect of this department with some exasperation.[17] It was an exaggeration, for the confraternities were characteristic only of some areas, such as Liguria or the city of Naples. But they offer an example of yet one more possibility of penetrating the obscure world of the poor.

There is always the danger of ascribing too uncritically to the poor, and particularly the deserving poor, the values of the society which enveloped them. In the final analysis, it is probably impossible to distinguish the values accepted by the poor from those they put forward as most likely to stimulate sympathy and charity from their wealthier neighbours. Nor indeed were such values – such as dowries for poor girls – often so crudely separated, except with deliberate intent to deceive. But it must surely be true that whatever values a poor individual or family professed differed in interpretation, or at least in intensity, according to the level or position they occupied within the confines of their world: 'honour' and 'shame', for example, could not have signified the same for a *vergognoso* and a vagabond. It is through the inner structures of the various groupings of the poor – both formal structures such as the confraternities and less formal ones such as family and neighbourhood – that it may prove possible to test these values. But this is a separate problem, which extends far beyond the history of pauperism in Italy during the period of French rule and hence beyond the limits of these brief remarks.

Notes

1 P. Piasenza, '"Povertà", costruzione dello stato e controllo sociale in Francia: alle origini del problema', *Rivista di storia contemporanea*, IX (1980), p. 13 and passim. This useful and interesting article is, in my view, vitiated by a failure to appreciate the conceptual difference between these two aspects.

2 ASF, Arno, 322, 25 June 1812.

3 See chapter 4 in this volume, 'The reliability of Napoleonic statistics'.

4 Lists of the temporarily destitute are to be found in the archives of the Congregazione di San Giovanni Battista, in the Archivio di Stato, Florence. For the descriptive statistics of rural migrations, to be found in the Archives Nationales, Paris (F20 434 and 435), see C. Corsini, 'Le migrazioni stagionali di lavoratori nei dipartimenti italiani del periodo napoleonico (1810–12)', in *Saggi di demografia storica*, Florence, 1969; the replies on which these statistics are based, in the individual prefectoral archives, would merit examination. For the *monti di pietà* and 'economic soups' in Tuscany, see chapter 3 in this volume, 'The treatment of the poor, pp. 92–3.

5 See the figures and maps making such comparisons for *ancien régime* France in O. Hufton, *The Poor of Eighteenth-Century France 1750–1789*, Oxford, 1974, pp. 151, 174–6.

6 See chapter 4 in this volume, 'The reliability of Napoleonic statistics', and G. Assereto, 'Aspertti dell'assistenza pubblica a Genova nei primi anni dell'Ottocento' in G. Politi, M. Rosa and F. Della Peruta (eds), *Timore e carità. I povere nell'Italia moderna*, Cremona, 1982, p. 349, n. 7.

7 L. Cajani, 'L'assistenza ai poveri nell'Italia del Settecento', *Transactions of the Fifth International Congress on the Enlightenment*, Oxford 1981; S. Rotta, 'Idee di riforma nella Genova settecentesca', *Il*

movimento operaio e socialista in Liguria, VII (1961). L. Ricci's attack on charitable institutions offers the most famous example of such criticism.

8 ANP, AF IV, 189, no. 1217, 3 nivôse an 14 (24 December 1805).

9 G. Ricci, 'Povertà, vergogna e povertà vergognosa', *Società e storia*, V (1979), p. 328; B. Pullan, 'The old Catholicism, the new Catholicism and the poor', in Politi, Rosa and Della Peruta (eds), *Timore e carità*.

10 G. Ricci, 'Da poveri vergognosi a ex nobili poveri. Privilegio nella povertà e discesa sociale nella Toscana napoleonica', in Politi, Rosa and Della Peruta (eds), *Timore e carità*.

11 D. Maldini, 'Pauperismo e mendicità a Torino nel periodo napoleonico', *Studio piemontesi*, VIII (1979), p. 53; for Florence, see chapter 7 in this volume, 'Charity, poverty and household structure'.

12 E. Grendi, 'Ideologia della carità e società indisciplinata: la costruzione del sistema assistenziale genovese (1470–1670)', in Politi, Rosa and Della Peruta (eds), *Timore e carità*; D. Lombardi, '1629–1631: crisi e peste a Firenze', *Archivio Storico Italiano*, 137 (1979). The Florentine Congregazione di San Giovanni Battista, an early eighteenth-century foundation, was created to assist those of menial status, but with the necessary requisites to qualify as shamefaced.

13 See chapter 3 in this volume, 'The treatment of the poor', pp. 103–9; C. Ciano, 'Il problema della mendicità nella Toscana napoleonica', *Bollettino Storico Pisano*, 42 (1973); D. Maldini, 'Il *dépôt de mendicité* del dipartimento del Po: analisi di una struttura assistenziale nel Piemonte', in Politi, Rosa and Della Peruta (eds), *Timore e carità*; G. Assereto, 'Aspetti dell'assistenza'.

14 Assereto, 'Aspetti dell'assistenza', p. 350, no. 11.

15 C. Duprat, 'Punir et guérir. En 1819, la prison des philanthropes', *Annales historiques de la révolution française*, 228 (1977); L. Panzeri, 'L'Ospizio della Senavra di Milano da asilo per alienati a manicomio (1781–1876)', in Politi, Rosa and Della Peruta (eds), *Timore e carità*.

16 *Compte rendu à S.M. l'Impératrice-Reine et Régente protectrice et présidente de la société de la charité maternelle, par S.A. Em. le secrétaire gén. et S. Ex. le trésorier gén. de la situation de la société, dans tout l'empire, et de l'emploi de ses fonds . . .*, Paris 1813, p. 3. For a reference to the wealthy 'who habitually subsidize poor families of the city of Florence': ASF, Arno, 322, 4 July 1812.

17 ANP, F15.489, 29 May 1810.

6

❦

Language and social reality:
job-skills in Florence
in the early nineteenth century

The study of popular culture has always presented particular difficulties to the historian because its most crucial source and overwhelming bulk of evidence is necessarily oral. The problem, well known to anthropologists and historians of non-literate (usually extra-European) societies, is how to interpret written evidence that claims to collect and report information about the day-to-day life or habitual practices of 'ordinary folk'. Such written evidence suffers from the original sin that it is recorded by literate, often learned, individuals, whose purpose – whether pedagogic, moral, practical or simply recreative, aimed at a contemporary audience – is anything but that of providing materials for future historians. The literati who collected such evidence were not only separate from the 'people' (as we all continue to be), but assumed their own superiority, not unnaturally, given the absence of any relativistic concept of culture. Hence, as Natalie Zemon Davis has recently argued so convincingly in a discussion of popular proverbs, this written evidence cannot be accepted at face value, but needs to be assessed in terms of why and for what purposes it was recorded, how the information was acquired, whether it was altered, and what function it was understood to play in the life of the people.[1]

Precisely because of the paucity and this deceptive quality of direct evidence about the ordinary, everyday life and culture of the 'people', the most brilliant and imaginative work of historians in recent years has resulted from the study of the exceptional, whether in terms of sources or of events. Thus inquisitorial records have proved particularly fruitful, because of the searchlight they focus, almost incidentally, on the beliefs, customs and practices of those suspected of heresy, such as the *benandanti*, the miller Menocchio or the villagers of Montaillou.[2] The exceptional has also attracted the historian in the sense of episodes that represented an interruption of the normal, day-to-day pattern of life (often leaving additional, usually judicial records) – such as the safety-valve recurrent festivities or charivari or the wholly exceptional riot.[3]

What then are we to make of the source discussed in this essay, the self-description of their skills professed by the respectable poor of Florence in the early nineteenth century? Historians have noted the growing separation and detachment of sophisticated, 'civilized' culture from that of the people between the sixteenth and eighteenth centuries, a central component of the increasingly rigid restructuring of western European societies which gouged a deep divide between the propertied and labouring classes.[4] But, despite this divide, job-skills and their description, particularly in a pre-industrial society of limited dimensions, could be regarded as common terrain to both educated and uneducated, in that they were manifestations of the economic activities through which the society functioned. The parish priest, innkeeper or other local notable, even the local lord (if resident) in village or small town, would be fully conversant with the language of agricultural or domestic industrial practices, and indeed would probably speak the local dialect. As the dimensions and complexity of a (usually urban) society increased, specialization of functions would diminish familiarity with the language of its economic mechanisms among those not directly involved. In contemporary societies, the growth of specialist, sectorial languages, whether imposed by the requirements of precise technical argument or deliberately cultivated to exclude the non-initiated, is a phenomenon well known to linguists.[5] But it is normally studied in the context of specific groups within the dominant class – bureaucrats, scientists, military, technicians, etc. – and reflects that specialization of function which is the essence of modern society. Arguably, a process of separation of language between dominant and popular classes, analogous and parallel to that broader division among social strata within western societies, might be said to develop over the centuries.

This process, affecting the language of communication between the dominant and subordinate classes, can be seen as operating in both directions. On the one hand, it led to the imposition of a uniformizing 'national' language, separate from and superior to regional dialects,[6] a language rendered surely the more incomprehensible to the 'people' in its most official manifestation as an expression of authority and power – such as the publication of decrees and regulations – by the utilization of a legal administrative-bureaucratic terminology. On the other hand, it may be connected to that retreat into extremely localized, secret slang or *argot* of restricted groups among the 'people', defensively strengthening the bonds of solidarity of shared profession or trade.[7] It would be interesting to trace the periods when such secret languages consolidated themselves among these closed, highly corporative groups, not just the picturesque thieves, vagabonds, tricksters or *cerretani* from the fifteenth and sixteenth centuries, but the labouring classes, the respectable artisans and traders, such as the masons of Bologna, the umbrella- and chair-makers, the chimney-sweeps and ambulant pedlars, or the nineteenth-century London costermongers or Parisian market porters who reversed the spelling and pronunciation of words.

These *argots*, while offering invaluable evidence to the historian of popular culture, precisely because of the specificity of their social and geographical location, nevertheless must be regarded as extreme cases because of their self-conscious intent of excluding not only the *padroni* but also almost the entire popular society in which they functioned. But while extreme, they could also be regarded as indicative of that broader and longer-term social process of linguistic separation. In a negative way, as confirmation of this process, one can point to one of its end-results – the fearful but compulsive curiosity of the middle classes of mid-nineteenth-century London or Paris about the 'dangerous classes' who ensured the day-to-day functioning of their cities. If religious philanthropy, combined with or leading to an almost sociological interest in the popular way of life, can explain the motivation of an investigator such as Henry Mayhew, it is inadequate to account for the apparently unending demand for real or fictitious accounts of the street and garret life of these denizens of an underworld metropolis, catered for by a Mayhew, a Dickens, an Hugo, or their multiple, often scandalistic imitators.[8] That this curiosity was compounded by ignorance is evidenced as much by the detailed descriptions of the professions (and their nomenclatures) of these labouring (and Fagin-type) poor as by the dictionaries of trades and their technical terms that appeared during the course of the century.[9]

Our source on economic activities and skills in early nineteenth-century Florence may be set in this context. The purpose for which these details were recorded was as part of information about family circumstances which the resident poor of Florence were obliged to provide, when applying for assistance to the major outdoor relief institution, the Congregazione di San Giovanni Battista. During the years when Tuscany was annexed to France (1808–14), the application forms to the Congregation were standardized and printed; they have survived for the period up to April 1812 (after which date the Florence flood of 1966 destroyed them). In all, there are 5284 applications; as details of every component member of each household were included, the evidence on these forms entered under the column 'trade' related to about 15,000 individuals.[10] From the handwriting it is not clear how frequently the information on these forms was written directly by a member of the household. But even if one assumes that it never was (given limited literacy), there is little reason to doubt that the words employed to describe the particular skills were those of the applicants themselves. Thus we are confronted with a source containing the self-description of their activities by a particular stratum of the labouring classes, the respectable poor qualifying for assistance according to various criteria, of which the ostensible possession of a skill was one. From a linguistic point of view, the source is more limited and less picturesque than *argot*, as our poor defined their professions often by a single noun, rarely in more than a few words. But this very sparseness of description sharply limits the likelihood or possibility of distortion in order to curry favour with the educated philanthropists who would read and adjudicate upon the applications. Hence the multiplicity of the occupations listed may reasonably be assumed to offer evidence about how these particular groups of Florentine *popolino* saw their daily activities.

I have analysed elsewhere the breakdown by broad groupings of these descriptions of job-skills.[11] It is enough to note here that, as one would expect in this city once renowned for its manufacturing, textiles (especially silk) dominated, accounting for approximately 50 per cent of occupations, while 15 per cent declared handicraft skills, 15 per cent called themselves petty traders and 10 per cent were in services. There was a marked sexual division of skills: nearly 93 per cent of those claiming textile skills were female, while 96 per cent of those in handicrafts were male; regular servants ('domestic', 'coachman', 'groom', 'servant') were almost all men, but casual domestic work – 'does cleaning', 'does housework', or 'scullery work' – was the domain of females, the charwomen of yesteryear.

Work and earnings were a family affair, as only collectively could the household unit hope to maintain itself at the level of subsistence. Precisely because the Congregation's forms required a description of 'work', only the babe-in-arms or dotard were not assigned such attributes, and even the latter usually attracted some comment about the quality of his or her disablement ('blind', 'poor health', 'maimed', 'insane' or – definitive evidence of incapacity, abandonment and ultimate condemnation to death – 'in hospital'). Thus, at the two extremes, negating the very concept of a trade, we can find a 5-year-old girl, third of five children, described as 'cradling' her two younger brothers, and an 80-year-old widow defined antonomastically 'poor woman' (*la povera*). But these are exceptions. The old or disabled are normally described as begging – 'mendicant', 'beggar', 'living off alms' – usually with a badge ('begs with a licence'), sign of the Congregation's authorization. Children, from the age of 6, are usually described as learning a skill – 'learning to starch', or 'to sew', 'goes to dressmaking school', or 'to milliner's . . .', 'stocking . . .', 'ribbon . . .', 'embroidery school' – where 'going to school' did not necessarily imply any physical displacement, as instanced by the girl who 'goes to school with her mother', i.e. 'learns from her mother' to 'work silk'.

How far particular skills were acquired within the family – as the conventional image of 'learning through doing' would lead one to expect – is far from clear. There are examples of the mother who 'teaches how to work silk'; or the three daughters who prepare the bobbins of the weft for the mother employed in a workshop; or the woodchopper with his son assisting him. But the types of jobs declared by most of our poor by their very nature argue against inherited expertise, as they were essentially unskilled and casual – the earlier stages in the production of silk or other textiles, street-selling or labouring jobs. Nor apparently even where (usually male) jobs were more or less skilled, were those who professed them fully qualified, describing themselves frequently as *garzone*, apprentice or assistant, to the cobbler, gilder, baker, carter, pot-maker, decorator, etc. Apart from handicrafts, there were few skills to be learnt. Street-trading, for example, does not often seem to have been a family affair. But, then, nor was it in London: Mayhew, in his discussion of costermongers' employment of children to shout their wares, never suggests they employed their own kin, although it is evident that the children came from the neighbourhood.[12] Among our Florentine poor, we can identify a market poulterer who employed a boy living a few houses away. Formal training was probably never significant; but family and neighbourhood ties presumably played their role in the search for employment.

For employment was almost always uncertain. Although 64 per cent of our entire population aged over 6 declared some job-skill, only 54 per cent stated that they were actually earning. The basic explanation is to be found in the self-selective character of our population, since those in regular employment presumably rarely had to turn to an institution for assistance. Indeed, to cite an unusual example, the vegetable seller who asked for charity was denied it as, though it was impossible to estimate her weekly earnings, her very ability to buy and sell meant that she earned enough to live on. But far more frequently, comments such as 'when there is any work' or 'with little work' are attached to the description of a job-skill. Uncertainty of employment derived from many causes and remained the fundamental reason for inadequate earnings. The French annexation of Tuscany marked the culmination of a prolonged period of intermittent political crisis, dating back to Peter Leopold's departure in 1790, and itself accentuated the economic crisis through the British blockade of silk exports. The change of regime led to the loss of jobs, for a bellringer, an amanuensis, a clerk, an overseer, but especially within the bureaucracy, as witnessed by the fairly numerous references to their suppression, in which the act was usually personalized, transferred from the function to the holder: 'abolished employee', 'abolished salt guard'. Households reduced their staff, dismissing servants, coachmen, grooms, stable boys. Ill-health was another cause of irregular and uncertain employment, for the wife who 'suffers from pains and is a seamstress when she is able', or the woman who 'reels silk poorly', or the laconically described 'indisposed barber'. As among the casual poor of late nineteenth-century London studied by Gareth Stedman Jones,[13] seasonality of employment was clearly of major importance. Although never stated in direct terms, such seasonality was implicit in many descriptions of jobs, like the woman who 'busies herself in making silk ribbons when able to', or the mother who reels silk 'when she has some'.

In an economy where putting-out and sweated labour were the norm, most work involving some form of manufacture was carried out at home. Sometimes this was stated, as with the 'hair-spinner at home', or the innumerable silk-spinners and reelers 'at home'. But unless otherwise specified, such domestic industry can be assumed to be the case, whether the (male or female) artisan was working for a merchant (rarely mentioned) or private individuals ('winds' or 'spins for individuals'). Employment in a workshop (*a bottega*) is usually stated, possibly because it offered the likelihood of more continuous employment; although, in the extremely unusual instances of silk-weaving by machine ('works silk by machine', 'makes ribbons by machine'), the undoubted location in a workshop is not always specified, presumably because it was regarded as self-evident. When we turn from manufacturing to commerce and services, the place of employment is sometimes specified, as with the pedlar who 'sells on the Ponte Vecchio', or the boy who 'works for Pampaloni in the market' or the domestic in a Jewish household ('serves the Jew Borghi'). But most revealing is the repeated qualification of a trade or skill as being exercised 'round and about', for example by a woodchopper or a tanner, but above all by pedlars or charwomen. It is one more confirmation of the casual and uncertain nature of employment, the result of which was the discrepancy we have noted between declaration of skills and earnings. For the 10 per cent without earnings usually described themselves as 'unemployed', 'without employment', 'without work', or most frequently 'at leisure' (*a spasso*), a phrase whose prevalent present-day meaning reflects the change in mentality from a society of frequent, often seasonally enforced unemployment to one in which the concern about lack of work was (until very recent years) increasingly displaced by the organized, continuously encouraged preoccupation with leisure.

By far the greatest number of terms utilized by the poor to describe their work come from the textile sector. The precision of the terminology, in this as in all fields of employment, reveals in exemplary fashion that division and specialization of labour identified by Adam Smith and the political economists as the essence of the production process. Not surprisingly among this urban population, there is no mention of cultivating silkworms, an exclusively rural occupation. But once the cocoons were bought by the merchant, the successive phases of production can be traced through these descriptions of skills: from the silk-spinner who 'spins silk', 'makes crude silk' and perhaps also the less precise 'makes silk', to the extremely numerous silk-winders, the throwsters and reelers. The complexity of the process of silk cloth-production emerges clearly. On the one hand, the male tool-makers of heddles and reel-winders; on the other hand, the female warper, the preparer of bobbins for the weft and threads for the loom, the loom assistant, all necessary but subordinate tasks preceding that of the actual weaving. Florence's role had been transformed from one of finished cloth manufacture to that of exporter of crude and semi-worked silks. So it is not surprising that silk-weaving seems barely to have existed, except for ribbons ('makes ribbons', 'works ribbons', 'ribbon-maker'), and even these may have been spun rather than woven, as was the case with flax ribbons.

Alongside silk, flax, wool and hemp were the fabrics mostly worked by our poor: the female flax-weaver, spinner, ribbon-maker, the spinner of wool, the hemp-spinner and rope-maker. The preparation or dressing of flax was a male occupation, like the tanning of hides, and dyeing or starching of fabrics.

The range of male handicrafts confirmed the high level of

consumption in a city of 75,000 inhabitants which, although in economic decline compared to its former glories, remained an important administrative centre, with resident Court and aristocracy. Even the highly skilled, once renowned handicrafts were represented among our poor, with assistants or apprentices to goldsmiths, silver- and bronzesmiths, jewellers and clockmakers, as well as painters, sculptors, engravers, printers, miniaturists, precious stone-cutters. But far more common were the artisans producing for more general consumer demand – the coppersmiths, nail-makers, horse-bit- and pack-saddle-makers, the braziers and tinsmiths, the cabinet- and chair-makers, the wig-makers and furriers, the upholsterers and case-makers, the coach- and trunk-makers, the gilders and varnishers, the glass-blowers and glaziers, the umbrella- and mattress-makers, the candle- and lamp-makers, the shoe-last-makers and cobblers, the flask-blowers and coverers, the hatter and hat-lining fixer. To read these descriptions, it is almost as if, as the skill becomes more humble, the precision of description increases in proportion.

A similar impression results if we list the female skills employed in the service of the wealthier citizens of Florence. Alongside the lacemaker lives the stocking-knitter, the laundress near the ironer. The seamstress and linen-stitcher, the knitter and dressmaker, the milliner and straw-hatter, are accompanied by the old-clothes adjuster, the trimmings sewer, the button-holer. Some women called themselves cap-seamstresses, but others specified that they knitted woollen caps or sewed hide caps.

But it is at the level of the poor servicing the poor or cleaning the streets that the self-description of jobs becomes rich, even exuberant. The petty trader or ambulant pedlar describes himself by different variants on the theme of selling – 'seller', 'hawker', 'small shopkeeper', 'sells at the market', 'retails in the square' – each presumably describing a precise function in the mechanism of the market, now difficult to recover, but analogous, perhaps identical to the varieties of street sellers discussed by Mayhew. But, unlike Mayhew's 'general dealers',[14] there are not many who diversify the range of their foodstuffs, perhaps partly according to season, like the 'foodstuffs, vegetables and bread seller'. Most Florentine pedlars seem to specialize in selling a single type of product. Some practise well-acknowledged trades – the miller, the baker, the fruiterer, the poulterer, the mutton butcher, the haberdasher, the rag and bone man. But among the victuallers there are those whose specialities are virtually self-explanatory about both clientele and climate – the tripeseller, the chicken plucker, the food frier, the pastry-cook or seller, the cocoa grinder, the ambulant wine seller (to be distinguished from the vintner), the soft-drink-seller, the ice-seller, the tinder-seller.

A similar wealth of nomenclatures exists for those responsible for maintaining the urban infrastructure. There is no evidence that our Florentine poor were organized and employed by contractors, as in Mayhew's London,[15] for they state their trades as if they were wholly independent. The more fortunate were employed by the municipality as firemen or lamplighters. A far greater number earned their living as roadsweepers or dustmen. Once again, it is at the humblest level that we find the most vigorous expressions: the Florentine equivalent of the London 'pure-finder' (dog's droppings used by tanners)[16] is the collector of horse dung, the 'manure gatherer', the teenager who 'scrapes together the gravy' or 'collects the rather liquid stuff for manure'; but presumably he is also the man who describes his work uniquely as 'grinding valonia for tanning, near the mint'.

It would be easy to continue with this exploration of the terminology of the multiple ways in which the poor of Florence 'picked up a crust' (to use the expression of the London poor, according to Mayhew).[17] I have not mentioned, for example, the barber or the shoeshine, the hat-cleaner or buyer of ashes; nor the whole sector of transport, the porters and unloaders, the wagon-drivers and carters. Some of the trades and skills remain obscure today: does the description of occupation as *gira la ruota* mean a knife grinder? What technique is used by the soapmaker *a pesto* (with a pestle?)?

But to return to our initial enquiry – what, if anything, does this evidence tell us about popular culture? It would be tempting to develop the elements of a theory of a popular language independent of that of their superiors. But we are not discussing one of Whorf's Meso-Indian tribes, nor an isolated primitive community, such as those favoured by anthropologists, nor even a closed group with its own secret slang. The terms used to describe job-skills are those employed by a segment of the labouring classes of Florence, a stratum of urban society closely tied, even integrated to the propertied classes on which it depended for both employment and (in the present instance) charity. The very purpose for which these descriptions were listed negates the possibility of a 'separate' language.

But they may offer some clues about the channels of thought of the Florentine poor. The very brevity of the descriptions may be misleading. For it is a brevity imposed by the form to be filled in, and does not necessarily correspond to the exercise of possibly a greater range of skills than the one declared. Taken by themselves, these applications for charity in early nineteenth-century Florence cannot resolve this apparent contradiction. On the one hand, versatility (in contrast to specialization) of skills is usually regarded as one of the defining characteristics of a non-modern society. In this sense, one would expect our poor to adapt to whatever jobs were available, even while declaring (because that was what was asked of them) only one specific trade; and among the adolescents or at the lower levels (and the two often went together) of spinners, pedlars, charwomen, muck-collectors, this may have been the case. But on the other hand, our evidence points very definitely to a highly developed sense of specialization. We can only leave this as one of the puzzles of this tantalizing source. But at the very least, we can conclude that these descriptions of job-skills point to an extremely close identification with the concrete, material experience of day-to-day work. And, at the humblest level, we are also offered a glimpse of a language rich in variety of expression, with an undertone of earthy humour. Perhaps these are the qualities we should like to identify with popular culture.

Notes

1 'Proverbial wisdom and popular error', in N.Z. Davis, *Society and Culture in Early Modern France*, London, 1975, pp. 227–67. See also, 'Oral history: fra antropologia e storia', *Quaderni storici*, 35 (1977).
2 C. Ginzburg, *I Benandanti*, Turin 1966; *The Cheese and the Worms*, London, 1980; E. Le Roy Ladurie, *Montaillou*, London, 1978.

3 N.Z. Davis, 'The reasons of misrule' and 'The rites of violence', in *Society and Culture*; E. Le Roy Ladurie, *Le Carneval de Romans*, London, 1980; L. Barletta, *Il Carnevale del 1704 a Napoli*, Naples, 1981.

4 P. Burke, *Popular Culture in Early Modern Europe*, London, 1978, for further bibliographical references.

5 G.L. Beccaria (ed.), *I Linguaggi settoriali in Italia*, Milan, 1973; M. Cohen, *Pour une sociologie du langage*, Paris, 1956.

6 M. De Certeau, D. Julia, J. Revel, *Une Politique de la langue. La révolution française et les patois*, Paris, 1975; T. De Mauro, *Storia linguistica dell'Italia unita*, Bari, 1963.

7 P. Camporesi, *Il Libro dei vagabondi*, Turin, 1973; G.L. Beccaria, *I Linguaggi*, pp. 36–7; E. Ferrero, *I Gerghi della malavita dal '500 ad oggi*, Milan, 1972; H. Mayhew, *London Labour and the London Poor*, London 1861, vol. 1, p. 23; E. Partridge, *A Dictionary of the Underworld*, London, 1949; A. Boudard, L. Etienne, *La Méthode à mimile (l'argot sans peine)*, Paris, 1974; E. Esnault, *Dictionnaire historique des argots français*, Paris, 1965.

8 H. Mayhew, *London*; G. Stedman Jones, *Outcast London*, Oxford, 1971, pp. 14–15; L. Chevalier, *Classes laborieuses et classes dangereuses à Paris pendant la première moitié du 19e siècle*, 1973. See, for example, *The Mysteries of London: Containing Stories of Life in the Modern Babylon*, published for the booksellers, London, n.d.; or C. Grant, *Stories of Naples and the Camorra*, London, 1897.

9 G. Carena, *Prontuario di vocaboli attenenti a parecchie arti, ad alcuni mestieri, a cose domestiche, e altre di uso comune; per saggio di un vocabolario metodico della lingua italiana*, Turin, 1851–3.

10 ASF, Congregazione di San Giovanni Battista, ser. IV, filze 2–43.

11 See below, pp. 174–7.

12 Mayhew, *London*, vol. 1, pp. 33–5.

13 Stedman Jones, *Outcast London*, pp. 34–41.

14 Mayhew, *London*, vol. 1, p. 91.

15 ibid., vol. 1, p. 136f.

16 ibid., vol. 2, pp. 142–3.

17 ibid., vol. 1, p. 3.

7

Charity, poverty and
household structure: Florence
in the early nineteenth century

The study of the history of the poor is conditioned by the nature of
the evidence, generated by the institutional mechanisms elaborated
by society for charitable or repressive purposes. Such evidence is
rarely produced by the poor themselves and, even when it is, it
cannot facilely be accepted at face value because of our uncertainty
about the audience to whom it was addressed or the purpose for
which it was prepared. Even more, the identification or categorization of the poor is (and always will be) elusive, partly because the
concept itself is not absolute but relative (poor compared to whom
or what?). But it is also elusive because society – and possibly most
of the poor themselves – regarded poverty as a temporary status, an
affliction imposed by destiny or moral weakness, more likely to
occur at certain phases of the life-cycle or the year, but rarely to be
recognized as a permanent condition. The fact that a substantially
greater number of the poor were 'conjunctural' rather than 'structural' (to use Gutton's terms) has directed historical attention
towards the causes rather than the condition of poverty. It is
arguable that historians, like other social scientists, by concentrating wholly on the processes of impoverishment have lost sight of the
poor themselves.

Be that as it may, there can be little doubt that the institutional
structures developed by western societies in the early modern

period incorporated a similar fundamental conviction that if a state of poverty was the likely lot of the greatest proportion of the population at certain, possibly repeated periods of life, it remained a passing phase, which could be relieved or even resolved through the assistance of society; whereas permanent poverty, except for very specific and restricted groups (above all the aged without family), was an indication of deliberate choice. The practical consequences of such a value system, particularly within Catholic societies, was the creation by each local society, usually at the level of the township, of a highly elaborate and sophisticated structure of specialized institutions, geared to assisting or repressing clearly identified individuals or families unable or unwilling to maintain themselves above the level of subsistence. Who these individuals were, how they survived through the organization of kin or household, what skills they possessed, what mechanisms they devised to alleviate if not escape from their poverty, what they expected from society, how society identified the individuals or families it regarded as deserving of help, are some of the questions that usually remain unanswered. The source we have utilized – applications for assistance to a major charitable institution of Florence during the years when Tuscany was annexed by Napoleonic France (1808–14) – offers at least partial explanations.

I The source: the Congregation of San Giovanni Battista

The Congregation of San Giovanni Battista, founded in 1701, was the Florentine variant of a late seventeenth-century Jesuit model of charity, exported from France to Piedmont and the Papal states, as well as Tuscany.[1] While retaining some of the elements of the ideology of *renfermement* – in its powers to imprison beggars and its organization of manufactures – the Florentine organization, unlike its Turin or Naples counterparts, was as much concerned with outdoor relief as with institutional segregation. From its outset it licensed beggars as well as imprisoning vagrants, and practised a putting-out system besides transferring the poor from the streets to its own workshops (significantly and symbolically removed to the Fortezza da Basso in 1785) or other institutions. Its productive activities (primarily woollen, but also linen, cotton, hemp cloths and ribbons) were on a large scale, employing 2700 in 1790, but were consistently deficitary, only surviving through grand-ducal subsidies; in 1812 it was forced to close its woollen manufactory. For a short period (1737–42), an attempt was made to remove licensed begging by allowing the Congregation to place the needy poor in hospitals or pay subsidies to those living with relatives. But the failure of this system (through overcrowding in the hospitals) led to a new policy of systematic outdoor relief (1767), which grew in scale until by the 1790s it cost an annual average of over 52,000 lire and more during the years of French rule.[2]

The Congregation's functions were thus composite; or, more precisely, it sought (or was requested) to meet the needs of the poor in a variety of ways. Besides outdoor relief, direct employment and licensing beggars, it paid for the board and training of orphans (twenty-seven in 1809, placed in three institutions). It acted as the financial intermediary between the government and the highly secretive institution for the 'shamefaced poor', the Buonomini di San Martino. In 1711 and again in 1790, when the Florentines rioted, the deputies of the institution were called upon by the government, together with the archbishop, to act as peacemakers. It is hardly surprising that during the famine winter of 1812 the French authorities should have turned to it to organize the distribution of 'economic soups'.[3] For the Congregation of San Giovanni Battista occupied as central a responsibility for outdoor relief as the arcispedale of Santa Maria Nuova for hospitalization.

But if the Congregation's activities were multiple, they were confined to limited sectors of the poor. Traditionally, in all western societies, the poor were divided between those who merited assistance and the non-respectable individuals, at best layabouts, at worst criminals, who were to be punished. Our Congregation's concerns were exclusively with the deserving poor (with the single exception of its repressive powers over unlicensed beggars, which it lost by the early nineteenth century). But even among the respectable poor the Congregation restricted its assistance to specific groups, displaying a specialization of function characteristic of the charitable institutions. There were three main criteria it employed to identify those it was prepared to help, criteria which emerge clearly from the printed forms completed by applicants: respectability, attested by the parish priest; an ability to work, identified through the possession of a skill or trade and of a normal state of good health; and residence at Florence, officially for at least five years. Given the generally accepted significance of immigration for urban demography, the exclusion of migrants or transients through the residential criterion could be argued to reduce the Congregation's significance to an extremely limited segment of the Florentine population. But in this instance there is a marked congruence between the statements of our applicants and the evidence of the 1810 census of the overall population of Florence. Of the 50 per cent of petitioners who answered the query about residence, over 90 per cent claimed that they had 'always' or 'for many years' been resident in the city; in a sample of nearly 7000 from the contemporaneous census of the entire city, 82 per cent were born in Florence or its immediate surrounds.[4]

The Congregation thus restricted its scope to the urban labouring classes. But the manner in which it chose to assist them leaves no doubt that it saw its purpose as offering only temporary help to overcome conjunctural difficulties. Assistance was rarely granted more than once. The requirement to specify state of health was evidently intended to exclude the more seriously incapacitated, for whom the hospitals were responsible. Only a very limited number of forms of assistance were provided – tools, beds, bedclothing, bread, cash, personal clothing and dowries. The principal concern of the Congregation was thus to assist families who had fallen on hard times for reasons outside their control and which were regarded as temporary, because they represented passing stages of the family or economic cycle: 'indigent families of our city who, despite applying themselves to work, do not earn enough for their entire subsistence, because of their numerous family and the presence of infants, or because an adult is sick, or for some other of those critical circumstances which often accompany the misery of the poor'.[5]

Given these self-imposed limitations, it is important to arrive at some estimate of the representativeness of the Congregation's activities among the urban working population of Florence. By the late eighteenth century, Florence, like almost all the Italian cities and the entire peninsula, had long since declined from its medieval peak. Once internationally pre-eminent, Italy had become an area dominated by an agrarian economy, mostly structured around peasant subsistence and ever more firmly controlled by the cities, which depended heavily on the transformation of agricultural produce. The rural population had begun to increase again by the later eighteenth century, albeit at a slower rate than in northern Europe, increasing the pressure on food supplies. By the Napoleonic years the overall population of Italy was somewhat over eighteen millions. The urban economies had declined sharply since the late sixteenth century, leading to both a contraction and a shift in employment. As the high quality woollen industry declined, the silk industry replaced it, but quantitatively at a lower level and qualitatively as a primary product, crude or semi-finished silk becoming the major export of northern and central Italy. By the eighteenth century, although the primary stages of textile production retained their leading role within the cities, employment had shifted around to artisan luxury goods, often for tourists on the Grand Tour, alongside services, food-processing and building for the nobility, church and princely bureaucracies.

Florence's population had once reached 120,000 (1340) and fallen through plague to as low as 40,000 (1427). By the mid-sixteenth century it had recovered to about 60,000, rising slowly and irregularly to around 75,000 by the 1760s, and then more steadily to 81,000 by 1794. The following years of political disturbance and economic difficulties led to a decline in the number of inhabitants: in 1810 there were 77,750. With the Restoration the population was to increase rapidly from 82,000 in 1818 to 96,000 in 1833.[6]

The shift towards silk production in Tuscany in the late sixteenth–early seventeenth centuries had not compensated for the drastic reduction of woollen manufacture: although by about 1650 the value of silk production was over double that of wool, their combined value had fallen to barely half that of 1565. By 1662 15,208 workers were reported as employed in the silk industry of Florence, with 5364 in the woollen sector. According to a census in 1766, there were 12,351 jobs in silk, 1018 in wool, 4915 in linen, hemp and leather and 9661 in services and food-processing.[7] The political troubles and then the Continental blockade seriously affected the level of textile production and hence employment. In 1811 the French prefect of the Arno department, Fauchet, estimated that export of woollen caps and silk ribbons to the Levant, a traditional market, had fallen from three million to 500,000–600,000 francs. Nevertheless, he claimed that the silk industry in the city of Florence (where production was concentrated) employed 20,000 in spinning and throwing and a further 5000 in weaving. Figures provided by the mayor of Florence in the same year estimated employment in the city as 23,000 in the silk industry and 5500 in woollen manufacture. Alternative and probably more realistic figures, produced at regular intervals from 1810 to 1812, oscillated around 10,000 for the silk sector.[8] The period to which our evidence relates were undoubtedly crisis years, not just of trade, but with high cereal prices in 1811 and 1812, the suppression of some jobs with the restructuring of the administration by the French, the direct burden of conscription and the indirect effect of increased taxation.

Florence was accustomed and relatively well equipped to assist its poor. Censuses carried out by the parish priests, together with the deputies of our Congregation of San Giovanni Battista, counted 26,192 in need of alms in 1750 and 29,301 in 1767, or slightly over one-third of the city's population. In the troubled years of the 1790s, with poor harvests and political disturbance, the deputies made a new count of those requiring bread coupons and reached the astonishing total of 56,918, or over 70 per cent; an 1812 count stated 23,455, or just under a third.[9] The figures are high but not out of line with the estimates of Gutton, Pullan or Hufton for the 'conjunctural' poor, of one-third of urban populations rising at moments of harvest crisis to two-thirds.[10]

One consequence of Napoleonic rule, in Florence as elsewhere, was the production of numerous and detailed accounts of the existing charitable institutions. The figures inevitably vary, but the Congregation of San Giovanni Battista (one of five institutions) was responsible for between 33 per cent and 45 per cent of overall expenditure on outdoor relief in 1808–9, for an average of 47 per cent for two trimesters in 1810 and still for an average 33 per cent for 1812. According to figures provided by the mayor of Florence in

1809, over 50 per cent of the Congregation's own expenditure was for assistance to poor families.[11] Let us turn from expenditure to numbers of those assisted. The surviving applications to the Congregation number 5284 over the period February 1810 to April 1812, an average of 195.7 per month or 2348 in a year. A register was kept in order to check repeated applications, which seem to have been extremely infrequent. The applications were always for an entire household; given the average size of household of 3.69, we can conclude that the Congregation was assisting an annual average of over 8600 individuals. This compares to an average (daily) presence in the hospitals of Florence of 1600 individuals (excluding foundlings).[12] Even allowing for an irregular flow of applications and hence an over-generous estimate (unlikely over twenty-seven months), the Congregation was helping over one-third or (if we include the 2700 to whom it gave employment) nearly one-half of the estimated poor of Florence. As a first approach, it seems reasonable to conclude that the applications provide information which is amply representative of the respectable poor of Florence.

Petitions to the Congregation were standardized on printed forms in the French period. After the surname, address, period of residence and domicility, the applications contain a list of all resident members of the household, starting with the head, followed by the spouse, children, other relatives and non-relatives. The name, relationship to the head of household, age, state of health, skill, employer and weekly wage (if any) is listed for each individual, followed by the form of charity requested. On the back of the form the parish priest wrote a supporting testimonial; two deputies of the Congregation, after a personal visit to the applicant's home, made their recommendation about the most appropriate form of assistance (or its refusal); the final decision belonged to a (rotating) group among the seventy-two deputies.

For administrative purposes, and to encourage a closer contact between the individual deputies and the parishes, the Congregation had divided Florence into six *sestieri*. Originally there were sixty-six files containing the petitions, but approximately one-third were lost in the Florence flood of 1966, effectively breaking the run in April 1812.[13] For this study, a sample was coded, containing all the applications from the second *sestiere*; this amounted to 1219 applications, or 23 per cent of the surviving run. For reasons which are not clear, the sample, while covering all twenty-seven months, was biased towards 1810 (79 per cent of all applications), but in all other respects it can be regarded as fully representative. It is worth noting that 1810 was a year of normal cereal prices.

The second *sestiere* covered an area of Florence north of the Arno, mostly within the *quartiere* of Santa Maria Novella, but also including part of the cathedral quarter of San Giovanni. The quarter of Santa Maria Novella in 1551 contained 17.5 per cent of the city's population, in 1632 21.8 per cent, by 1745 it had declined slightly to 19.3.[14] The actual streets of our sample extended from Borgo Ognissanti and Via Palazzuolo on the west to the area around the great church of Santa Maria Novella, and then east to the maze of small streets around the present-day central market and the Basilica of San Lorenzo. There can be no doubt that our sample is representative of the area of popular habitation at Florence.

The data contained in these applications can be subjected to various objections of a methodological nature. The details about family and household suffer from the limitations inherent in all cross-sectional data: on the one hand, they represent a single moment in time and place and hence may merely reveal a temporary conjuncture rather than a longer-run condition; on the other hand, their information about household structures, in terms of size, age, composition and cycle, cannot be assumed necessarily to equate with those of the family. The debate over the past decade about census data has clarified many of the ambiguities implicit in the identification of household and family. Censuses, of whatever sort, were drawn up by bureaucracies which did not always possess adequate knowledge, skills or personnel to ensure the veracity or, more commonly, the completeness of the information written down by the census-taker. At a deeper level, the very concept of the 'household' was derived from the state, because of its functionality for purposes of taxation, conscription, etc., and does not necessarily reflect accurately the ties – of neighbourhood, friendship or service, as well as kin – that lie behind such co-residential units. Family and kin can only be perceived in so far as they appear within the possibly constraining and certainly excessively crystallized recorded framework of the household. Precisely because of the identification of households as separate units, relationships (of whatever nature) crossing the boundaries between households are absent from the record. Hence household data may both exclude the wider network of family and kin and impose a false appearance of inner cohesion as a unit on a group of individuals who reside under the same roof. The imperfect match between household and family is increasingly revealed as the evidence is pressed to yield information about the family as an ongoing process, and about the ambiguity of the function of the household as a unit of reproduction, of consumption or of co-residence.[15]

It is evident that such criticisms apply in part to the data contained in our applications for charity. The information could be false. But this is unlikely, except in minor details, given that it is verified by the parish priest (a source habitually accepted by historians as reliable) and checked by the Congregation's deputies through a visitation. The information could be incomplete. But this is also unlikely, if it related to the members of the household listed on the form, as it would be to their advantage to include more rather than fewer individuals to support their appeal for assistance. At most, it may have led to an under-statement of earnings; and even this can be partly checked by comparing earnings within the sample. Most seriously, the data is likely to be incomplete in that it excludes information on relationships with other households. There are no means of checking whether applicants for charity were contemporaneously receiving help from kin or neighbours outside the household. Their very concentration in specific streets could be argued in support of some form of mutualistic economic behaviour, rendering less distinct the boundaries between households. It has even proved possible to discover traces of a street network in one instance, where a boy was employed by his neighbour at a poultry stall at the market.[16] As for kin, one can only note that the absence of family in a position to help was an *a priori* condition for assistance, almost always confirmed by the parish priest; and that, in the eyes of society (the charitable institution), the level of earnings and needs of the household as a unit remained the crucial test for assistance, rather than the existence of other kin. Indeed, occasionally the applications spell this out, noting the existence of non-resident kin but excluding any role of economic support, as they were themselves *miserabili*.[17] At this level of subsistence, in urban society at least, the ongoing process of family formation, with the departure of children at marriage to set up other households, created separate domestic units, any of which might be judged worthy of assistance.

One further criticism needs to be taken into account. It can be argued that the applicants to the Congregation of San Giovanni Battista constituted a very specific, self-selective group and hence are unrepresentative not only of the general population of Florence, but even of its poor. Given the specialized functions of the various charitable institutions and the criteria employed by our Congregation, the petitioners were certainly self-selective: for example, no vagabonds applied, as they lacked the prerequisites of respectability, residence and job-skills; equally, it was both pointless to turn to the deputies to take charge of a new-born infant and superfluous since the foundling hospital of the Innocenti was the appropriate quarter. But it does not follow from this that our petitioners are unrepresentative, not only because of the very broad range of circumstances which were recognized as constituting legitimate reasons for assistance by the Congregation, and the number of applications (representing an annual average of over 10 per cent of the entire urban population), but ultimately because the respectable labouring classes, almost by definition, cannot but be regarded as representative of an urban population.

In short, the applications can tell us nothing about the world of the non-respectable poor, the layabouts, vagrants, thieves and others. But among the respectable poor, quantitatively and qualitatively our petitioners represent a central segment. Precisely because they were respectable wage-earners, their need of charity marks them as at the borderline between independence and indigence, and hence as deserving further study as a step towards a more precise understanding of the causes and likely frequency of the decline into dependent poverty within their life-cycle. The Congregation regarded them as conjunctural poor. Analysis of the information provided by the applications, on household composition, skills and level of earnings, points to a different conclusion.

2 Household structure

In what respect the applicants to the Congregation differed in their household structure from that of the overall urban population of Florence will only emerge when Professor Santini has completed his analysis of the census of 1810. At present we can note that the sex ratio of our sample of 4498 individuals is significantly out of line with that of the overall population. Whereas the 1810 census sample gave a ratio of 100 males to 111 females, our applicants show a ratio of 100:133. Unlike many early census figures, there can be no question of any under-reporting of females, as one may assume that expectations of obtaining charity were related, at least in a general but consistent way, to size of family. If the overall figures are broken down by age (and the distorting presence of widows removed), the imbalance is locatable to the years of adolescence and early adulthood: a ratio of 100:149.4 among our poor for the cohorts aged 15 to 39, compared to 100:128.4 for the general population (cohorts aged 16 to 35). The applications obviously offer no explanation for this marked absence of young men except for a number of references to sons serving in the Napoleonic armies. Conscription (counting effective enrolment and deserters) in the department of the Arno rose between 1810 and 1813 from around 1000 a year to nearly 2000, drawn from the cohorts aged 20 to 25, the contingent raised from the city of Florence in 1812 was 205.[18] It seems reasonable to conclude that this obligatory removal from the household by conscription increased (by an unknown quantity) the voluntary departure of young men in search of work, while the disparities in the ratios would seem to indicate that the proportion of young males leaving home was greater among the poor than among the overall population.

In terms of age distribution, the applicants for charity again differed from the general urban population. These poor families contained a disproportionate number of young, both infants under 5 (14.7 per cent compared to 9.9 per cent for the census sample) and children aged 6 to 15 (21.1 per cent compared to 15.5 per cent). At the other extreme, the proportion of the elderly poor is low – only 14.5 per cent aged over 50 compared to 23.1 per cent in the census sample; only 5 per cent of the poor were aged over 65. Perhaps life-expectancy was shorter among the poor. Certainly a likely consequence of growing old without family support was hospitaliz-ation: an annual average of 400 old men and women lived and died in the hospitals of Florence in these years.[19]

The data on household composition contained in our appli-cations for charity are extremely rich. They can also be regarded as highly reliable, not just because they are vouchsafed by the parish priest, but even more because of the care taken in listing members of the household according to their hierarchical location within the family and between families: after the head of the household, children followed adults, primary kin preceded secondary, extra-neous individuals or secondary family units were all identified clearly. Thus, alongside the most common entries of husband, wife and children listed by age, it is possible to find an extended household in the following order: widow (aged 50), unmarried son (28) and daughter (16), married son (29), daughter-in-law (29) and their child (7). The only exception, which reflects the social view of the order of authority within the household, by effecting a displacement within the family hierarchy, is the relegation to the end of the list of a parent (usually a widow), once she ceased to act as head of household: husband, wife, children, parent.

The distribution of these households according to their size shows the very substantial proportion of small households – over 80 per cent contained no more than five persons, with households of between two and four comprising over half the total number:[20]

Table 4 Distribution of households according to size

Size of household (no. of persons)	1	2	3	4	5	6	7–11
Percentage (no. of households: 1219)	14.1	16.5	18.6	19.5	13.2	9.8	8.1

But this image of an overwhelming predominance of small households is somewhat modified if the distribution of the population within these households is taken into account. For the most common experience of these Florentine poor as individuals was to live in households of four, five or six; over half (50.9 per cent) lived in households of five or more.

Of these households, over a third (35 per cent) were headed by women, the greatest proportion of whom (87.3 per cent) were widows. These women became heads of household at a substantially later age than their male counterparts: nearly half (45 per cent) of the female heads were aged at least 55, compared to under a quarter (23.3 per cent) of the same male cohorts. It is not surprising that the mean size of these female-headed households was significantly smaller than those headed by men – 2.46 compared to 4.37. For by the time women became heads, there was every likelihood that some children would have left the household. In fact, the mean size of male-headed households reached its peak of five individuals with the male cohort aged 30 to 39 and only dropped beneath four (3.95) when the male head was over 60, whereas female-headed households only included more than three individuals when the women were aged 45 to 49 and then declined steadily to 1.87 for women over 65. The drift towards truncation of the household, through the departure of children, was markedly greater in the absence of a male head; which perhaps helps explain the high incidence of remarriage among men, only 2 per cent of whom (in good part aged over 60) remained widowers, compared to 17 per cent of widows.

In the developmental cycle of these families, the pressures towards dissolution of the family unit were considerable. The rental of single rooms imposed a rigid spatial constraint. Presumably it accounted for the minuscule presence in these households of non-relatives, nephews, nieces or cousins (0.6 per cent). Both sons and daughters left their families relatively early to earn their independence. By the age of 20 only 15.7 per cent of sons and 21.1 per cent of daughters still lived at home; by the age of 24 the figures had dropped to 6.9 per cent and 9.3 per cent respectively. Given the almost total absence of lodgers, we can deduce that such departures, to learn a trade or accumulate a dowry, were not in the neighbourhood; we have no means of knowing whether these children could turn to kin further afield, in the city or the countryside. But a calculation of the singulate mean age at marriage – 27.4 years for men, 26.15 for women[21] – indicates a gap of some four to six years on average between the time sons and daughters left their parents' household and when they set up on their own.

The smallness of these urban households – a mean size of 3.69 – is not surprising. With no landed property and few, almost derisory movables, one would not expect to find much evidence of the stem-family structure of landowning families, while even kinship ties within the nuclear family might appear weak. Our households consist overwhelmingly of two-generational nuclear families – 94.6 per cent. They consist of nuclear families in the most classic sense – parents and unmarried children without other relatives. Barely 3.2 per cent consists of married men or women living with their parents, and hence forming the core of a three-generational structure. If we isolate households of two members, 43.8 per cent consists of husband and wife, and a further 44.3 per cent of widow or widower and child. If we take together the two largest groups of households – those of three and four – 63.2 per cent consist solely of an adult couple and their child or children, while another 24.3 per cent contain a single parent and children.

But it is as nuclear households that they are also particularly vulnerable. For of 1219 families, 172 or 14.1 per cent consisted of single persons; of these, 83 or 48.2 per cent were aged 60 or more. These single-member households, in fact, were dominated by widows (122 or 70.9 per cent), followed by a far smaller number of unmarried children (24 or 13.9 per cent), very few of whom (6) could be described as orphans in their teens.

This minute number of orphaned households offers a clue towards detecting the inner structures of familial defence against the strong pressures towards fragmentation. For although the nuclear family appears to dominate, with small households as its corollary, it is necessary to recall that 31 per cent of all households contained from five to eleven persons, comprising in all some 51 per cent of our entire population of poor. It is in these larger households that more complex family structures are to be found. These structures are not those of the stem-family, traces of whose organization can barely be seen: only fifty-eight families, or 1.3 per cent of the total population, included a married child, a retired parent or a retired widower, the categories which clearly identify a stem-family organization, according to Berkner;[22] only 9 of the 1219 families are multiple. What are visible are the signs of extended family organizations. In part, they consist of those relatives identified by Berkner as belonging to such an organization (parents, unmarried siblings or, alternatively, married children). Young married sons frequently form part: 62 per cent of all married men who were not heads of household lived in families of five or more; 44 per cent of these were aged under 30; 60 per cent under 35. But in part these extended structures belong to a different organization, which brought kin together in a household where the 'normal' partner was missing: orphaned grandchildren living with their grandparents, widowed or abandoned sisters or sisters-in-law with children, even brothers or brothers-in-law widowed or abandoned by their wives. The essential element, in all instances, is the presence of a child or children; sometimes, but not necessarily, these complex family structures are three-generational. They are structures that can be regarded as characteristic of these Florentine poor families without property, vulnerable and prone to fragmentation, and responding to the threat by bringing together within the household those most exposed by the loss of an adult partner. Within this group, the characteristic male dominance as head of household loses its significance. Indeed, among these propertyless poor urban families, the female, usually widowed, head plays a disproportionate role. Because our sample is limited in size, the numbers are unfortunately small, so that the figures can only be regarded as indicative. But as can be seen from Table 5, when broken down by age, in these larger families of five to eleven members the extended family organization can be seen most clearly among the under-forties and over-sixties, where they represent between 19 per cent and 28 per cent of the age-groups.

It is possible that this particular organization of the household represented a temporary response to the conjunctural pressure of these years. But it offers one more, indeed the most convincing indication of the relatively fluid and shifting composition of these households of the poor. With one in three individuals under the age of 15, an unusually large number of young men absent from the

Table 5 Composition of extended group in relation to head of household (male and female) in families of five to eleven

Age											
	20–9		30–9		40–9		50–9		60 and over		Total
Composition of extended group	No.	%	No.	%	No.	%	No.	%	No.	%	No.	%
1. Parents or unmarried siblings	4	19.0	18	18.8	9	7.0	2	2.4	1	2.2	34	9.0
2. Married child	—	—	—	—	3	2.3	5	5.9	7	15.2	15	4.0
3. Three-generational, or relative with child	1	4.8	—	—	2	1.6	2	2.4	5	10.9	10	2.7
	5	23.8	18	18.8	14	10.9	9	10.7	13	28.3	59	15.7
Nuclear	16	76.2	78	81.2	114	89.1	75	89.3	33	71.7	316	84.3
Total	21	100.0	96	100.0	128	100.0	84	100.0	46	100.0	375	100.0

household, most children departing by the age of 20 or soon after, a substantial proportion of households headed by ageing widows, a significant number of people living alone, and the formation of extended family organizations among particularly vulnerable kin as a shield against economic pressures, it would be tempting to conclude that our applicants were poor because of their household and family structures. Tempting but premature. For ultimately it will only prove possible to test whether these structures were the cause or the consequence of our applicants' poverty by analysis of the census of the overall urban population. In the meantime, our evidence on skills and earnings allows us to arrive at more precise estimates of the household as an economic unit and the identification of some of the reasons for the slide beneath subsistence to dependence on charity.

3 Family skills and earnings

Given the Congregation's requirements for assistance, it is not surprising that virtually all the families of applicants (97.5 per cent) declared at least one member with a job-skill. More interestingly, three-quarters (75.1 per cent) of the entire population from the age of 6 (3837) claimed some form of skill or training; and even though those admitting to any earnings were significantly fewer, they still amounted to 64.4 per cent. Hence unemployment as the cause of the dependence on charity would seem inadequate by itself as an explanation – although not underemployment or casual, discontinuous employment.

The distribution of skills among our population displays in almost 'classic' fashion the profile of a pre-industrial urban economy (Table 6).[23] Textiles (especially silk) dominated, with half the total number of those declaring skills. The sexual division of labour was absolute, not only in the female domination of the textile sector (92.9 per cent) and the male monopoly of handicrafts (96.3 per cent), but in services and commerce: the garment industry and charring were women's work, while victualling, costermongering, peddling, porterage and street-cleaning were male preserves. The male monopoly of regular domestic service (94.6 per cent) can perhaps be explained in terms of outdoor jobs (groom, stable-boy, etc.), whereas female servants tended to live in.

But beyond these broad categories, the applications are reticent about the relationships between skills and family organization. Work began young, from the age of 6. We can find individual examples of 'learning through doing', such as the mother who 'teaches how to work silk', or the three daughters who prepared the bobbins of the weft for their mother employed in a workshop, or the woodchopper with his son assisting him. But statistically it is difficult to detect any particular patterns of transmitted skills within the families.[24] The unskilled and casual nature of most of the jobs – preparation of the early phases of silk or other textile production, street selling, labouring, etc. – and above all the subordinate role as apprentices or assistants of two-thirds of those in the handicrafts and services sectors presumably meant that there were few skills to be learnt or inherited.

The applications are far more forthcoming about earnings, which are always given as a weekly figure. It seems likely that they relate to the moment when the applications were made, or at most to an impressionistic estimate of earnings averaged over a limited number of weeks. Of all the information contained in the applications, earnings are the most liable to error. It is possible that they were distorted by the seasonality of the applications, heavily (and inexplicably) biased in our sample to the months between May and August (78 per cent). One can assume, because only cash earnings were reported, that perquisites in kind were ignored. Deliberate under-reporting, in order to sharpen the appeal for charity, was probable and difficult, within limits, for either parish priest or deputy to detect. But such limits are revealed fairly clearly by the consistency of the levels and hierarchy of earnings declared for the specific skills, even though we know nothing of the number of hours worked or quantity of material produced. Female silk-reelers, for example, declared earnings ranging from $\frac{2}{3}$ to $1\frac{1}{2}$ lire, linen-spinners declared between 1 and $1\frac{1}{2}$ lire, ribbon-weavers between 1 and 2 lire; whereas male dyers declared between 1 and 2 lire, barbers, tailors or house-painters 4 lire, tanners and carpet-makers 6 lire. Thus the range of earnings, particularly for the poorest paid jobs, could vary enormously, even doubling or more (presumably according to the quantity reeled or spun). But the hierarchy of earnings between different skills imposed rigid parameters, effectively delimiting the boundaries of under-

Table 6 Occupational skills by sex and marital status

	Male					Female					Total	
	Single %	Married %	Other %	Total No.	Total %	Single %	Married %	Other %	Total No.	Total %	No.	%
Textiles	3.3	3.8	0.1	111	7.1	30.8	40.4	21.7	1450	92.9	1561	50.2
Handicrafts	44.8	49.3	2.2	430	96.4	0.4	2.9	0.2	16	3.6	446	14.3
*Services, commerce	25.7	43.0	2.1	551	70.9	16.2	6.0	6.8	226	29.1	777	25.0
'At school'											244	7.9
Miscellaneous											82	2.6
Total									3110	100		
*Services, commerce												
Pedlar, shopkeeper, seamstress, embroiderer, etc.	26.4	21.0	0.4	141	47.8	37.6	8.5	6.1	154	52.2	295	38.0
Services (barber, dustman, cobbler, employee, etc.)	26.7	60.9	3.7	147	91.3	4.3	2.5	1.9	14	8.7	161	20.7

Regular domestic service (groom, servant, stable-boy, etc.)	20.8	72.2	1.4	68	94.4	2.8	1.4	1.4	4	5.6	72	9.3
Casual domestic work (charring)	3.7	1.9	1.9	4	7.5	9.3	29.6	53.6	50	92.5	54	6.9
Victualling (baker, miller, tripe-, cake-, pasta-, water-ice-seller etc.)	36.0	61.3	1.8	113	99.1	—	0.9	—	1	0.9	114	14.7
Professions (teacher, dancer, singer, etc.)	31.2	37.5	18.7	14	87.4	—	—	12.6	2	12.6	16	2.1
General porterage (custodian, errand-boy)	21.7	69.6	8.7	23	100.0	—	—	—	—	—	23	3.0
Transport (carter, muleteer, unloader, etc.)	10.0	80.0	—	9	90.0	10.0	—	—	1	10.0	10	1.3
General services ('helps in market')	31.3	65.6	3.1	32	100.0	—	—	—	—	—	32	4.1
Total	25.7	43.0	2.2	551	70.9	16.3	6.0	6.8	226	29.1	777	100

estimates: no silk-reeler, for example, could earn as much as a tailor.

The mean weekly earnings of individuals declaring an income (2470) was 59.3 soldi (2 : 19 : 4 lire), equivalent to 2.50 francs. What this signified in terms of subsistence can be estimated, however approximately and crudely, in various ways. The average daily cost for the sustenance of an adult patient in the Florentine hospitals rose between 1810 and 1813 from 1 to 1.30 francs, making a weekly expenditure of 7 rising to 9.10 francs. When houses of correction (*dépôts de mendicité*) were set up in Tuscany in 1811, the daily diet of the inmates was given as 600 grammes of meat, a half-litre of wine and two quarter-litre soups; at Florence prices of 1811–13, the cost can be calculated as 50–70 centimes, or 3.50 to 4.90 francs per week. In fact, the accounts of the San Gimignano *dépôt* (which was reputed to be worse than a prison) show that the real cost was substantially lower between 1811 and 1813, ranging from 24 to 40 centimes a day (according to season), making an overall weekly average of 2.25 francs. Interestingly, genuine prisoners of Florence in 1809 cost the administration the slightly higher figure of 43 centimes a day or 3 francs a week. During the famine winter of 1812 the administration decided to distribute Rumford's 'economic soups' made of cheap vegetables, estimating that two daily soups would substitute, in terms of minimal nutrition, for a *livre* of bread (normally 400–500 grammes), generally accepted as rock bottom for survival; the average cost of each soup at Florence (where over 22,000 were distributed) was 10 centimes, so that the weekly cost was 1.40 francs.[25] While not too much weight should be placed on the precision of these figures, they converge towards the same conclusion: the weekly cost of food at a minimum subsistence level for an adult at Florence in these years was of the same order of magnitude as the average weekly earnings of the applicants to the Congregation of San Giovanni Battista. Even if we allow for systematic under-declaration of earnings, and for supplementation of a non-monetary kind (such as perquisites or scavenging by children), this relationship remains.

Within our population, the distribution of earnings was markedly splayed, reflecting both the sexual division of labour and the life-cycle of the individuals (Table 7). Over half our applicants (56 per cent) earned less than the mean of 60 soldi, or minimum

Table 7 Individual earnings by sex and marital status (weekly)

Income (soldi)	0–19 %	20–39 %	40–59 %	60–79 %	80–99 %	100–49 %	150 + %
Unmarried men (no. = 403)	38.7	12.7	17.2	12.4	15.2	10.4	6.7
Unmarried women (no. = 518)	42.3	23.5	22.7	22.8	14.5	6.0	—
Married men (no. = 573)	2.3	3.3	7.9	19.9	39.0	66.5	88.0
Married women (no. = 591)	8.0	35.5	28.3	32.9	22.1	10.8	2.3
Widowers (no. = 18)	—	0.2	0.3	1.7	1.7	0.6	2.3
Widowers (no. = 324)	8.7	22.0	20.3	9.2	7.5	4.1	—
Unknown status (no. = 43)	—	2.8	3.3	1.1	—	1.6	0.7
Total							
Male (no. = 994)	41.0	16.5	25.4	34.3	55.9	78.2	97.7
Female (no. = 1433)	59.0	83.5	74.6	65.7	44.1	21.8	2.3
Total	100.0	100.0	100.0	100.0	100.0	100.0	100.0
(no. = 2470)	(300)	(631)	(453)	(347)	(290)	(316)	(133)

subsistence. Amongst the lowest paid, adolescents and young unmarried adults dominate: of the cohorts under 20, 76.3 per cent earned less than 20 soldi, with only 15.5 per cent earning more than the mean. Married women tended to earn more than unmarried women, but women as a category remained bunched in the lower earnings brackets, where they constituted 75.3 per cent of those earning less than the average. Females, in fact, dropped dramatically at the highest levels of earnings, with only 72, or 16 per cent, showing more than 100 soldi income. By contrast, nearly all married men (88.8 per cent) earned more than the average, with a particularly marked presence in the two highest brackets (78 per cent and 98 per cent). But as they aged, the earnings of both men and women began to fall: of the cohorts over 60, only 18.4 per cent earned more than the mean and nearly half (45.5 per cent) earned substantially less, under 40 soldi. If we compare earnings in the different sectors of economic activity, these trends are confirmed. In terms of gender divisions, it is hardly surprising that women tended to earn less, if we bear in mind that the textile sector was the poorest paid, comprising 69.7 per cent of those earning beneath the average of 60 soldi. If we look at the life-course of our poor, we can note that the 17.5 per cent in the handicrafts sector earning less than 20 soldi were young, unmarried apprentices, whereas the 38.1 per cent in the highest brackets, earning over 100 soldi, were both their elders and hierarchical superiors, often describing themselves as masters (an ambiguous term by these years).

The analysis of individual earnings thus sketches in a clear outline the life-course of our Florentines: learning but often not earning at all as children, their wages remained usually far beneath subsistence level in their adolescence. As they matured and married, their wages rose, with more than half earning above the mean of 60 soldi from their twenties to their forties; thereafter, as they aged, their earnings fell, although rarely to as low a level as the starting point of the young apprentices, barrow-boys or textile girls. Within this cycle, men – usually in the better paid handicrafts or services sectors – earned consistently more than women.

To turn from individual earnings to collective household income allows us to identify more precisely the differences and relative weaknesses and strengths of the family structures. For the self-sufficiency of a household – regarded by the charitable institution (and presumably by its members) as an economic unit – depended upon its size and the earning capacities of the individuals composing it.

The mean weekly income of our households was 120 soldi. Just over half the households (51.8 per cent) earned less than this mean. As a first approach, a comparison of the size of household with its income (Table 8) argues for an intrinsically strong relationship. Thus in the lowest income bracket (under 60 soldi), the vast majority of households (78 per cent) contained only one to three members; while in the next income bracket (60 to 119 soldi), a similar proportion (73.3 per cent) came from households of two to four; of households with a middling income level (120 to 239 soldi), 77 per cent contained three to six members, while the incomes above 240 soldi were the near monopoly (87.6 per cent) of households of at least four, and heavily dominated (66.9 per cent) by those of five or more.

But while the relationship between income and size of household is evident, it is not directly proportionate, because of the variable number of individuals with earning capacities. As we can see in Table 9, the average number of earners remains significantly lower than the corresponding size of household. Thus, at one extreme, there were twice as many households with only one earner as single-member households; and at the other end, only one-fifth of the households of five or more members had at least five earners. The relationship between size of household and number of earners, strongest in three-member households, grew progressively weaker as households increased in size. For, irrespective of size, virtually no household contained more than four members with earning capacities. Taking our population as a whole, given the mean size of household of 3.69, the mean number of earners was only 2.02, while the mean number of dependants was 1.67.

This disproportion between the number of earners and size of household was accentuated by the considerable differences in earning capacities. As we have seen, sex and age could affect earnings negatively. Hence we can conclude that the earnings of single-member households were likely to fall beneath the subsistence mean of 60 soldi, since widows constituted 79 per cent of such

Table 8 Household income by size of household

	Income in soldi					
Size of household	0–59 %	60–119 %	120–79 %	180–239 %	240–99 %	300+ %
1 (no. = 176)	41.4	8.7	1.1	—	—	—
2 (no. = 201)	20.3	24.2	14.6	8.3	3.8	7.3
3 (no. = 227)	16.3	26.7	20.5	15.5	10.0	2.4
4 (no. = 238)	9.9	22.4	24.9	24.9	27.5	7.3
5 (no. = 161)	5.1	8.3	20.9	17.6	25.0	22.0
6 (no. = 120)	4.5	6.1	10.3	19.2	21.2	12.2
7–11 (no. = 98)	2.5	3.6	7.7	14.5	12.5	48.8
Total	100.0	100.0	100.0	100.0	100.0	100.0
(no. = 1219)	(355)	(277)	(273)	(193)	(80)	(41)

Table 9 Household size and numbers of earners

Household size		Earners in household	
Number of persons	*Percentage*	*Number of earners*	*Percentage*
1	14.3	1	30.1
2	16.5	2	32.5
3	18.6	3	15.8
4	19.5	4	15.0
5–11	31.1	5–11	6.6
	100.0		100.0

households, and nearly half the widows (48.2 per cent) were aged over 60. In similar manner, the presence of children was likely to limit the household income, as not all were old enough to earn and even those who were belonged to the lowest earning categories. Given the proportion of single-parent families we noted above, it is not surprising that the presence of child earners should have been significant even among the smaller households. In fact, children constituted one-third of earners in households of two, rising steadily to nearly three-quarters in the largest households of seven to eleven (Table 10).

What conclusions can be drawn from these figures? We have already seen that the earning capacities of these poor, whether they are considered as individuals or, more realistically, as economic

Table 10 Households with child earners

Household size	Number of earning children	Earning children as a percentage of total number of earners
1	9	5.1
2	64	31.8
3	90	39.6
4	116	48.7
5	88	54.7
6	64	53.3
7–11	70	71.4

units identified in the household, were constantly on the edge of subsistence. Three structural elements inhibited their ability to generate larger incomes: the differential level of wages imposed by sex and age; the growing proportion of child earners, with necessarily low earnings; and the absolute ceiling on the number of earners irrespective of the size of household.

The consequences of these inbuilt limits can be demonstrated unequivocally by comparing household income to subsistence needs. It is evident that, as earning capacities varied, so did consumption requirements: a child or an aged widow, for example, did not eat as much as a man in his prime. The weekly figure of 60 soldi, calculated above as approximating to minimum subsistence, referred to adult males. We have employed a set of age- and sex-specific consumption schedules elaborated for contemporary peasant societies and recently adopted by Wrigley and Schofield[26] in order to calculate the needs of our poor. Although the precise applicability of these coefficients to the urban poor of the early nineteenth century can be criticized, the results (Table 11) are not open to doubt. For almost three-quarters of the households (73.7 per cent), whatever their size, income fell beneath subsistence

Table 11 Households with less than subsistence income

Size	Household Number	Percentage
1	171	73.6
2	201	62.7
3	227	72.7
4	238	70.2
5	161	73.9
6	120	84.0
7	50	86.0
8	24	83.0
9–11	24	100.0
Total	1216	73.3

needs; families of two were relatively the best equipped to achieve a balance, the largest households were the most vulnerable.

The scale of inadequacy of these households to cover their subsistence needs reinforces the conviction that the earnings stated in the applications were under-declared and ignored other supplementary forms of income. The families must necessarily have elaborated additional strategies of survival, whether of a non-monetary kind, such as 'waste' from their work or scraps of food picked up by the children in the market, or temporary loans raised by pledges to the *monte di pietà* (communal pawnshop), or possibly by tapping other sources of charity, both institutional and private. But even if such additional sources of revenue could be demonstrated, the evidence of structural poverty remains. The Congregation of San Giovanni Battista saw its task as assisting families in conjunctural difficulties. In one sense this representation of the social reality remained accurate, for the dependency ratio within the family cycle directly affected the ability to generate adequate income: small families (excluding families of one) were better able to achieve self-sufficiency not only because there were fewer young children or aged, but because the earnings levels of mature adults (roughly between the ages of 25 and 55) were substantially higher. But precisely because the economic equilibrium of these farmilies was so fragile, the negative conjunctural stages of the family cycle had become a structural element. Alongside the immigrants to the city, these pauperized families formed a constant part, possibly the core, of the labour force of Florence, and were able to reproduce themselves, but only at the price of transmitting their pauperization. What we cannot tell, because of the limited time-span of our documentation, is whether this condition merely reflected the particular conditions of these years, or was part of a long-term phenomenon, the consequence of stationary wages in a declining urban economy stretching back across the eighteenth century or earlier.

4   Strategies of charity

The exclusive purpose of the applicants to the Congregation of San Giovanni Battista was to obtain charity. Details about family, skills or earnings, essential to obtain consideration of the application, contained factual responses with relatively little margin or purpose for error or guile. This was not necessarily true of the specification of the form of charity requested, as the applicant enjoyed some freedom of choice, within the objective constraint of the restricted number of items the Congregation was entitled to distribute and the subjective limitation of his assessment of his needs and the likely outcome to a request. How consciously applicants were aware of these possibilities is unknowable; but it is worth enquiring if any relationships exist between the types of request and household size and income, as they could reveal a strategy towards charity on the part of the respectable needy.

The applications to the Congregation were essentially limited to five objects: beds (of three dimensions), bedclothing (usually sheets, but occasionally blankets or even mattresses), cash subsidies, female clothing and bread.[27] Presumably a separate procedure existed for dowries; the absence of requests for work-tools may also point to a different administrative method. The most frequent requests, each amounting to 29 per cent of the total, were for beds and cash subsidies; beds and bedclothing accounted for nearly half the requests (45.8 per cent) (Table 12). The justification for asking for beds, constantly repeated, was the need to separate children from parents or sister from brother, as the girl (or occasionally the boy) reached puberty. Concern about sexual mores, whether justified or not, where the entire family almost invariably slept in a single bed,[28] can be seen as powerful motivation for such requests.

In broad outline, the pattern of requests can be explained by that correspondence between size and income of household we noted earlier. Although the overall distribution of applications among all households up to five is fairy regular, it is heavily biased towards families with the lowest incomes (under 180 soldi) (Tables 12 and 13). The relationship can be demonstrated if we compare the number of single-member households which requested charity – 14 per cent – to those with under 60 soldi income – amounting to 29 per cent – and recall that of all single-member households 72 per cent earned less than 60 soldi.

In terms of specific requests, the demand from the smallest and

Table 12   Form of charity requested by size of household

Size of household	No. of households	Beds %	Bedclothes %	Subsidies %	Clothes %	Bread %	Total %
1	171	5.7	16.9	16.0	17.4	23.7	14.2
2	198	5.1	26.8	17.1	21.1	23.0	16.4
3	226	14.5	22.9	20.5	21.7	15.8	18.7
4	236	24.2	17.9	18.5	14.4	19.4	19.6
5	160	21.4	6.0	13.1	9.9	7.9	13.1
6	119	16.0	7.5	8.5	6.8	5.1	9.9
7–11	93	13.1	2.0	6.3	8.7	5.1	8.1
Total	1203	100	100	100	100	100	100

Table 13   Form of charity requested by household income

Income (soldi)	No. of households	Beds %	Bedclothes %	Subsidies %	Clothes %	Bread %	Total %
0–59	351	15.4	34.8	34.9	27.6	42.4	29.1
60–119	271	21.4	26.4	19.9	27.6	20.2	22.5
120–79	272	26.2	20.9	23.9	17.8	18.0	22.6
180–239	192	23.6	13.9	13.4	13.5	8.6	15.9
240–99	80	10.3	3.0	4.5	7.4	7.2	6.6
300+	40	3.1	1.0	3.4	6.1	3.6	3.3
Total	1206	100	100	100	100	100	100

poorest households (single-member, under 60 soldi) was spread over all the possibilities, but with a fairly marked preference for bread – an item reflecting a condition of immediate need. The exception to this pattern was the very small number of requests for beds, understandably enough for small families of one or two; by contrast, the demand for beds was highest from households with incomes between 60 and 240 soldi (overwhelmingly those of between two and five members). Apart from beds, no clear picture emerges from the requests for bedclothing, cash subsidies or personal clothing. Once households reached a certain size (five to six) or level of income (240 soldi or more), the proportion of requests steadily declined, possibly reflecting a fall in expectations of success; but even among these large and less poor households, the request for beds remained substantially higher than for other items. The strategy of requests for charity, whatever the level of self-awareness, seems to have matched the relative strengths and weaknesses of the household in terms of size and income.

To turn from the requests to the grants of charity is to move out of the world of the daily needs of the labouring poor into that of the society enveloping them. The analysis of grants raises questions about the criteria employed by the deputies of the Congregation in selecting the families and forms of assistance, and the assumptions which underlay their assessment of self-sufficiency. That perceptions of need could differ fundamentally depending on the visual angle of respectively recipients or donors is demonstrated unequivocally by the rate of rejection and choice of form of charity decreed by the deputies (Table 14).

Less than half the requests (45.3 per cent) were accepted, over a third (38.3 per cent) were rejected, and the remainder (16.4 per cent) were modified by the donors. In terms of specific items, cash subsidies were the most likely to be rejected (54 per cent), beds the least likely (28.5 per cent). As an indication of a conscious choice deliberately imposed on the applicants the category of modified grants is particularly interesting. At first sight the choice seems haphazard; why give bedsheets when bread is requested, or personal clothing in place of a cash subsidy, or a bed instead of clothing? But out of the apparent arbitrariness of the juggling between items of charity two criteria appear clearly – an extreme reluctance to make grants of money, and a strong inclination to provide bread, almost as a universal solace. In fact, while only 11.4 per cent of all applicants requested bread (and 5.2 per cent of these were granted it), a total of 15.3 per cent were given bread whatever they asked for.

What strategy and assumptions underlay these choices? We can test some possible explanations by returning to the size and income levels of our households. As one might expect, the grant rate rises as households grow larger: for beds and clothing, from 40 per cent (for households of one and two) to over 70 per cent (for those of six and seven); while the smallest households of one and two were the most

Table 14 Requests and grants of charity

Requests	No.	%	Rejected (467) %	Accepted (552) %	Modified (199)				
					Beds	Bedclothes	Subsidy	Clothes	Bread
Beds	351	28.8	28.5	65.5	—	5	—	5	11
Bedclothes	201	16.5	32.3	39.8	3	—	—	13	40
Subsidy	352	28.9	54.0	20.2	8	11	—	22	50
Clothes	163	13.4	30.1	58.3	4	4	1	—	10
Bread	139	11.4	36.7	54.7	3	3	—	6	—
Others	12	1.0	100.0	—	—	—	—	—	—
Total	1218	100	38.3	45.3	18	23	1	46	111

likely to be granted bread, whether or not they requested it. Beds were given particularly to families of four and five (49 per cent), cash subsidies were more easily granted to households of three and four (47 per cent). The absolute level of household income, more surprisingly, seems to bear little direct relationship with the decision to make a grant, until we link it to the number of members in the household actually earning; at this point, the higher the number of earners, the greater the likelihood of being granted a bed (presumably because some of the earners were pubertal children); the fewer the earners, the more probable a grant of bread. Thus the policy of the deputies of the Congregation would appear to be biased in two respects: bread for small households, with few earners and hence at the lowest income levels; approval of middling size families of three to five, to whom beds and even cash subsidies were granted with disproportionate ease. We can add that, except for cash, the deputies displayed a higher propensity to make grants to families with daughters than to those without, and that this was most marked in the grant of beds and personal clothing (Table 15).

How can we explain these choices? Like Oxfam, the High Commission for Refugees or any other humanitarian or charitable organization, present or past, the deputies, confronted by a world of misery, could not assist all who met their conditions, but were forced to select. They could justify their choice by adherence to the strict institutional qualifications for grants: sheets were normally only given to the sick (as a measure against infection); personal clothing was meant for children of larger families so that they could

Table 15 Grants of charity, as a percentage of requests, according to presence or absence of daughter

	Without daughter (no. = 734) %	*With daughter (no. = 445)* %
Bed	51.8	77.5
Bedclothing	38.1	43.3
Subsidy	21.0	17.6
Clothes	38.1	71.0
Bread	53.0	59.0

go out and learn a trade; beggars licensed by the Congregation were not entitled to further assistance; families were rarely allowed a second grant, even for a different item. Not all these regulations were applied with equal severity, and there were evidently differences of judgement and opinion within the sphere of discretion allowed the deputies. One deputy recognized that a widow (aged 87), licensed to beg, was not entitled to a subsidy to help her with her rent, but he still recommended that she be granted bread, given her age; another recommended that a widow with two adult daughters, earning altogether 7 lire, be granted thirty days' bread because of the ill-health of the mother and a daughter. Both were rejected, the former as a licensed begger, the latter because of the level of income. As against this, a family of five, including three adult children, earning a total 13.66 lire, received clothing for the 19-year-old daughter (in place of the subsidy requested).[29] In general, the deputies actually visiting the applicants' homes seemed more inclined to stretch the rules than those responsible for the decision.

Alongside or behind these discretionary judgements certain preferences seemed to operate in the selection of both persons and objects of charity. Among the applicants, a distinction was made between ability or disability to earn: hence the youthful and healthy were the least likely to receive grants, even if their earnings were very low; 'unencumbered, young, healthy and able to procure greater earnings' was a recurrent phrase used to justify rejection. Among the items of charity, cash, bread and beds stand out. There was an evident reluctance to make grants of money, presumably through fear that it would not be put to good purpose. The period and amount of bread was usually not specified; where it is noted, it seems to vary from 1 to 3 *livres* daily, for two to four weeks. It seems to have been recommended almost as a matter of course by the deputies visiting homes as a form of immediate, albeit temporary aid for the particularly vulnerable, the old, the incapacitated, the (aged) widows. The grant of beds derived from ethical rather than practical values – fear of incestuous relations. As Luigi Passerini, the historian of the Congregation (writing in 1853) paraphrased the mayor of Florence's 1809 explanation, beds were given 'to prevent those improprieties that are born of inappropriate closeness between persons of different sex'.[30] There is no evidence of incest. Indeed the French prefect of the department, Fauchet, was sceptical, maintaining that 'most of those who solicit assistance of this sort sell the beds they possess to reduce themselves to the right state for what they hope to get; hence the children, of either sex, find themselves in the same condition as they were before'. Even the deputies had moments of self-doubt, threatening to punish those who hocked the Congregation's beds or bedclothing.[31] But, in this instance, arguments of morality contradicted and even pre-empted those of economic ability, as beds were also given to families whose adult members were physically capable of earning.

Whom the Congregation thought it was helping, and how, are questions that bring us back to our initial concerns. The deputies of the Congregation unquestionably saw themselves as assisting a particular category amongst the poor – the respectable labouring classes of Florence, temporarily in difficulties. Other institutions existed for long-term help, for infants and children, the aged and ill. Even within their chosen field of outdoor relief, boundaries were marked out by the allocation of responsibilities to separate institutions, with the inevitable consequence of demarcation disputes. The shamefaced poor technically appertained to the Buonomini di San Martino, but the Congregation's clients could be (and on occasion were) described by the same term. For its definition of those within its remit was both the narrowly defined positive one of 'shamefaced poor by birth or by the profession they exercised or exercise in the service of the Prince', and the far more extensive negative one of those 'who are of the class of the shamefaced poor because they do not beg, nor are agricultural labourers by birth or condition'.[32] In the event the matter was of no practical importance, as the Congregation merely excluded those already in receipt of assistance from the other institution.

Even among the category of the poor for whom they assumed responsibility, the deputies made further distinctions in their manner of treating them. Begging licenses were only granted to the old (usually over 70) and the blind[33] – and were regarded as a sufficient means of subsistence, disqualifying other forms of aid. Youth and health in childless couples were assumed to equate with ability to increase earnings. Both the very vulnerable (the aged, the single, the sick) and families with one to three children were seen as particularly meritorious.

Underlying all the distinctions made by the deputies, the assumption persisted that only temporary assistance was needed. It permeated the deputies' explanations of their recommendations; but it equally accounts for the willingness to lend small looms or reeling spools[34] or the grant of dowries. There was a profound and genuine horror at the living conditions of the labouring poor, as well as of their potential consequences, whether immorality or disease. The causal link between such conditions and inadequate earnings was acknowledged: 'the bed on which these miserable creatures lie can best be described as a dog's-rest . . . it seems natural that such wretched people, who have no other resource in the world besides the labour of their own hands, should necessarily languish if their work stops or even (let us be clear) if it diminishes a lot'.[35] On occasions, but infrequently, the deputies acknowledged that, besides food, other items such as rent or clothing could prove too much: 'such earnings are not enough to provide for living expenses and house rental, in short for those other necessary things besides food'.[36] In short, the recognition that earnings could prove inadequate for reasons outside the control of the individuals was a *raison d'être* for the existence of the Congregation.

Nevertheless its manner and choice of action bore only an anachronistic relationship to the problems of the poor it assisted. The time-scale of assistance was apparently arbitrary and could deny the very urgency of the need, for between ten days and six weeks could pass between the date of an application and a decision. The choice of items was inappropriate or too brief: a family needing cash might not consider a dress for a daughter as essential; two weeks of bread would not solve unemployment. Part of the explanation for this contrast between needs and forms of charity can be found in the Congregation's legacy of outdated practices. This seems the most likely explanation of the frequent donation of bread, a symbolic gesture of compassion whose futility (like that of token dowries) was to be recognized by the Congregation's historian, Passerini, forty years later, as pointless or worse. It was also caught up in moral assumptions which conflicted with the evidence of economic needs, assumptions both old and new – that sexual licence was potentially ubiquitous, that money would be dissipated, that unemployment was a matter of choice. But ultimately the deputies of the Congregation would seem deliberately to have limited their intervention to the conjunctural effects for the family cycle, most visibly in the rejection of requests from young, childless couples, and in the facility of grants to aged widows and to families with pubertal daughters aged 10 to 15. Underlying such self-imposed restrictions (besides the undoubted financial constraints, especially under French rule) was the tacit assumption that these poor families would turn elsewhere, to the *monti di pietà* or perhaps to private benefactors.[37] We can only conclude that a fundamental contradiction existed between the objects and methods of charity employed by the deputies of the Congregation of San Giovanni Battista towards the deserving poor of Florence and the structural weaknesses of these pauperized households, which worked against the likelihood of their achieving economic self-sufficiency.

Notes

1 L. Cajani, 'L'assistenza ai poveri nell'Italia del Settecento', *Transactions of the Fifth International Congress on the Enlightenment*, Oxford, 1981.

2 L. Passerini, *Storia degli stabilimenti di beneficenza e d'istruzione elementare gratuita della città di Firenze*, Florence, 1853, pp. 61–97.

3 ibid., pp. 69–72, 79; ASF, Arno, 508, 26 April 1809; Arno, 158, accounts, July–December 1812. Already in 1808–9 the head of the French junta reorganizing Tuscany, the ideologue and philanthropist De Gérando, had used the Congregation to distribute his stipend among the poor of Florence (Passerini, *Storia della stabilimenti*, p. 88).

4 The analysis of the 1810 census is being prepared in machine-readable form at the Department of Statistics, University of Florence, under the direction of Professor A. Santini and Dr G. Gozzini. I wish to thank Professor Santini for the preliminary results he has made available to me, based on a sample of 6887 persons.

5 ASF, Arno, 508, 26 April 1809.

6 E. Repetti, *Dizionario geografico fisico storico della Toscana*, vol. 2, Florence, 1833, pp. 273–5; D. Herlihy and C. Klapisch-Zuber, *Les Toscans et leurs familles*, Paris, 1978, pp. 173–7. A table of population, birth and death rates, in ANP, F20.165, gives the 1809 population as 77,156 and that for 1810 as 77,696.

7 P. Malanima, 'Industria e agricoltura in Toscana tra Cinque e Seicento', *Studi storici*, 21 (1980), pp. 290–1; A. Zobi, *Storia civile della Toscana dal MDCCXXXVII al MDCCCXLVIII*, Florence, vol. 2 (1850), Appendix 5.

8 ASF, Arno, 476, 2 July 1811; ANP, F16.990, 8 March 1811; F12.1602.

9 Passerini, *Storia della stabilimenti*, p. 87; ASF, Segreteria di Gabinetto, 154, no. 10; ANP, F15.509.

10 J.P. Gutton, *La Société et les pauvres en Europe (XVIᵉ–XVIIIᵉ siècles)*, Paris, 1974, pp. 72–3; *La Société et les pauvres: l'exemple de la généralité de Lyon 1534–1789*, Paris, 1971, pp. 51–3; B.S. Pullan, 'Poveri, mendicanti e vagabondi (secoli XIV–XVII)', *Storia d'Italia. Annali 1, Dal Feudalesimo al Capitalismo*, Turin, 1978, p. 989; O. Hufton, 'Towards an understanding of the poor of eighteenth-century France', in J.F. Bosher (ed.), *French Government and Society. Essays in Memory of Alfred Cobban*, London, 1973, p. 145.

11 ASF, Arno, 508, 4 March 1809, 26 April 1809, 23 November 1809; Arno, 83, for accounts of the *bureau de bienfaisance* for September–December 1810; Arno, 508, for accounts for March–August 1810; Arno, 403 and 158, for accounts of the *bureau de bienfaisance* for 1812, which underestimate the Congregation's full income and expenditure (the 'economic soups' have been excluded from this calculation). All the figures are lower than the average expenditure calculated by Passerini (p. 87) for the 1790s.

12 ANP, F15.509.

13 The applications for assistance are in ASF, Congregazione di San Giovanni Battista (henceforth SGB), ser. IV, 2 to 43 (1810–12), 66 and 67 (1814); a batch of applications was sent by De Gérando to Paris: ANP, F15.508 (August 1808–October 1809).

14 Repetti, *Dizionario geografico*, vol. 2, pp. 273–5. The figures for 1632 have been provided by Professor Santini, of the University of Florence, whom I wish to thank.

15 The literature on the household–family debate and census material is now considerable. See, primarily, T.P.R. Laslett (ed.), *Household and Family in Past Time*, London, 1972; L.K. Berkner, 'The use and misuse of census data for the historical analysis of family structure', *Journal of Interdisciplinary History*, 5 (1975); 'The stem family and the developmental cycle of the peasant household: an eighteenth-century Austrian example', *American Historical Review*, 77 (1972); R. Wheaton, 'Family and kinship in Western Europe: the problem of the joint family household', *American Historical Review*, 80 (1975); K.W. Wachter, E.A. Hammel and P. Laslett, *Statistical Studies of Historical Social Structure*, London, 1978. It is worth noting that most of the debate has been concerned with rural families.

16 ASF, SGB, ser. IV, 17, Giuliano Boni and Salvatore Spini, 20 June 1810, residents in Via Case Nuove, civic numbers 3580 and 3559.

17 ASF, SGB, ser. IV, 17, e.g. Giuseppe Valenti, 20 June 1810; Caterina Pagni, 18 June 1810.

18 ANP, F9.159, Arno, especially 2 November 1812. Poor families deprived of sons or brothers through conscription were offered subsidies by the end of 1813: ANP, F1A.29, 12 December 1813. It is generally recognized that conscription affected the poor disproportionately, as wealthier families were able to pay for substitutes: cf. J. Godechot, *Les Institutions de la France sous la Révolution et l'Empire*, Paris, 1968, pp. 600–2.

19 ANP, F15.509.

20 Gutton (*La Société et les pauvres*, pp. 54–6) found the same small size of households of respectable poor assisted by the Société Philanthropique, with an average 2.61, and average minimum and maximum (based on streets) ranging from 1.57 to 4.25.

21 J. Hajnal, 'Age at marriage and proportions marrying', *Population Studies*, 1953, Appendix 3. Since a sizeable group of men aged 15 to 39 is missing from our data (see p. 168), one would expect the actual singulate age of marriage for both men and women to be lower than reported.

22 Berkner, 'The stem family', pp. 406–7.

23 For a more detailed discussion of these skills, see above, 'Language and social reality: job-skills at Florence'.

24 Of the cohort aged 6 to 9, 57 per cent were described as learning a trade 'at school', or as working. 70 per cent of daughters worked in different sectors from their mothers, although there is a relatively high proportion (45 per cent, or 121) of mothers and daughters working within the textile sector itself; 72 per cent of sons worked in different sectors from their fathers, with only a moderate proportion (36 per cent, or 44) of fathers and sons working in the handicrafts sector. In contrast to this near-absence of inter-generational transmission of skills, there is some indication of related activities between husband and wife in textiles, where 84 per cent (47) of the few husbands in this female-dominated industry worked in the same sector. But the figures are too small to draw any firm conclusions.

25 ASF, Arno, 97; ANP, F15.509 (hospitals); ASF, Arno, 504; ANP, F16.540A (*dépôt*), with prices calculated from ANP, F11.468; F11.1161 and F11.1171; ASF, Arno, 512 (prisons); ASF, Arno, 158; ANP, F11.706, F15.2877–8 ('economic soups').

26 E.A. Wrigley and R.S. Schofield, *The Population History of England 1541–1871*, London, 1980, pp. 444–6.

27 A handful of applications, excluded from the analysis, requested a combination of these five items.

28 The deputies' descriptions consistently refer to a single bed or straw mattress. Such an arrangement was normal in rural areas: J.L.

Flandrin, *Familles: parenté, maison, sexualité dans l'ancienne société*, Paris, 1976, pp. 97–101.

29 All examples come from ASF, SGB, ser. IV, filza 19, and do not necessarily refer to the second *sestiere*.

30 Passerini, *Storia della stabilimenti*, p. 95; ASF, Arno, 508, 26 April 1809.

31 ASF, Arno, 323, 27 September 1813; Arno, 83, 13 September 1810.

32 ANP, F15.508.

33 ASF, SGB, ser. I, filza 7, 101–7.

34 ibid., ser. I, filza 108.

35 ANP, F15.508.

36 ASF, SGB, ser. IV, filza 19, Giovanni Gucci, 4 July 1810.

37 See chapters 3 and 5 in this volume: 'The treatment of the poor', and 'Problems in the history of pauperism'.

8

❦

Charity
and
family subsistence

Charity implies choice; and choice, in turn, usually requires some method of checking. If we leave aside casual or indiscriminate distribution of alms (say, of small change to beggars outside a church, or soup to the needy at the convent gate), the regular and above all the continuous exercise of charity has always necessitated discrimination because of the permanent disproportion between resources and demand. In this sense, charitable institutions in the past functioned in similar manner to contemporary departments of social security, elaborating mechanisms to identify preferences: personal and family information was demanded and classified, such information was checked against anticipated norms or even by direct investigation, and on this basis either rejection or an appropriate level and form of assistance was decided. The distinction habitually made between charity and the welfare system is that, for the latter, need is the sole criterion giving entitlement to assistance (at least until the attacks on the welfare state of the past few years), whereas for the charitable organizations of early modern and modern Europe value judgements of worthiness accompanied assessments of need. In fact, as the literature on the persistence of poverty in the welfare state has amply demonstrated,[1] assessments of need are often difficult to arrive at, even with the imposing statistical back-up of modern government, and easily contain value judgements. What is common to contemporary social security organizations and earlier outdoor relief charities is that because both work from the premiss of family needs, they are obliged to elaborate models, or at least Weberian ideal-types, of different family structures or different phases in the family cycle, in relation to their relative earning capacities, against which to test needs and upon which to draw up their regulations. It is this identification by an early nineteenth-century Florentine charity of family structures, cycle and subsistence needs that is the main concern of this chapter.

The Congregation of San Giovanni Battista was the main outdoor relief organization of Florence, to which a third or more of the poor turned for assistance – an annual average of 8600 in 1810–12, or over 10 per cent of the urban population.[2] By statute, it only assisted the labouring poor of the city, excluding not only non-Florentines, but citizens unable to prove their domicile, some job-skill (however rudimentary) and moral conduct. It was also statutorily limited in the outdoor relief it could offer, which consisted of five objects – cash subsidies, beds, bedclothing (sheets, occasionally blankets), clothes and bread – some of which were subject to further conditions. These limitations derived from the highly specialized organization of charity in Florence (as in most Italian and western European cities), by which individual institutions assumed specific responsibilities (such as hospitals for foundlings, conservatories for orphan girls, etc.). But our Congregation played a central role in Florence of the eighteenth and nineteenth centuries, as it existed to support the fundamental unit of social life – the family in its home – at moments of particular crisis. Permeating all its assistential activities was the concern to underpin the independence of the family as a unit, to prevent individuals or entire families from becoming permanently dependent on institutional support (for instance, in hospitals, workhouses or asylums), or alternatively from adopting strategies of survival disapproved of by society (theft, prostitution, unauthorized begging, etc.).

In chapter 7 I suggested, on the basis of a statistical study, that the Congregation concentrated its efforts on critical moments of the family cycle.[3] The purpose of the present chapter is to explore this conclusion on the basis of a non-statistical analysis of the descriptions and comments made by the deputies of the Congregation about each application for assistance. As in chapter 7, the evidence is based on a sample consisting of all the applications from a single *sestiere*, numbering 1219 family units (4498 individuals) or 23 per cent of the series. This second *sestiere* covered the *quartiere* of Santa Maria Novella and part of the zone near the market of San Lorenzo, typically popular areas of Florence, densely inhabited by artisan and street-trading families.

In order to request assistance, the Congregation required applicants to fill in a printed form, listing information about each individual living in the household: name, relationship to the head of household, age, state of health, job-skill, employer and weekly wage (if any); underneath these details, the applicants specified the form of assistance they hoped for. At the back of the form, the parish priest was asked to confirm the information and add his own comments, which were followed by those of two deputies of the Congregation. It is worth dwelling briefly on these procedures of acquiring information, as it was solely on their reliability that the individuals, units or categories to be assisted could be identified. Four aspects can be noted.

First, the quantity of information demanded was considerable and can be compared, without impropriety, to that required by contemporary social service offices. In a substantially illiterate society, the compilation of these forms must have frequently (usually?) required the collaboration of someone outside the household (parish priest? Deputy of the Congregation? A neighbour or relative?), whose very participation can be read by us ambivalently as implying either a check on the veracity of the information or collusion with the supplicant (or both). But, perhaps more importantly, the quantity of information required must have discouraged the casual applicant (that Florentine yesteryear equivalent of the 'scroungers' living off social security, so useful to our English and American neo-liberal critics of the welfare state). It could have been no light matter applying to the Congregation, not something to be tossed off, like a football pools coupon, on the off-chance of a useful supplement to one's income; but a desperate measure, often a final resort, in the face of total indigence, destitution or worse. Indeed, the humane, upright and conscientious deputies of the Congregation must have reinforced this austere impression by their automatic dismissal of applications 'because of inadequate information', or its 'improper presentation', not only by the supplicants, but by the parish priest ('because of the limited information provided by the priest', 'because the curate has written his usual general phrase'). Full presentation of this substantial corpus of information was thus a bureaucratic prerequisite, failure to comply with which risked the chilling response of one deputy: 'Refused in that providing little information implies no great need.'[4] Only the genuinely needy or skilled rogues (our present-day 'scroungers') were likely to go to the trouble of applying. And the latter, although they did not know it, were rapidly identified in the deputies' registers and rejected, if they had ever before obtained assistance ('already assisted other times').[5]

The second point to be noted about the applications is the character of the data demanded. The information about family relationships and age (common to many census-type sources) was essential to the deputies, in a general sense to set against their ideal-type families, and in an immediate sense to judge the nature and urgency of their intervention (e.g. separation of pubescent daughters from the parental bed). State of health and job-skills were more unusual, both serving (like weekly earnings) as component elements towards a composite judgement about levels of vulnerability; but also useful as discriminatory information, both negative and positive: to decline responsibility for those without any job-skills (another statutory prerequisite), to elicit information about alternative supplementary benefits (was the applicant in receipt of 'the usual subsidy for new-born babes from the Innocenti hospital'?), to recognize the drastic consequences of the illness or even worse the hospitalization of a head of household ('the grave and serious illness of the head of the family').[6] Earnings, both individual and of the household unit, obviously represented a crucial element in the deputies' decision and (as we shall see) were subjected to some scrutiny.

The third aspect we must note is the procedure of visitations. A few families were at once excluded because they lacked the parish priest's confirmation of good conduct: 'the family is not of good morals and for this reason has not been visited'.[7] On receipt of an application, two of the seventy-two deputies proceeded to a visit of the room in which the applicants lived. Such personal contact was an essential ingredient of nineteenth-century Catholic charity, shortly to be fixed in its definitive mould by De Gérando in his best-selling *Le Visiteur du pauvre* (1820) as the most effective method 'of recognizing true indigence, and rendering alms useful to both donors and recipients'.[8] In practice, the visitation permitted the deputies to assess the applicants' living conditions (although presumably not to verify earnings). A negative judgement from the deputies ('very poor, but not of the most needy') was virtually equivalent to rejection.[9] Following the comments of the visitor-deputies, another deputy, acting as rapporteur, wrote his proposal for a decision, which was then submitted to the Congregation's bureau (six deputies, acting in rotation). This rapporteur's proposal was almost always clear-cut, accompanied by a brief explanation. But on rare occasions he expressed uncertainty and left the decision to the bureau, as in the case of an unauthorized beggar (technically disqualified from further assistance) whose family lived 'in great and extreme misery', or the wife, forced by her husband's hospitalization to change to a cheaper but totally empty room, asking for a bed and bedclothing which the regulations did not permit.[10] Applications were occasionally rejected in the absence of adequate information from the visitor-deputies ('given the little verification of the request by the deputies'), even through their failure to check the age of a starving widow.[11] An obligatory requirement for a subsidy to pay for a wet-nurse was a visit by a doctor, sometimes (always?) the Congregation's doctor, whose report occasionally led to refusal.[12]

This complex procedure based on personal knowledge brings us to the final point – verification of the veracity of the information. Here the most delicate item was the declaration of earnings. There were no direct means by which the deputies could check the amounts earned from intermittent (mostly textile) putting-out work or street peddling; nor, in this instance, could they rely on the parish priest, little better able than they to check and more likely to confirm than to deny (and hence ensure the rejection of) the declarations of worthy and genuinely needy parishioners. The deputies, in fact, were suspicious and rejected a fair number of applications on the explicit grounds of 'greater earnings than those declared', 'must earn more than declared', 'untrue declaration of personal earnings', 'false declaration of earnings', and similar verdicts. Usually we do not know on what evidence they based their conclusions. But on occasion they point to specific skills, such as the silk-weaver's (where work was not lacking and hence earnings must be higher than declared) or the coach-builder's (who must be earning something); or deny that it is possible for a family to declare no earnings; or comment that the age and good health of the individuals mean that they must be earning more than they declare.[13] There can be no doubt about the scepticism of the deputies over the precise earnings declared, nor about their direct knowledge of wage levels. But not only is the proportion of applications rejected on these grounds minimal (perhaps 60 out of the total 1219); more important is the statistical evidence that the declared earnings of three-quarters of all applicant families provided less than minimal subsistence, so that even substantial under-declarations would not have removed them from the most vulnerable category of poor.[14] At best, gross or inept under-declaration of earnings served the deputies as a further means of discrimination amidst a multitude of desperately needy families.

That the deputies were aware that virtually all applicants were not only poor but in critical circumstances is evident from the terminology they employed. 'Poor' (*povero*) described a permanent condition, 'wretched' (*miserabile*) a state of urgent need, a 'poor' family was presumed able to find the means of ensuring its subsistence, a 'wretched' one was clearly beneath the poverty line. For the families themselves, the distinction between *povero* and *miserabile* was tenuous and mobile, a continuum rather than a contrast, for both labels not only included families practising the same (usually low level) skills and living in the same houses, but could describe the same family at different moments of its cycle. For the Congregation, the distinction was definitive: 'Poor to the utmost, but not of the most needy. Rejected'.[15] The operative words for serious consideration by the deputies – which applied to the overwhelming majority of applicants – were 'wretched' or 'needy' (*bisognoso*), around which was woven a miniature tapestry of qualifications: 'wretched enough', 'very wretched', 'extremely wretched', 'most wretched', 'state of wretchedness', 'truly needy', 'state of extreme need', in short, appurtenance to what was significantly called 'the class of the wretched'. Given these variations on the term *miserabile*, visitor-deputies were obliged to employ alternative signals to highlight the most urgent cases, such as 'maximum indigence' or 'total destitution'.[16]

It is evident that such terminological distinctions served a function of discriminatory choice, in exactly the same way as the rejections through inadequate information. The deputies never explain what they mean by 'poor', at most affirming that the applicants earn or, given their condition, could earn enough for their subsistence. It is rare to find so explicit a statement as 'not appropriate to be assisted, as sufficiently provided with everything'.[17] In like manner, and far more frequently, the deputies took refuge behind their regulations. A substantial number of rejections (38 per cent of all applications were rejected) were justified generically as 'contrary to the regulations'. In specific instances the refusal might be because the application was for something not included among the Congregation's items for outdoor relief – a dowry for a daughter, assistance to train a son as coach-driver. Alternatively, the application would be rejected because it came from a beggar, whose licence to beg from the Congregation automatically precluded further assistance. Families applying for blankets in the summer were not granted them as it was not yet the right season.[18] Yet again, the rejection might be based on the non-conformity of family conditions with the specifications of the items requested – the fact that a mother was actually suckling her new-born baby, even though she was starving, when the regulations stipulated a physical inability to breast-feed; clothing for adults, even when they were literally in rags, as only children were statutorily entitled; refusal of a bed, because the children were too small to require separation, even if there were many of them.[19] As one would expect, some rapporteurs were more meticulous than others in their interpretation of the rules. It is possible to point to extreme cases of bureaucratically-minded deputies who had lost sight of the human distress staring out at them from the applications, such as the refusal of a wet-nurse subsidy because the baby's incapacity to suckle (as distinct from the mother's to feed) was not foreseen in the regulations. Red tape most clearly smothered the direct contact on which the charity operated on those rare occasions when the rapporteur decided primarily or exclusively in terms of maintaining a rough balance of charity between the parishes: 'refused, given the multiplicity of subsidies needed by this parish [San Lorenzo]', 'granted, given the few subsidies that this parish [Ognissanti] has obtained'.[20]

But it would be misleading to place too much weight on a legalistic approach to the requests of these needy families. The deputies were not only compassionate, but were prepared to interpret the rules broadly, even in special cases to go against them. Mothers denied the wet-nurse subsidy were often granted nappies instead. Single old women were frequently given at least bread. Very large families, with four, five, and up to nine children, were granted beds even if the children were not of the statutory age. But even small families could reasonably hope for a bed, if their living conditions were particularly shocking ('they are all sleeping together on a straw mattress on the damp floor', 'sleeping on boards', or 'on a chest', 'on straw', 'more than a bed, it seems like a dog's kennel', 'on the bare floor'.[21] Grants were occasionally made despite inadequate declarations, 'because of the information provided by the parish priest'. A wet-nurse subsidy was granted, although not within the regulations, 'given the wretchedness of the family and the lack of employment'; a family, 'wretched to the utmost', denied a bed, was given an alternative subsidy. A bed was granted, even though it was noted that the father was an authorized beggar; or where father and son were sleeping on the bare floor, 'even though it is known that this family already got a bed from the Congregation, which perhaps was sold'. A wife about to give birth was often sufficient justification for the grant of a bed. Most revealing of a willingness to interpret the rules in order to fit the human case are two examples of beds which should have been refused as the daughter was marrying. In the first case, it was noted that the bed was the property of the daughter, whose marriage would have left her father and sister bedless; in the second instance, having observed that the daughter was about to marry and could not do so as she was the only earner in the family (and hence unable to buy a bed), it was decided, casuistically, that a bed could properly be granted to separate her from her parents and not because she was marrying.[22] If the regulations were sometimes used as a means of negatively determining choice, if individual rapporteurs could sometimes display deeply hostile suspicion and reject applications perhaps in a bout of irritability, there is abundant evidence that for the most part the deputies utilized the evidence they had assembled so carefully in order to assess the relative degrees and urgency of need of the families they had visited.

What did the deputies look for? What criteria did they employ to guide their choice? The comments they wrote on the applications provide us with a fairly definitive picture which – bearing in mind that the information was based on face-to-face contact – can reasonably be accepted (at least for those aspects which they noted) as an accurate description of family and living conditions in these lower, more unfortunate levels of the poor.

Three parameters can be identified, within which the deputies located their entire discourse – the presence of kin, the level of earnings and the size of family. All three, separately or in various combinations, were repeatedly employed as a means of explaining why a family was *miserabile* (and hence meritorious), or why it should not receive help. The washerwoman, living alone, was denied help as her son, even if not living with her, could provide for her subsistence; the aged widowed mother, with low earnings, merited assistance as her only son was about to leave her in order to marry; the old, mentally ill widow, living in the same house as her married daughter, was granted aid as her son-in-law (himself an applicant for a bed) was not able to help her. A conscripted son was a guarantee for a grant, precisely because conscription implied enforced absence of kin (even worse, of male kin) and hence a sometimes drastic diminution of earnings.[23] The quintessential prerequisite for an application was inadequate earnings, repeated in virtually all applications, whose counterproof is to be found in the systematic refusal to grant aid because in the deputies' judgement the family earned enough. Size of family functioned in similar dualistic manner: 'maximum indigence' was the alarm-bell sounded for big families (nine, even eleven members) 'because of their large number and low earnings'; whereas the single individual, even female, was refused aid 'because she is healthy and of an age to earn her living'.[24] Within these three parameters, state of health provided a crucial supportive function, rarely sufficient of its own to justify assistance, but a clinching argument in combination with one of the three permanent conditions. Thus the ageing man of limited health was rejected because he had no family to support; the family of three headed by a sick father was assisted because of inadequate earnings; husband and wife were given a grant, as the husband's earnings, normally adequate, were insufficient to pay for all the medicines his wife needed during her prolonged illness.[25] Two ideal-type meritorious families, at the extremes of our continuum, were the single widow, alone in the world, aged, of uncertain health and hence unable to earn enough for subsistence; and the large, sometimes extended family, with children too young to earn, an aged parent, and one of the normal earners sick.[26]

A certain symmetry thus existed between family structures likely to provoke cool detachment and those certain to attract sympathetic attention among the deputies. A check-list of the former, destined to be refused assistance, would read as follows: 'excellent earnings' or 'sufficient earnings'; 'young, healthy and [hence] capable of earning'; a young couple without children; an adolescent of sufficient age to earn enough; a single young woman; an old but healthy man or widow; a female head of household aided by her children; a female with small children requesting a bed, or with a son old enough to buy one; a daughter leaving home to marry asking for a bed. Certain job-skills, judged as generating adequate income, were likely to justify rejection of those who declared them: female silk-weaving especially, but also washerwomen and an innkeeper; and servants, as they were expected to be looked after by the household that employed them.[27]

The counterpart to these types of families regarded by the deputies as self-sufficient was the family condition that merited particular attention. Single aged women, if ill, were almost certain to receive at least bread (if healthy, they might be rejected on the grounds that they could beg); orphans were guaranteed help, as were abandoned wives; the recent death of a husband could ensure assistance, as would the additional burden of an aged infirm parent. Children too young to earn, a deranged member of the family, serious or prolonged illness of a resident relative, and especially of the head of household, all guaranteed assistance; large families were almost equally sure of receiving a bed, not least because they were likely to include at least one pubescent daughter who had to be separated from her male relatives.[28]

It would be over-simplistic to conclude that the deputies of the Congregation restricted their help exclusively to the critical moments of the life-cycle and family cycle. Social and especially moral considerations played a not inconsiderable role. Families with some link with the Congregation or the parish priest were especially meritorious; recommendation from an influential person (the local police official, a high level bureaucrat) could prove decisive. Soldiers and officers, suddenly unemployed after twenty-five to thirty years' service through the vagaries of political change, were given sometimes substantial help. Professional skills – as a copper-engraver, a violinist, a teacher – deserved particular regard, as did the dismissed clerks of the former grand-ducal administration. Occasionally and imperceptibly such social considerations could merge into traditional and by now anachronistic concerns for social status, for the shamefaced poor (even though the legal responsibility for the shamefaced belonged to the separate institution of the Buonomini di San Martino). It is difficult to tell whether a dismissed clerk was genuinely destitute or merely unable to sustain his proper station. But there can be no doubt about the families described as of 'good birth' or 'civil condition', regularly granted assistance; nor about the family 'of noble birth', where the wife fell ill through having to do all the housework, so obliging the husband to pawn his possessions in order to pay for a woman to look after wife, three children and home.[29]

Once more, we must not exaggerate this handful of instances of social considerations reinforcing, and in rare cases even replacing, assessments of the economic condition of the families. Certainly more important were moral considerations. In extreme cases, usually of large families, an unruly child or one who refused to work would be removed from home and placed in the disciplinary Casa Pia.[30] Daughters were given clothes in order to go to church.[31] But above all beds were granted to separate the sexes, even when it meant going against the regulations or despite fears of fraud. Daughters entering puberty were the main concern, but sons reaching an age of sexuality (in one case noted as fourteen) also provided an impelling reason to grant a bed. The deputies were quite explicit: the daughters were of 'a dangerous age', it was 'a scandalous matter' for daughters to sleep together with young parents; on the contrary, a 6-year old girl could continue 'for some time' to sleep with her parents and maternal grandfather.[32] Potential sexual promiscuity was the more worrying as kin sleeping together extended beyond parents and children: orphan nieces needed to be separated from their uncle, a father-in-law and his son from the married couple, children and grandfather from the marital bed – while a pubescent niece was told to continue sleeping in the same bed as her uncle, given his old age and infirmity.[33]

Specific moral considerations thus coloured the deputies' judgements, though even in the case of sexual worries they did not often lose sight of the possibility for the family to buy its own second bed. Nevertheless, their prime concern remained the economic independence of the family throughout its cycle. This explains why they never refused to redeem the household possessions pawned by a family at the *monte di pietà*, as their sale by the *monte* marked a significant rent in the thin fabric of the family's autonomy.[34] The deputies were always sensitive towards negative conjunctures in the family cycle: illness, unemployment, an imminent childbirth, loss of a son through conscription or a husband through death were regularly accepted as justification for granting assistance. But, more importantly, they also displayed a clear awareness of the structural relationships between levels of earnings and, on the one hand, the individual life-cycle (in which age and gender were the determinants); and, on the other hand, the family cycle (in which income was limited not only by age and gender, but by the number of children and the small proportion of earning members).[35] Large families and single old women were given preference precisely because they were the least likely to earn enough for subsistence. But the most miserable job-skills, such as muck-raking or street peddling, were recognized as yielding 'uncertain earnings', or as unlikely to provide enough for a family.[36] Unequivocally the policy of the deputies consisted of intervention to underpin the most vulnerable family structures and the most critical moments of the family cycle, which they identified by direct impressions and experience, without need of the statistical evidence of subsequent historical research.

In a simple model of urban poverty, charity would thus have been channelled to discrete nuclear families, each comprising its own household. In chapter 7 I pointed to the practical identification of family and household: 94.6 per cent of the applications described two-generational nuclear families, and a mere 0.6 per cent included non-relatives or more distant kin.[37] Analysis of the deputies' comments, however, reveals a more complicated image, as a small minority of applications came from, or on behalf of, individuals living (and sleeping) with larger families. Although the identification of household and family remained overwhelmingly the norm, it was the abnormal cases that attracted disproportionate attention from the deputies, precisely because of the burden represented by the additional household members.

Among this limited number, the most frequent case is that of an aged parent: the mother living with her son's family of four, unable to support her, merited help, as did the son-in-law, unable to support his mother-in-law when she fell ill, even though she did not live in the same house.[38] The principle underlying these favourable decisions was that acceptance of family responsibilities could overstretch subsistence capacities; we can consider it as a variant on the assistance given to widows living alone, who did not deny that they had kin, but described them as in as wretched a state as themselves. Another variant was when the family was so poor that a newly married son or daughter could not afford to rent a separate room: bedding complications were created, in which not just sisters, brothers, mothers or fathers, but even fathers-in-law and brothers-in-law found themselves sharing the same bed, and appealed to the willing ear of the deputies.[39]

More complicated were the cases where blood-ties were less close or even non-existent. Orphans were the main group concerned: the niece sleeping with her married aunt, with husband and four children, was an obvious candidate for a bed.[40] But if the orphan was without relatives, the importance of finding a family ready to accept her (for almost only cases of girls are recorded) more than justified a bed.[41] There could be perfect consonance between the ideals of the Congregation and the applicant family, as with the widow Mazzaranghi, who had taken in the Braccini orphans, brother and sister, and 'it seems, is giving them an excellent education'.[42] But in other instances, the orphan might only be taken in because of the householder's need of assistance: widow Pestellini, old and ill, was obliged to take in a girl from the public orphanage (Bigallo) to share her work (and hence her insignificant earnings). The orphan Anna Chini, 'sick and infirm', lived with non-relatives, but in such wretched conditions that she was granted aid, 'given her pitiful situation'.[43] The examples of households containing more than the classical nuclear family are too few and the comments of the deputies too cryptic to deduce any elaborate significance about the implications of cohabitation at this level of subsistence, where space, beds and food were all in very short supply.[44] But it is evident that the Congregation's prime concern was to find a home for orphans and that it was prepared to listen sympathetically, even to stretch its rules in order to achieve this end.

What conclusions can be drawn from this study of charity and subsistence? There can be no doubt that the Congregation of San Giovanni Battista understood its duties of outdoor relief (*a domicilio*) in a very literal sense: the deputies saw their task as underpinning the independence of the family, both economic and residential, at moments of crisis. To achieve this end they were prepared to intervene at various levels of subsistence crisis (from a family's initial use of the pawnshop to its sudden awareness, through absolute lack of food, of the immediacy of starvation[45]), at different stages of the family cycle (orphans, large families, aged widows), and at particular conjunctural moments (sickness, insanity, unemployment, etc.), while deliberately excluding others (young couples, healthy adults, individuals with skills judged capable of ensuring adequate earnings). Precisely because of their overriding concern with the family in its home, they were particularly sensitive towards the problem of orphans, who lacked kin and consequentially also neighbourhood support. But equally, although they preferred to deal with entire families (and hence insisted on full information), they were prepared, wherever judged necessary, to intervene within households in order to assist a specific individual. The conviction of the deputies about the centrality of the social role of the economically independent family unit would be difficult to fault. At most, one may query whether the forms of charity they proposed were appropriate to the world of structural poverty which was their domain.[46]

Institutional sources offer little direct evidence about how families viewed and responded to the cyclical problems of daily existence at a permanent level of minimum subsistence. In this instance, application to the Congregation was evidently regarded as an aspect of the family strategy of subsistence, but only as a fall-back tactic, more or less the last resort of a family of good morals to meet an immediate crisis. It is unequivocally clear that the equilibrium between needs and earnings was always taut, as liable to snap through the absence of a bread-earner as through the presence of an additional member in the household. Our Congregation, probably like most outdoor relief organizations, offers us evidence about some cyclical needs. Another crucial aspect of poverty at Florence, which the Congregation failed to confront (presumably because it was not contained in its statutes) and hence which is only hinted at, was the high level of rentals, which explained the overcrowding and cramped habitations of these families. The problem remains to be explored, although the deputies' refusal in one instance to help pay a rent, on the specific grounds that 'these cases are too frequent', is an unambiguous indication of its importance.[47] Similarly, the whole issue of topographical concentrations of poverty (our contemporary inner-city ghettos) is ignored, although a cursory, impressionistic survey of the applications already indicates numbers of families giving the same address, as well as possibly family networks living in nearby houses.

For the moment these must remain open questions, pointers to other aspects of structural poverty and to the family strategies adopted to confront them. But it is worth recalling that by the eighteenth and nineteenth centuries (and earlier), if outdoor relief was of central importance in western Europe, because of the stress placed on economic independence by society, alternative (and indeed concurrent) strategies of survival were open to the poor, even though they could only have affected significantly smaller numbers. At one extreme, because of the moral taboo on allowing death through visible neglect, families or individuals could opt for a total and socially accepted dependence on institutional support, whether temporary (a period of *renfermement*, the deposit of a legitimate baby at the foundling hospital) or permanent (old-age residence in a hospital). At the other extreme, poor individuals and families could develop an abusive dependence on society by adopting social practices formally and usually juridically unacceptable to that society (such as prostitution, theft or begging). It is evident that the choices were rarely so stark and drastic. Indeed, it is most likely that within the life-cycle of the poor, use was made of various alternatives or combinations of them, depending on the nature of the relationships between each individual and the society in which he (or she) recognized himself (or herself); hence the importance of less formal ties of kinship or clientelism. But it is also possible to suggest that strategies of subsistence made more use of institutional resources by the eighteenth and nineteenth centuries precisely because the range and specialization of charitable (and repressive) institutions had widened as a response to a growing awareness of the complexity of society and the incidence of domestic crisis.

Notes

This study would not have been possible without the earlier assistance provided by the Social Science Research Council, grant HK 6583. I should also like to thank Anna Gozzini.
  1 P. Townsend and D. Wedderburn, *The Aged in the Welfare State*, London, 1965; P. Townsend, *The Concept of Poverty*, London, 1970; P. Townsend, *Poverty in the United Kingdom; a Survey of Household Resources and Standards of Living*, London, 1979; B. Showler and A. Sinfield (eds), *The Workless State; Studies in Unemployment*, Oxford, 1981; A.B. Atkinson, *The Economics of Inequality*, Oxford, 1983; A.B. Atkinson, A.K. Maynard and C.G. Trinder, *Parents and Children: Incomes in Two Generations*, SSRC–DHSS studies in deprivation and disadvantage, 10, London, 1983.

2 For a full discussion of the Congregation of San Giovanni Battista and the nature of the sources, see chapter 7 in this volume, 'Charity, poverty and household structure'.

3 See pp. 192–4.

4 ASF, Congregazione di San Giovanni Battista, serie IV, filze 2 to 43. All references and quotations in this article come from this source and will list the *filza* number, civic number of the habitation and surname of the applicant family. Although usually only one or two references are given, they are representative of substantially larger numbers. (Filza) 3: (civic number) 5106 Rossi; 17:5031 Cornamusi; 22:3730 Nannetti, and cf. 19:3405 Ricci; 10:3835 Fiorini; 12:5083 Chellini; and cf. 4:4148 Bruni, rejected 'because it is a matter of assisting a single individual, of unknown age'.

5 42:4802 Ferranti; 36:3401 Mochi. One deputy, while recommending the grant of a bed in 1810, noted that a bed had already been granted in 1803: 5:5291 Berretti; while another applicant who had already received two beds in the past ten years was refused: 2:4917 Aiazzi. The total number of repeated applications (forbidden by the regulations) only amounted to a few dozen.

6 6:3941 Socci; cf. 20:4940 Perini ('maintained by the hospital'); 16:4592 Coli ('the serious and dangerous illness of the head of household'). Illness or hospitalization of the head of household was a common justification for granting help, e.g. 18:5342 Agostini; 18:3517 Sonni; 3:3891 Bastianelli; 35:4982 Moschini.

7 15:3668 Puliti; 24:3728 Benini ('not of good morals, as not even their children are educated'); 19:4338 Bartolini.

8 J.M. de Gérando, *Le Visiteur du pauvre: mémoire qui a remporté le prix proposé par l'Académie de Lyon sur la question suivante: 'Indiquer les moyens de reconnaître la véritable indigence, et de rendre l'aumône utile à ceux qui la donnent comme à ceux qui la reçoivent'*, Paris, L. Colas, 1820. An English translation was published in 1833, an Italian one in 1834; by 1844 eleven French editions had been published.

9 25:3730 Saracini, and many others. There are some rare exceptions, where the visitor's negative recommendation was overturned: 26:3759 Miraceli, 14:3537 Manfriani, 28:3528 Bernini.

10 19:3367 Stiattesi; 22:4020 Nasi.

11 2:4709 Papi; 2:5154 Fossi; 4:4136 Borsacchi; 12:4088 Cheli. In one instance (4:4534 Zanoboni) an irritable rapporteur rejected the application on the grounds that the visitor-deputies had recommended a bed, whereas the request was for clothes: 'it's impossible to know what is the real need'.

12 31:4705 Bardini: 'the doctor who visited the applicant could find no reason why she cannot feed her daughter'; 32:4623 Cavazzani.

13 10:3582 Pampaloni; 25:4292 Giamberini; 10:4860 Chiaranti; 10:3808

Vanini; 2:4709 Bassilichi; 10:3889 Corsini; 6:4252 Fioravanti; 3:4835 Lolli; 6:5002 Cavini ('it's not possible that the applicants do not earn enough'); 6:5021 Buncioni. Many more examples could be given.

14 See p. 184.

15 8:3943 Bianchi.

16 16:3389 Corti; 20:3453 Tedeschi; 18:4075 Lanzi; 15:4389 Martini; 18:5342 Agostini, and many others.

17 19:4401 Cappelli.

18 For the total number of rejections, see pp. 188–9. 18:3519 Benvenuti (dowry 'refused, as against the regulations'); 12:4130 Nesi (coach-driver training); 19:4157 Bichi; 19:3714 Noccioli (beggars); 22:4215 Santi; 6:5027 Panazzoli (blankets).

19 In files 31 to 36, of 74 applications for a wet-nurse subsidy, only 26 were accepted. The visitor-deputies frequently referred to the mother's inability to feed through lack of nutrition ('incapable of feeding through poor nutrition': 36:4971 Conti). 27:4069 Giorgi ('among their other dire needs, we must also note their total lack of clothing'). 40:3393 Frassinesi (bed).

20 Particularly hard-nosed rapporteurs seem to be those in files 17 and 27, and a compassionate one in file 21. 37:3512 Boccaccini (wet-nurse). 12:4890 Fanti; 6:3769 Pichi (parishes); see also 10:3387 Sbrocchi.

21 36:4757 Coloretti; 34:4817 Gabbiani; 35:5038 Santoni (nappies). 3:4042 Ricci; 37:4977 Maglierini (bread). 39:6478 Maori; 18:3442 Guidi; 28:4465 Vestri (numerous children). 28:5075 Spe; 18:3954 Guarnieri; 28:3848 Ferroni; 23:4212 Massai; 18:4916 Giorgetti; 23:4075 Macciani; 10:4786 Albizzi (living conditions).

22 20:4642 Melani (parish priest); and cf. 20:3609 Manetti. 33:3610 Bellucci (wet-nurse subsidy). 15:3735 Fedi (alternative subsidy). 28:5052 Pani (begging). 6:4846 Lucheri (bed sold). 40:3961 Furillazzi; 3:3408 Vallesi; 4:4910 Conti (imminent childbirth). 19:3625 Petrini; 9:3760 Masetti (daughter's bed).

23 22:4503 Salvagnini (washerwoman); 27:3773 Galletti ('given that her son is about to abandon her in order to take a wife'); 18:3442 Vitali, Bartolini (widow and son-in-law). 18:3892 Lori; 3:4312 Piccini; 21:4902 Lippi (conscription); and cf. 21:5182 Sereni, a widow 'extremely wretched', because she had sold all her belongings to give some money to her conscripted son who had now been killed in battle.

24 15:4389 Martini; 42:3774 Parenti (large families). 6:4847 Galleri (single woman).

25 43:3791 Pelatti; 26:3772 Rossi; 18:3568 Rastrelli.

26 33:4600 Chini ('sick and incapable, she is allowed to continue living where she is out of charity'); 14:3471 Ghelardini, a family of seven, consisting of mother and two married sons, each with one infant (but all in good health); 26:4375 Mazzetti, a family of six, with the head of household unable to work and the eldest son deranged (*demente*).

27 3:3905 Farolfi; 22:5372 Fraschetti (earnings); 25:4409 Donzelli (young couple); 3:4074 Pezzati (couple without children); 6:5021 Buccioni (adolescent); 27:3414 Marchi; 12:4089 Seroni (single young woman); 27:4992 Bellucci (old woman); 27:4397 Ciappi (woman helped by children); 6:5042 Mori; 3:5027 Tafani (beds); 11:4968 Aiazzi (marriage); 12:4328 Falchi (silk-weaving); 27:4969 Monelli (washerwoman); 14:3391 (innkeeper); 20:4687 Ganti (servant); and cf. 13:4149 Franchi, considered as a servant even though she was not a domestic but 'does cleaning jobs' on a casual basis.

28 19:3982 Miglia (old woman); 27:4020 Nesi (orphan); 20:3909 Marchiana (abandoned wife); 3:5045 Delli (widowed); 40:3784 Bellebuone (recently widowed, with the additional burden of a married daughter who had fled from her husband); 25:3471 Conti (aged parent); 13:4710 Giannelli; 15:3370 Casati (young children); 20:4951 Pietrai; 11:5007 Bassi (insanity); I have counted seven cases of *dementi* in the total 4498. 26:3770 Segalari; 3:4705 Ferroni (illness); 18:5342 Agostini; 16:4592 Coli (illness of head of household); 40:3900 Massai; 3:4801 Ceccherini (large family).

29 9:5092 Ciabilli; 5:4444 Piamonti (close to Congregation or parish priest); 5:5000 Pini; 13:3348 Montefiori (recommendations); 26:3977 Bacchini; 7:4796 Galli; 12:4720 Cordernio (army); 6:3800 Marchini; 10:4330 Cantini; 23:4220 Albertini; 15:5137 Guarducci (professional skills); 40:4009 Aretini; 17:4756 Brandi (dismissed clerk); 24:4641 Vannetti; 19:4101 Baccini (good birth); 43:4806 Renard (noble).

30 3:3857 Borla ('as these two children are of vicious temperament'); 42:3759 Sacchi ('with a son who lives in the most total idleness, as he has no one to guide him'); all accepted into the Casa Pia.

31 10:3473 Landucci; 14:3655 Morosi.

32 21:3866 Bartolini ('but someone should keep check that the bed is not sold'); 14:3835 Scarlini; 11:5183 Covoni; 39:3925 Bianchi; 28:5066 Carotti ('as the parents are young'); 6:5042 Mori.

33 11:3413 Laghi; 6:4866 Paladini; 6:4897 Mori; 22:4859 Lascialfare.

34 40:3748 Mazzoni; 7:4085 Accioli; 4:4245 Belli ('as the sum is substantial', the deputies decided that only items 'of essential needs' should be redeemed).

35 See pp. 190–4.

36 33:3773 Bronchelli; 43:5016 Bettini; 20:4240 Cioni.

37 See p. 171.

38 16:3389 Corti; 23:3654 Giorgi; 12:3634 Picchi; 12:3833 Bianchi; 4:4449 Gucciardi; 14:3471 Ghelardini; 3:4611 Stefanelli (son's family of four); 43:3957 Martinelli (mother-in-law in another house).

39 28:5007 Galli; 6:4866 Paladini; 6:4897 Mori; 6:5033 Frangini.

40 12:4909 Gamberucci; 11:3413 Laghi.

41 23:4956 Pichianti (where the family insisted on a separate bed as the condition for keeping the orphan; the Congregation agreed, so long as it was her property); 21:4737 Giorgi, 27:4704 Giolli.

42 5:5094 Mazzaranghi.

43 14:3542 Pestellini; 33:4600 Chini.

44 For example, see the obscure explanation in 6:4861 Ferroni, where a bed was requested to separate the sister from a 'cohabitant'.

45 For the redemption of pawned possessions, see above, note 34. 22:4062 Teresa Grifoni ('very small weekly earnings [from spinning[which oblige her to fast on occasion').

46 See pp. 193–4.

47 27:4101 Meini.

Bibliography

This bibliography makes no claims to provide a full list of even the major works on poverty and charity in western Europe. Its purpose is to provide an introduction to the most important and most recent studies. Although works in English have been privileged, a considerable number of publications in other languages have been included, because they contain the results of important recent research usually ignored in English-speaking countries.

The bibliography is divided into sections on specific countries, followed by works which do not relate to one country and finally by a selection of what for me have been the most helpful works on the study of family structures and on poverty and welfare today.

Britain

Beier A.L., 'Vagrants and the social order in Elizabethan England', *Past and Present*, 64, 1974.

Beier A.L., *The Problem of the Poor in Tudor and Early Stuart England*, London, 1983.

Booth C., *Life and Labour of the People in London*, London, 1889–91.

Cavour C., *Extrait du rapport des commissaire de S.M. Britannique . . . sur l'administration des fonds provenant de la taxe des pauvres en Angleterre* (Turin, 1835), in F. Sirugo (ed.), C. Cavour, *Scritti di economia 1835–1850*, Milan, 1962.

Checkland S.G. and E.O.A. (eds), *The Poor Law Report of 1834*, Harmondsworth, 1974.

Coats A.W., 'The relief of poverty: attitudes to labour and economic change in England, 1660–1782', *International Review of Social History*, 21, 1976.

Bibliography

Crowther M.A., *The Workhouse System*. London, 1981.

Defoe D., *Giving alms no charity and employing the poor a grievance to the nation . . .*, London, 1704.

Eden F.M., *The State of the Poor*, London, 1797.

Fraser D. (ed.), *The New Poor Law in the Nineteenth Century*, London, 1976.

Hall C., 'The active age of charity: men, women and philanthropy, 1780–1850', unpublished working paper, University of Essex, 1980.

Hastings R.P., *Poverty and the Poor Law in the North Riding of Yorkshire, 1780–1837*, London, 1982.

Jones M., *The Charity School Movement*, London, 1964.

Jordan W.K., *Philanthropy in England, 1480–1660*, London, 1959.

Kussmaul A.S., *Servants in Husbandry in Early Modern England*, Cambridge, 1981.

Leonard E.M., *The Early History of English Poor Relief*, Cambridge, 1900.

Levine D., 'Industrialization and the proletarian family in England', *Past and Present*, 107, 1985.

McClure R.K., *Coram's Children: the London Foundling Hospital in the Eighteenth Century*, New Haven, 1981.

McKendrick N., 'Home demand and economic growth: a new view of the role of women and children in the industrial revolution', in N. McKendrick (ed.), *Historical Perspectives: Studies in English Thought and Society*, London, 1974.

Marshall J.D., *The Old Poor Law, 1795–1834*, London, 1968.

Mayhew H., *London Labour and the London Poor*, London, 1851.

Mitchison R., 'The making of the old Scottish poor law', *Past and Present*, 63, 1974.

Newman Brown W., 'The receipt of poor relief and family situation in Aldenham, Hertfordshire 1630–1690', in R.M. Smith (ed.), *Land, Kinship and Life Cycle*, Cambridge, 1984.

Nicholls G., *A History of the English Poor Law*, 3 vols, London, 1898–1900.

Oxley D., *Poor Relief in England and Wales, 1601–1834*, Newton Abbot, 1974.

Pearl V., 'Change and stability in seventeenth century London', *The London Journal*, 5, 1979.

Pearl V., 'Social policy in early modern London', in H. Lloyd Jones, V. Pearl and B. Worden (eds), *History and Imagination. Essays in Honour of H.R. Trevor Roper*, London, 1981.

Pound J., *Poverty and Vagrancy in Tudor England*, London, 1971.

Poynter J.R., *Society and Pauperism: English Ideas on Poor Relief, 1795–1834*, London, 1969.

Romanelli R., 'Ritorno a Speenhamland. Discutendo la legge inglese sui poveri (1795–1834)', *Quaderni storici*, 53, 1983.

Rose M.E., *The Relief of Poverty 1834–1914*, London, 1972.

Rose M.E., *The Poor and the City: the English Poor Law in its Urban Context, 1834–1914*, Leicester, 1985.
Salter F.R., *Tracts on Poor Relief*, London, 1926.
Slack P., 'Poverty and politics in Salisbury 1597–1666' in P. Clark and P. Slack (eds), *Crisis and Order in English Towns 1500–1700*, London, 1972.
Slack P., 'Poverty and social regulation in Elizabethan England', in C. Haigh (ed.), *The Reign of Elizabeth I*, London, 1984.
Snell K.D.M., *Annals of the Labouring Poor: Social Change in Agrarian England, 1660–1900*, Cambridge, 1985.
Trebble J.H., *Urban Poverty in Britain 1830–1914*, London, 1979.
Wales T., 'Poverty, poor relief and the life cycle', in R.M. Smith (ed.), *Land, Kinship and Life Cycle*, Cambridge, 1984.
Wales T., 'Poverty and poor relief in early modern England: a reassessment', unpublished working paper, n.d.
Webb S. and B., *English Local Government: English Poor Law History*, 3 vols, London, 1927–29.
Williams K., *From Pauperism to Poverty*, London, 1981.
Wrightson K. and Levine D., *Poverty and Piety in an English Village: Terling, 1525–1700*, London, 1979.

France

Berger P., 'Rural charity in late seventeenth century France: the Pontchartrain case', *French Historical Studies*, 10, 1978.
Bloch C., *L'Assistance et l'Etat en France à la veille de la Révolution . . . 1764–1790*, Paris, 1908.
Bloch C. and Tuety A., *Procès-verbaux et rapports du Comité de mendicité de la Constituante 1790–1*, Paris, 1911.
Chevalier L., *Labouring Classes and Dangerous Classes in Paris during the First Half of the Nineteenth Century*, New York, 1973.
Chill E., 'Religion and mendicity in seventeenth-century France', *International Review of Social History*, 7, 1962.
Coornaert E., *Les Compagnonnages en France*, Paris, 1966.
Davis N.Z., 'Poor relief, humanism and heresy', in N.Z. Davis, *Society and Culture in Early Modern France*, London, 1975.
Duprat C., 'Punir et guérir. En 1819, la prison des philanthropes', *Annales historiques de la Révolution française*, 228, 1977.
Endres R., 'Das Armenproblem im Zeitalter des Absolutismus', *Jahrbuch für Frankische landesforschung*, 34/35, 1975.
Fairchilds C.C., *Poverty and Charity in Aix-en-Provence, 1670–1789*, Baltimore, 1976.
Fontaine L., *Le Voyage et la mémoire. Colporteurs de l'Oisans au XIXe siècle*, Lyons, 1984.
Forrest A., *The French Revolution and the Poor*, Oxford, 1981.

Bibliography

Geremek B., *Le Salariat dans l'artisanat parisien aux XIIIe–XVe siècles* . . ., The Hague–Paris, 1968.

Geremek B., *Les Marginaux parisiens aux XIVe et XVe siècles*, Paris, 1976.

Gutton J.P., *La Société et les pauvres. L'exemple de la généralité de Lyon 1534–1789*, Lyons, 1971.

Gutton J.P., *L'Etat et la medicité dans la première moitié du XVIIe siècle*, St-Etienne, 1973.

Gutton J.P., *Domestiques et serviteurs dans la France du l'ancien régime*, Paris, 1981.

Higgs D., 'An aspect of French poor relief in the nineteenth century: the dépôt de mendicité of Toulouse, 1811–1818', *Annales du Midi*, 86, 1974.

Hufton O., 'Begging, vagrancy, vagabondage and the law: an aspect of the problem of poverty in eighteenth century France', *European Studies Review*, 2, 1972.

Hufton O., 'Towards an understanding of the poor of eighteenth-century France', in J.F. Bosher (ed.), *French Government and Society: Essays in memory of Alfred Cobban*, London, 1973.

Hufton O., *The Poor of Eighteenth-Century France 1750–1789*, Oxford, 1974.

Imbert J., *Les Hôpitaux en France*, Paris, 1958.

Jones C., *Charity and Bienfaisance: the Treatment of the Poor in the Montpellier Region, 1740–1815*, Cambridge, 1982.

Jones C. and Sonenscher M., 'The social functions of the hospital in eighteenth century France: the case of Nimes', *French Historical Studies*, 13, 1983.

Lallemond L., *Histoire de la charité*, 5 vols, Paris, 1902–12.

Norberg K., *Rich and Poor in Grenoble, 1600–1814*, Berkeley, 1985.

'Les Oeuvres de charité en France au XVIIe siècle', *XVIIe Siécle*, 90–1, 1971.

Piasenza P., '"Povertà", costruzione dello stato e controllo sociale in Francia: alle origini del problema', *Rivista di storia contemporanea*, 9, 1980.

Shapiro A.L., *Housing the Poor of Paris, 1850–1902*, Madison, 1985.

Vaux de Foletier F. de, *Les Tsiganes dans l'ancienne France*, Paris, 1961.

Italy

Aymard M., 'Villes laborieuses, villes oisives: l'Italie à l'époque moderne', in *La Force du travail dans les cités méditerranéennes du milieu du XVIIe au miliéu du XIXe siècle*, Université de Nice, Cahiers de la Méditerranée, 3, Nice, 1974.

Aymard M. and Bresc H., 'Nourritures et consommation en Sicile entre XIVe et XVIIIe siècles', *Mélanges de l'Ecole française de Rome*, 87, 1975.

Cajani L., 'Gli statuti della Compagnia dei ciechi, zoppi e stroppiati della Visitazione (1698)', *Ricerche per la storia religiosa di Roma*, 3, 1979.

Cajani L., 'L'assistenza ai poveri nell'Italia del Settecento', *Transactions of the Fifth International Congress on the Enlightenment*, Oxford, 1981.

Camporesi P. (ed.), *Il Libro dei vagabondi*, Turin, 1983.

Ciano C., 'Il problema della mendicità nella Roscana napoleonica', *Bollettino storico pisano*, 42, 1973.

Corsini C., 'Le migrazioni stagionali di lavoratori nei dipartimenti italiani del periodo napoleonico (1810–12)', in *Saggi di demografia storica*, Florence, 1969.

Corsini C., 'Materiali per lo studio della famiglia in Toscana nei secoli XVII–XIX: gli esposti', *Quaderni storici*, 33, 1976.

Delille G., *Croissance d'une société rurale. Montesarchio et la vallée Caudine aux XVIIe et XVIIIe siécles*, Naples, 1973.

Del Panta L., *Le Epidemie nella storia demografica italiana (secoli XIV–XIX)*, Turin, 1980.

Geremek B., 'Il pauperismo nell'età preindustriale (secoli XIV–XVIII)', *Storia d'Italia*, vol. 5:1. I Documenti, Turin, 1973.

Geremek B., 'Renfermement des pauvres en Italie (XIVe–XVIIe siècles). Remarques préliminaires', in *Mélanges en l'honneur de Fernand Braudel*, Toulouse, 1973.

Grendi E., 'Pauperismo e albergo dei poveri nella Genova del seicento', *Rivista storica italiana*, 87, 1975.

Grendi E. (ed.), 'Sistemi di carità: esposti e internati nella società di antico regime', *Quaderni storici*, 53, 1983.

Herlihy D. and Klapisch-Zuber C., *Les Toscans et leurs familles*, Paris, 1978.

Lombardi D., '1629–1631: crisi e peste a Firenze', *Archivio storico italiano*, 137, 1979.

Lombardi D., 'L'ospedale dei menticanti nella Firenze del seicento. "Da inutile serraglio dei mendici a conservatorio e casa di forza per le donne"', *Società e storia*, 24, 1984.

Maldini D., 'Pauperismo e mendicità a Torino nel periodo napoleonico', *Studi piemontesi*, 8, 1979.

Marcolin M., *The 'Casa d'Industria' in Bologna during the Napoleonic period: public relief and subsistence strategies*, Florence: EUI Working Paper 85/132, 1985.

Meneghetti Casarin F., 'La repressione dei vagabondi alla fine del XVIII secolo: il caso della Repubblica di Venezia', *Società e storia*, 18, 1982.

Meneghetti Casarin F., *I Vagabondi, la società e lo stato nella repubblica veneta alla fine del '700*, Rome, 1984.

Muratori L.A., *Della carità cristiana in quanto essa è amore del prossimo*, Modena, 1723.

Passerini L., *Storia degli stabilimenti di beneficienza e d'istruzione elementare gratuita della città di Firenze*, Florence, 1853.

Bibliography

Politi G., 'Introduzione' to M. Fantarelli, *L'Istituzione dell'ospedale di S. Alessio dei poveri mendicanti in Cremona (1569–1600)*, Cremona, 1981.

Politi G., Rosa M. and Della Peruta F. (eds.), *Timore e carità. I poveri nell'Italia moderna*, Cremona, 1982.

Pullan B.S., *Rich and Poor in Renaissance Venice*, Oxford, 1971.

Pullan B.S., 'Poveri, medicanti e vagabondi (secoli XIV–XVII)', *Storia d'Italia. Annali I. Dal feudalesimo al capitalismo*, Turin, 1978.

Pullan B.S., 'The old catholicism, the new catholicism and the poor', *Timore e carità*, Cremona, 1982.

Ricci G., 'Povertà, vergogna e povertà vergognosa', *Società e storia*, 5, 1979.

Ricci L., *Riforma degli istituti pii della città di Modena*, Modena, 1787.

Rosa M., 'Nota critica', in J.P. Gutton, *La Società e i poverti*, Milan, 1977.

Rosa M., 'Chiesa, idee sui poveri e assistenza in Italia dal cinque al settecento', *Società e storia*, 3, 1980.

Russo S., 'Potere pubblico e carità privata. L'assistenza ai poveri a Lucca tra XVI e XVIII secolo', *Società e storia*, 23, 1984.

Low Countries

Blockmans W. and Prevenier W., 'Poverty in Flanders and Brabant from the fourteenth to the mid-sixteenth century: sources and problems', *Acta historiae neerlandicae*, X, 1978.

Bonenfant P., 'Les origines et le caractère de la réforme de la bienfaisance publique aux Pays-Bas sous le règne de Charles Quint', *Revue belge de philologie et d'histoire*, 5, 1926; 6, 1927.

Bonenfant P., *Le Problème du paupérisme en Belgique à la fin de l'Ancien Régime*, Brussels, 1934.

Haesenne-Peremans N., *La Pauvreté dans la région liégeoise à l'aube de la révolution industrielle*, Paris, 1981.

Haesenne-Peremans N., *Les Pauvres et le pouvoir. Assistance et répression au pays de Liège (1685–1830)*, Kortrijk-Heule, 1983.

van Leeuwen M. and Smits F., 'Steunverlening en steuntrekkers in Amsterdam, ca. 1770–1800', *Skript*, 4, 1982.

Other countries

Briod A., *L'Assistance des pauvres dans le Pays de Vaud*, Lausanne, 1926.

Carbonell i Esteller, 'La beneficiència a Finals del s. XVIII: una aproximacio. La casa i hospital de misericòrdia de Barcelona', *Actes Primer Congrés d'Història Moderna de Catalunya*, Barcelona, 1984.

Dubler A.M., *Armen- und Bettlerwesen in der Gemeinen Herrschaft 'Freie Amter', 16. bis 18. Jahrhundert*, Basel, 1970.

Jimenez Salas M., *Historia de la assistencia social en España en la edad moderna*, Madrid, 1958.

Johansen H.C., 'J.G. Büsch's economic theory and his influence on the Danish economic and social debate', *Scandinavian Economic History Review*, 14, 1966.

Martz L., *Poverty and Welfare in Habsburg Spain: the Example of Toledo*, Cambridge, 1983.

Rau V. and Saez F. (eds), *A Pobreza e a assistencia dos pobres na peninsula ibérica durante a idade media*, 2 vols, Lisbon, 1983.

General

De Gérando J.B., *Le Visiteur du pauvre*, Paris, 1820.

De Gérando J.B., *De la bienfaisance publique*, Brussels, 1839.

Fatica M., 'Il "De subventione pauperum" di J.L. Vives: suggestioni luterane o mutamento di una mentalità collettiva?', *Società e storia*, 15, 1982.

Foucault M., *Folie et déraison. Histoire de la folie à l'âge classique*, Paris, 1961.

Foucault M., *Discipline and Punish: the Birth of the Prison*, Harmondsworth, 1978.

Geremek B., *Truands et misérables dans l'Europe moderne (1350–1600)*, Paris, 1980.

Grimm H.J., 'Luther's contributions to sixteenth century organization of poor relief', *Archiv für Reformationsgeschichte*, 61, 1970.

Gutton J.P., *La Société et les pauvres en Europe (XVIe–XVIIIe siècles)*, Paris, 1974.

Lis C. and Soly H., *Poverty and Capitalism in Pre-industrial Europe*, Hassocks, 1979.

Les Marginaux et les exclus dans l'histoire, Paris: Cahiers Jussieu, no. 5, Université de Paris VII, 1979.

Mollat M., *Les Pauvres au moyen âge*, Paris, 1978.

Mollat M. (ed.), *Etudes sur l'histoire de la pauvreté (Moyen âge–XVIe siècle)*, 2 vols, Paris, 1974.

Pullan B.S., 'Catholics and the poor in early modern Europe', *Transactions Royal Hist. Soc.*, 26, 1976.

Riis T. (ed.), *Aspects of Poverty in Early Modern Europe*, Florence, 1981.

Vives J.L., *De subventione pauperum*, Bruges, 1526.

Wilkinson R.G., *Progress and Poverty*, London, 1973.

Family structures

Anderson M., *Family Structure in Nineteenth Century Lancashire*, Cambridge, 1971.

Anderson M., *Approaches to the History of the Western Family, 1500–1914*, London, 1980.

Bibliography

Barbagli M., *Sotto lo stesso tetto. Mutamenti della famiglia in Italia dal XV al XX secolo*, Bologna, 1984.

Berkner L.K., 'The stem family and the development cycle of the peasant household: an eighteenth century Austrian example', *American Historical Review*, 77, 1972.

Berkner L.K., 'Recent research on the history of the family in western Europe', *Journal of Marriage and the Family*, 1973.

Berkner L.K., 'The use and misuse of census data for the historical analysis of family structure', *Journal of Interdisciplinary History*, 5, 1975.

Cipolla C.M., 'The plague and the pre-Malthus malthusians', *Journal of European Economic History*, 3, 1974.

Evans R.J. and Lee W.R. (eds), *The German Family*, London, 1981.

Goubert P., 'Family and province: a contribution to the knowledge of the family structure of early modern France', *Journal of Family History*, 2, 1977.

Hajnal J., 'European marriage patterns in perspective', in D.V. Glass and D.E.C. Eversley (eds), *Population and History*, London, 1965.

Hajnal J., 'Two kinds of pre-industrial household formation system', in R. Wall *et al.* (eds), *Family Forms in Historic Europe*, Cambridge, 1983.

Hareven T.K., 'Family time and historical time', *Daedalus*, 1977.

Hareven T.K. (ed.), *Transitions: The Family and the Life Course in Historical Perspective*, New York, 1978.

Laslett P., 'The characteristics of the Western family considered over time', in P. Laslett, *Family Life and Illicit Love in Earlier Generations*, Cambridge, 1977.

Laslett P., 'Family and household as work group and kin group: areas of traditional Europe compared', R. Wall *et al.* (eds), *Family Forms in Historic Europe*, Cambridge, 1983.

Laslett P. and Wall R. (eds), *Household and Family in Past Time*, Cambridge, 1972.

Levine D. (ed.), *Proletarianization and Family History*, San Diego, 1984.

Manoukian A., *I Vincoli familiari in Italia*, Bologna, 1983.

Mitterauer M., 'Familiengrösse – Familientypen – Familienzyklus, Probleme quantitativer Auswertung von österreichischen Quellenmaterial', *Geschichte und Gesellschaft*, 1, 1975.

Mitterauer M. and Sieder R., *The European Family*, Oxford, 1982.

Smith R.M., 'The structured dependence of the elderly as a recent development: some sceptical historical thoughts', *Ageing and Society*, 4, 1984.

Smith R.M. (ed.), *Land, Kinship and Life Cycle*, Cambridge, 1984.

Smith R.M., 'Transfer incomes, risk and security: the roles of family and the collectivity in recent theories of fertility change', in D. Coleman and R. Schofield (eds), *The State of Population Theory*, Oxford, 1986.

Wachter K.W., Hammel E.A. and Laslett P. (eds), *Statistical Studies of Historical Social Structure*, New York, 1978.

Wall R., Robin J. and Laslett P. (eds), *Family Forms in Historic Europe*, Cambridge, 1983.

Wheaton R., 'Family and kinship in Western Europe: the problem of the joint family household', *American Historical Review*, 80, 1975.

Wheaton R. and Hareven T.K. (eds), *Family and Sexuality in French History*, Philadelphia, 1980.

Wrigley E.A. and Schofield R.S., *The Population History of England, 1541–1871*, London, 1981.

Poverty and welfare today

Abel-Smith B. and Townsend P., *The Poor and the Poorest*, London, 1965.

Atkinson, A.B., *Poverty in Britain and the Reform of Social Security*, Cambridge, 1969.

Atkinson A.B., *The Economics of Inequality*, Oxford, 1975.

Atkinson A.B., Maynard A.K. and Trinder C.G., *Parents and Children: Incomes in Two Generations*, London, 1983.

Beckerman W., 'The measurement of poverty', in T. Riis (ed.), *Aspects of Poverty in Early Modern Europe*, Florence, 1981.

Blockmans W., 'Circumscribing the concept of poverty', in T. Riis (ed.), *Aspects of Poverty in Early Modern Europe*, Florence, 1981.

'Comment identifier un peuple sans connaître son histoire', *Quart Monde Igloos*, No. 99/100, Pierrelaye, 197.

Commissione di indagine sulla povertà. Primo rapporto alla Presidenza del Consiglio dei Ministri, Rome, 1985.

Higgins J., *The Poverty Business: Britain and America*, Oxford, 1978.

Jordan B., *Poor Parents: Social Policy and the 'Cycle of Deprivation'*, London, 1974.

Lewis O., *Five Families: Mexican Case Studies in the Culture of Poverty*, New York, 1959.

O.E.C.D., *Public Expenditure on Income Maintenance Programmes*, Paris, 1976.

Orshansky M., *Counting the Poor: Another Look at the Poverty Profile*, Washington, D.C., 1966.

Rowntree B.S., *Poverty: a Study of Town Life*, London, 1901.

Sen A., 'Issues in the measurement of poverty', *Scandinavian Journal of Economics*, 81, 1979.

Sen A., *Poverty and Famines: An Essay on Entitlement and Deprivation*, Oxford, 1981.

Showler B. and Sinfield A. (eds), *The Workless State: Studies in Unemployment*, Oxford, 1981.

Bibliography

Sinfield A., *The Long-term Unemployed: A Comparative Survey*, Paris, 1968.

Titmuss R.M., 'The social division of welfare', in R.M. Titmuss, *Essays on the Welfare State*, London, 1958.

Townsend P., *Poverty in the United Kingdom: A Survey of Household Resources and Standards of Living*, London, 1979.

Townsend P. (ed.), *The Concept of Poverty*, London, 1970.

Townsend P. and Wedderburn D., *The Aged in the Welfare State*, London, 1965.

Walker R., Lawson R. and Townsend P. (eds), *Responses to Poverty: Lessons from Europe*, London, 1984.

Waxman C.I., *The Stigma of Poverty: A Critique of Poverty Theories and Policies*, New york, 1977.

Young M. and Wilmott P., *Family and Kinship in East London*, London, 1957.

Young M. (ed.), *Poverty Report 1974: A Review of Policies and Problems in the Last Year*, Institute of Community Studies, London, 1974.

Index

Index

5

DATE

SESTIERE | UFIZIO AUSILIARE DI BENEFICENZA | 18

Secondo

CURA
DI
Ognissanti

Signori Componenti l'Ufizio di Beneficenza
della Città di Firenze

Num.

Delib. a

la Famiglia *Vallesi* abitante nella Cura di *Ognissanti*
Sestiere *Secondo* nella Casa al Piano *Terreno* in via *De Canacci* al Num. *5798*
nativa in Firenze, domicillata da ed abitante in questa Cura
è composta come appresso

	Nome	Età Anni	Sano Malato Impotente	Mestiere che esercita	Con chi stà impiegato a lavorare	Guadagno Settimanale
Capo Casa	*Vincenzio*	76	*pescatore di Povero*		2	
glie	*Caterina*	64	*Sana*	*Incannatora di Seta*		2
li {	*Novziata*	42	*Sana*	*Incannatora di Seta*		2
	M.ª Angiola	91	*Sana*	*con Sopra*		
ri nti {						
nei {						

Essendo questa Famiglia di buoni costumi, e poveri, nè potendo sostenersi senza qualche ajuto,
supplicherebbe di ottenere *Sussidio*